363.25   Micheels, Peter A.
MIC
          The detectives.

4 WEEKS

$21.95

DATE			

5/94

BAKER & TAYLOR BOOKS

THE

DETECTIVES

ALSO BY PETER A. MICHEELS

BRAVING THE FLAMES
HEAT

THE

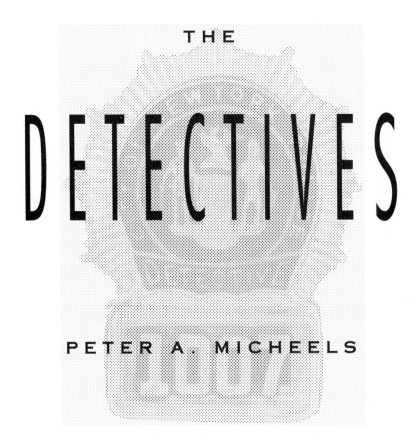

DETECTIVES

PETER A. MICHEELS

ST. MARTIN'S PRESS NEW YORK

Editor: Jared Kieling
Production Editor: Richard Klin
Copyedited by Lynne Wood

Library of Congress Cataloging-in-Publication Data

Micheels, Peter A.
    The detectives / Peter A. Micheels.
      p.   cm.
    ISBN 0-312-09785-0
    1. Detectives—New York (N.Y.)—Case studies. 2. Criminal investigation—New York (N.Y.)—Case studies. I. Title.
HV7914.M53   1994
363.2'5'097471—dc20   93-42693
                                     CIP

First edition: April 1994

10 9 8 7 6 5 4 3 2 1

This book is dedicated to all

those members of the NYPD

who were killed or seriously injured

in the line of duty.

It is also dedicated to my father,

who would have loved to

have been a detective.

CONTENTS

AUTHOR'S NOTE

Because I have allowed these men and women to speak in their own voices, there may be some terms with which the reader is not familiar. The glossary at the end of the book explains these terms. An asterisk next to a name means that a pseudonym is being used to protect a person's identity.

ACKNOWLEDGEMENTS

This book could not have been written without the gener-
ous support and cooperation of the men and women o' t e
New York City Police Department's Detective Bureau no
so candidly told me their stories. I also owe a special d t of
gratitude to Detective First Grade Brian Mulherer ind
Lieutenant Raymond O'Donnel for giving me access   the
NYPD, because without their help this book would s l be
just an idea. Sergeant Jack Casey, Detective Second (tade
Christopher Johnson, and Detective First Grade Jack
McCann were invaluable in giving background inforn tion
about the world of New York City detectives. I also w it to
thank Donna Anderson and Dominick Palermo, assistant
curator, and John R. Podracy, curator, New York City Police
Department Museum, for their help with my research.

Jared Kieling, senior editor at St. Martin's Press, and
Ensley Eikenburg deserve nothing less than my heartfelt
gratitude for believing in this book and for continuing to
make me a better writer. I would also like to thank production editor Richard Klin, copy editor Lynne Wood, and Joe
Rinaldi for his commitment to publicizing this book.

•

My agent, Richard Curtis, deserves more appreciation than he knows, and I would like to thank him for his help with this book and with my writing career.

Barbara Gallay gets my deep appreciation for all her support and encouragement.

I would also like to thank the Bellevue crew: Mike Duffy and Bernard Salzman, for their help.

A special note of appreciation is due to my uncle Charles Byars.

As always, I would like to thank my mom and the staff of the Franklin Square Public Library for fostering my love of books.

INTRODUCTION

The woman who called 911 wouldn't give her name, but her complaint was serious enough to send a patrol car to check it out.

The central Brooklyn neighborhood had seen better times. Many of the three-story attached houses needed repair. A few had char marks on the bricks above the windows—a sign that fire was no stranger on this street. The cops in the patrol car spotted the new, four-door black Mercedes parked halfway up the block. Prior to the introduction of crack, the only way you would find a car like that in this neighborhood was if someone had stolen it because they needed a ride home.

A twenty-one-year-old black man, wearing an expensive leather coat and a green cotton turtleneck, was in the front seat of the Mercedes, indifferent to the cop knocking on the side window. He was also indifferent to the fact that he was sitting in a pool of his own blood.

The young police officer went back to his car and radioed the dispatcher to have the detectives respond to the scene forthwith.

•

New York is a city of crime. In 1990, its seven million people reported over half a million felonies: burglary, extortion, fraud, grand larceny, robbery, felonious assault, kidnapping, forcible rape, manslaughter, murder, and a host of other crimes, repeated over and over again like a malignant litany.

It is the perpetrators and victims of this gruesome catalog of cruelty, deceit, and greed who are dealt with on a daily basis by the members of the Detective Bureau of the New York Police Department (the NYPD). These detectives form the main line of resistance against the forces of chaos and injustice that threaten the city.

The Detective Bureau formally dates back to May 17, 1882, when the state legislature passed a bill authorizing the Board of Police to establish an investigative body within the New York City Police Department.

The first chief of detectives was Thomas J. Byrnes. He was an immigrant from Ireland who had the reputation of being a tough and innovative cop. Byrnes successfully curtailed crime in the Wall Street area by dramatically establishing a prohibited zone, marked by an invisible barrier called the "death line." He ordered his detectives to arrest anyone with a criminal record who crossed that line. Byrnes also created the morning lineup, so that detectives could view those arrested the night before and familiarize themselves with new faces.

Since its inception, the Detective Bureau of the NYPD has been involved in an incredible number of colorful and thrilling cases, many of which have received considerable attention in books, films, and the media. Some of the highlights include the Stanford White case, in which the famous architect who had designed the original Madison Square Garden was killed in a love triangle, and the Rubel's Ice House robbery of the 1930s, in which thieves armed with submachine guns stole almost a half million dollars and made their escape by motorboat. There was also the case of

Willie Sutton, who said that he robbed banks "because that's where the money is." In the 1950s George Metesky, better known as the "mad bomber," had the city terrorized until his capture. The city also knew terror when serial killer David Berkowitz, better known as Son of Sam, was using a .44 magnum pistol to kill couples parked in various lovers lanes. One Murph the Surf added a touch of glamour by stealing the Star of India diamond. More recently there have been cases such as the Central Park Jogger—a talented investment banker who was brutally gang-raped and left for dead by a bunch of young men who were out for a night of "wilding."

In 1992, the bureau had approximately 3728 third-grade, 415 second-grade, and 107 first-grade detectives assigned to various precinct detective units and special divisions. All wear the coveted gold shield. The detective bureau also has a number of sergeants and lieutenants who are part of the command structure of the police department.

A detective is the working level of the police department, according to Captain John Gorman, commanding officer of the Bronx district attorney's squad. The detective is the one who does the work. He or she is assigned a case, no matter how big, and if the police commissioner wants to know about that case he's got to talk to that detective, because that detective knows more about the case than anyone else and is responsible for it.

Prospective detectives undergo a lengthy selection process in which their work as patrol officers is carefully evaluated. All new members of the bureau are required to successfully complete the criminal investigation course, which is taught by experts from within the NYPD. Many detectives also take the chief of detectives' homicide investigators course, and other specialized courses. The NYPD is considered to have one of the most sophisticated detective training programs in the country.

Women now comprise an important part of the detective

•

bureau, although that was not always the case. In 1891, prompted by concern about the treatment of female prisoners in police precincts, Governor Hill signed a bill that mandated the hiring of police matrons, and the establishment of separate cells for men and women under arrest.

Gradually women took on other roles within the police department, but until 1965 women could only secure promotion through the detective division. Even though Isabella Goodwin had achieved the rank of detective first grade in 1912, very few women followed. Those who did often worked among women in situations where the presence of a man would be noticed. There was considerable resistance to giving the gold shield to policewomen. One policewoman, for example, served twelve years in the Missing Persons Bureau before being designated a third grade detective.

In 1950, ten women were third grade detectives, another ten were second grade, while only four women held the rank of detective first grade. Then in 1978, the Policewomen's Endowment Association and the police department entered into an agreement to increase the number of female detectives.

Since its inception the detective bureau has made a number of enhancements, in addition to integrating women into its areas of specialization. For example, the bureau started the Bomb Squad around 1910.

When the Bomb Squad was first organized, it was known as the "Italian Squad," because it handled so many bombs planted by the Black Hand, later to become the Mafia. At the time there were many immigrants coming in from Italy, and the Black Hand was extorting money from Italian merchants on the Lower East Side. When people wouldn't pay up, they might find one of these bombs in their stores.

In 1972, the Sex Crimes Liaison Unit was started to counter the low conviction rate the bureau had with these types of crimes.

•

Following a bungled bank robbery, which was made infamous in the film *Dog Day Afternoon,* the police department saw the need for a hostage negotiation unit. Fortunately, the detective bureau was able to build on work already started by Lieutenant Frank Bolz and Detective Harvey Schlossberg. After the riot at Attica State Prison, and the assassination of the Israeli athletes at the Munich Olympics, Lieutenant Bolz thought that an organized approach to hostage recovery would save lives. He contacted the director of the Munich police to find out what they had learned about the disaster. Then, with the help of Schlossberg, who was also a clinical psychologist, they formulated guidelines to establish a distinct capability within the bureau to deal with hostage situations.

The Technical Assistance Response Unit, TARU for short—grew in part out of the need of the Hostage Negotiation Unit to establish contact with "the person behind the door." The twenty-eight members of TARU also handle the bureau's electronic and photo surveillance needs. For example, in sting operations TARU will wire up stores with video cameras and microphones so they can be used as police fronts for buying stolen property.

In the 1990s, the men and women of the Detective Bureau of the NYPD are faced with the unprecedented challenge of solving crimes that occur with phenomenal frequency. What follows are the stories of how a unique group of men and women meet that challenge by waging a fascinating, dangerous around-the-clock war.

1

•

LIEUTENANT

PHIL

PANZARELLA

I n 1971 I was assigned to the Narcotics Division, which at that time was still in the Detective Bureau. I was a white-shield detective. It's like an embryo detective; you're really not a detective, but you are. You're working towards your gold shield.

I was only in narcotics a short time. But for the length of time that I was in narcotics, I worked on major violators. We had a book called "the top major violators," which was comprised of one hundred violators with their photos and pedigree. Most detectives would be familiar with the names of the guys at the front of the book, but for some reason I also looked at the names, which were in alphabetical order, at the back of the book.

One day in 1973, Detective—now lieutenant—George Pagan, and Detective Shelley Wasserman, and I were riding in George's private vehicle down Columbus Avenue, and as we made the turn on Seventy-first Street to go over to Broadway, we saw people looking down the block. And as we drove down the block we observed a male Hispanic bleeding profusely from the

•

head. And he was pointing towards this man, who was later identified as Martin Yamin, and he was yelling, "He's got a gun! He's got a gun!" in Spanish. Thank god George spoke Spanish.

We chased this individual into a building. We had our guns out. But when we got up to the third-floor landing, Mr. Yamin was standing partially over the guardrail pointing a revolver down at the three of us. He had a detective shield in his hand and a detective's gun—a "detective special"—in his other hand. We weren't really expecting it because we were on a charge up the staircase at the time. When I first saw him I think I had to change my underwear, to tell you the truth. We kept asking him, "Are you a cop? Are you a cop?" But he wouldn't answer us.

He gave us only a quarter of his body to shoot at. He leaned over the rail with the gun in his left hand instead of his right, but he couldn't pull the trigger back, and that prevented the gun from firing. And basically the only reason that we were alive or not seriously injured was the fact that Yamin had hit the complainant in the head with the gun. The complainant was collecting rents, and Mr. Yamin was going to rob him of the money. The man resisted, so Yamin hit him on top of the head with the gun—which pushed the trigger guard into the trigger.

George and I shot him. We were thankful that we were alive. Yamin was also still alive. We called for an ambulance.

He had on a wig, phony eyebrows, and a fake mustache. And as we searched him we retrieved an envelope that said MARTIN YAMIN.

I said, "George, this guy's a major violator. And we just shot him. Holy Christ!" Yamin's name was in the back of the "the major violators" book. Yamin was also doing a lot of ripoffs, and a lot of robberies. He had robbed an art dealer of 90,000 dollars a few weeks before. He had previously been a circuit-court judge, but had been arrested in

•

Baltimore. Apparently he had hired somebody to kill his wife. I think he was convicted, but he was released from prison. And somehow he was hooked into somebody in the diplomatic scene who was alleged to be bringing heroin into this country in the courier bags from Yugoslavia.

Several years later he died of a kidney infection.

Not long after my involvement with Yamin, I got promoted to detective, and was assigned to the Queens district attorney's office. And while I was there, we worked a lot of cases with Alcohol, Tobacco and Firearms.

The ATF guys were great people. They knew what they were doing and they always brought enough people to do the job. We get along very well with them.

I bought drugs and guns with them. One funny incident was where I bought pills from this individual. It was a cold night and I had a cold. I had a shabby coat on and my nose was running, so I did look like a junkie. Alex D'atri, an ATF agent, introduced me to him on Woodhaven Boulevard, and I made the buy.

He hadn't seen me in a suit and tie before, so subsequently when we locked him up he didn't believe it was me. He said, "No. No, that's not—I didn't sell to this guy, no way would I sell to this guy, this guy's a cop." And the guy until the day he was sentenced never believed that I was the guy he sold to. So I could get over on them.

Several times I also posed as a dealer buying illegal guns. I had one particular case with D'atri and Dominick Polifronte, where we bought over 150 guns right out of JFK Airport. Alex, who had done exclusively undercover, was excellent at this work. D'atri is still in the ATF. Now he is one of the top supervisors in Washington, D.C. Dominick is a supervisor in New Jersey.

The ATF had made a connection into JFK with several Italians over in the 106th precinct area in Queens, and we had made a deal to buy three cases of guns from them. I think they were .38's and .357 magnums.

•

We set up a meet at a particular house. I was to be the money man. The backup team was in a van half a block away.

The car pulled up, and the guys we were buying from got out and opened the trunk. We then opened one case to make sure that we had guns and not water pistols. I gave the signal for the backup team to move in.

The backup team consisted of Jay McGowan, the brother of Hugh McGowan, Jack Leonard, and several other detectives. To show that they weren't fooling around, they started running towards us with these shotguns in their hands.

One of the guys we were buying from had a .25 automatic in his belt, but he couldn't get rid of it. He kept jumping around, trying to get rid of the gun. I said, "Holy shit, they're going to shoot this guy." Then I said, "Our guys are going to kill me instead of killing this other guy." But the gun finally got through his pants. And it worked out okay—we seized three cases of guns. That was really a nice takedown—a nice arrest.

Undercover work is very dangerous. You have got to be able to play a very unique role, in that you have to watch what you say all the time, so that you don't talk like a cop. You have to talk like a street person, and that's hard.

When you're in that role as a bad guy you're thinking like a criminal. You can't think like a regular person. You have to be always conniving on these guys to gain their confidence. You have to be a little bit sleazy to get over on them, because they have to think that in dealing with them you're as sleazy as they are.

It's very hard to go away from what you've been doing your whole life and assume this new role, but you change right back when it's over. I wasn't doing it every day, so it's a little bit different for me than for someone who's in deep cover. Every day they make buys, so after a while it becomes second nature for them.

•

I wasn't exclusively an undercover, so I had to perform a little bit harder to make it work. I was a detective, but I always looked the youngest, so they always picked me. I bought drugs, I bought guns, I bought stolen checks, and I bought a whole credit card scam that led to a big investigation recovering better than 150 stolen cards.

We had an interesting case where we were going to purchase silencers. One of the individuals we were buying from wanted us to hit the people making the silencers, and then we would have the money and the goods. So I was brought in as the hit man. However, the guy didn't like me because of the way I had talked to him—he thought I was a little too wacky to do it. He thought I would do it right then and there in the restaurant. He said, "No, I don't want this guy. I don't trust this guy. He's liable to do me too."

So I had really gotten over on this guy. Sometimes you can really get into it and it throws them off because they're not really that high up on the criminal ladder and they get a little frightened. Basically, these are people on the fringes of organized crime. They are wanna-bes. They would do the little jobs instead of the heavy-duty ones. Very few of them get up to that so-called soldier level in organized crime.

On that case we just went and made the arrest rather than pursue it any further.

In 1977 we had a case involving a corrections officer who worked in the Queens House of Detention. We had an informant that turned us on to him. She was supposed to meet him every once in a while and he would get sex. In return she would deliver narcotics to him and he would take it in to her boyfriend.

On this particular night she had placed the drugs under the fender of a car parked by the Queens House of Detention, and the corrections officer had come out and taken it. Once he put it in his pocket we arrested him. He was convicted for possession of narcotics and he lost his job.

I worked in the DA's office from 1973 to 1982. Sometimes

•

it was good and sometimes it was bad. When I first got there I worked for Mike Armstrong, who was second in charge of the Knapp Commission. And the people that were there were very, very qualified. And we did a lot of cases. It was good working for Armstrong and for Judge Nick Ferrara. You were able to talk to them, and it was a good training facility.

I was still a young detective, and although I knew the law, I got to know the criminal justice system on the inside as far as how the courtroom, the lawyers, and the district attorneys operated, along with deepening my understanding of wiretaps and search warrants.

You come to realize that the justice system lacks because of the multitude of cases that they have to deal with. I'm not saying that every case can go to trial, but there's too much plea bargaining in cases. For example, they just started a program throughout the city where they will be establishing zones around where shootings have occurred to see if they can make gun arrests and make them stick, so that these people will be sentenced to heavy jail time. Now, you are supposed to get a mandatory year for the illegal possession of a gun, but a year is nothing. They do nine months and they're back out. They should do what the charge is. I mean if it's a D felony that's what they should serve—which means seven to fifteen years.

There just isn't enough judges, and there isn't enough jails. If they had more jails maybe crime would go down.

The criminal justice system has more or less tied the police officer's hands, in the sense that they've put all these safeguards of individual rights into effect. I'm not saying that individual rights shouldn't be safeguarded, but there came a time when they just went overboard with it. I mean, to the extent that if a defendant who we arrested had an open case, we couldn't talk to him about the case we arrested him for even though it had nothing to do with his prior case. Anything that you gleaned from talking to him

•

6

would be thrown out. If you made another case against him it too would be automatically thrown out. They recently reversed that decision when the Court of Appeals came down with the "Bing decision," so now you can talk to that individual even if he has an open case.

When we interview people, nobody gets hosed anymore and there's no more so-called "backroom justice." The good guy-bad guy routine does work at certain times in the interrogation. But you're dealing most of the time with career criminals, and they know how to play the game. So in order for you to get a confession, which I've gotten quite a number of, you have to appeal to their better sense. Everybody wants to tell you, it's the psychology of the thing. For example, we had someone as a serial rapist. But he couldn't tell us about the rapes right away because it's not a good crime. It's not a criminal's crime. It's a crime that nobody really wants to talk about, because in jail it's frowned upon. The other inmates' mentality is, it could have been my wife, or it could have been my sister, or it could have been my mother that was raped.

Nobody wants to go to jail for rape because most of the time they're segregated from the open population. And once they get in population they usually get the shit kicked out of them by the other inmates when they learn that he's in for a rape. And it's the same for a child abuser.

There's a certain code in criminality that you just don't do these type of crimes.

To get people to confess, you sit and you talk to them, and you try to relax them and you try to gain their confidence. Ninety percent of the time they want to tell you, they want to get it off their chest.

There is a certain amount of remorse. They realize that they're captured and there's nowhere to go. And at that particular time you're the only friend they have.

I've had people tell me before they confessed, "I can't live with what I gotta tell you." And there are others that I've sat

•

and talked with for four or five hours and they never told me anything. Sometimes the guy wants to go to the bathroom, and while he's doing his business he'll decide, all right, I think it's time I talked to you.

My position has always been that he didn't do anything to me, so I'm not going to do anything to him. We see a lot of people come in who think they're going to get beaten up by the detectives, or somehow they're going to be forced to tell. But we don't do that. You want to tell us, you tell us. We got the case already. The confession just makes the case stronger.

Usually we interview these guys in the station house, in an interview room. It's a very bland room. It just has a desk, a two-way mirror, a couple of chairs, and a bench. Nothing on the walls.

You have to gain their confidence. What usually happens is you'll give them cigarettes, coffee, or soda, and you relax them, and a good percentage of the time they'll tell you what you want to know. They don't always tell you the truth in a confession. They'll give you bits and pieces. A lot of times they'll tell on each other. If you have one, they'll always say the other guy did the shooting. "I was just there."

When you get the other one, he will say, "Well, I didn't do the shooting, he did it." And that's the way it works out most of the time when you have two or three different players—particularly in the game of homicide.

What was bad about working in the DA's office is that after a while you become stale, especially if the DA doesn't want to do too much investigation of crime in his borough.

In 1981, Richard Konzi stuck up a drugstore on Metropolitan Avenue, in Queens, and was running down Union Turnpike. At that time, I was with a detective, who is now a lieutenant assigned to Mayor Dinkins's security, Alicia Parker. We saw him running while he was discarding his clothes. I said, "Alicia, something's wrong here. That guy has done something. I don't understand why he's doing this." We made a U-turn and came back around. But he made us—he saw that we were police. So he ran over to a car stopped at a traffic light and dragged this woman out and threw her on the ground. Then he got in the car. I approached him and I told him, "don't move." I started fighting with him to pull him out of the car. He was much, much bigger than I was. At one point he grabbed the barrel of my revolver and we were struggling for the gun. He was pointing it at me now, and he started pulling me into the car. I was halfway in the car. He took one hand off the revolver and put the car in gear. The car jerked. The gun went off and struck him in the chest. He died. He fell forward and the car proceeded about a block and crashed into two or three parked cars.

Even though I had been in several shootings before, it took a half an hour just to get the adrenaline down and to get my composure. At the time, even though it is a bad scene, you're overjoyed that nothing happened to you. Like I've told people many, many times, "I'm the guy going home and he's not. Unfortunately, he caused his own demise, not me."

The complainant that he robbed was okay. They got him out of the drugstore, and he came and made the identification at the scene.

A lot of times what people don't realize is that you're so hyper after it happens. They criticize the department for sending you right after a shooting to a hospital to get checked out. I truly believe it's a good thing because you're so emotional at that point, and it's not every day you fire your gun. I fired my gun quite a bit in the early part of my career. It's not a nice feeling to kill somebody. You think about it and believe me, you dream about it. Absolutely.

I shot a guy in 1969 in the 30th precinct in Manhattan. What had happened was two drug dealers were shooting at each other, and a 26th precinct car had gotten in between

•

them, and they had called a 10-13 on themselves. This is early in the morning, two-ish, or somewhere around there.

Donnie McIntyre, who was my partner, and I responded down Broadway to 141st Street. A civilian I knew told me, "Phil, Phil he went that way, he's got a gun." We went back up Broadway the wrong way. But we had lost him. So we started down 144th Street towards Riverside Drive. It's a one-way street. I was driving. I had my revolver out. With my peripheral vision I caught a glimpse of this individual leaning over the hood of a car pointing a .45 at us. So I put the revolver up to the glass and shot through the windshield of the radio car.

The bullet split in half. One half went god-knows-where and the other half went out and hit him in the nose. And he dropped the .45 caliber automatic, which was loaded. We got out of the car and handcuffed him and took him into the precinct. We were really hyper because this was a very dangerous situation.

I had a captain by the name of William Lakeman, who was there talking to a lieutenant, Fred McBride. Now, I owe a great deal to Freddie McBride for teaching me how to be a police officer, and how to apply the laws in the proper way. But he was a yeller and screamer and everybody feared him. I didn't fear him because I stood up. If you stood up to him, he'd take care of you, but if you were a namby-pamby type person, he'd get on you because he wanted to make you a better policeman. His only concern was that you didn't get hurt in the street. And being that I made a large quantity of arrests, I was always dealing with him. And he'd point out the mistakes. He was very gruff and a lot of people didn't understand that was just his nature. But I loved him. I love him to this day. Freddie McBride, in a sense, was like my guardian angel on the job. He'd always berate me when I was wrong, but I knew in reality he was trying to make me a better policeman.

The thing was that I had to go and tell him that I just blew

•

the radio-car window out from inside. So I go over and I said, "Lou, I have to talk to you about something."

He said, "Yeah, take it upstairs."

"I have a very important thing to tell you."

"Well, I can't talk to you now. They want you to go back to the scene."

So I get a hold of McIntyre and we go back to the scene, where another civilian tells me, "Phillie"—they used to call me Phillie because I always smoked cigars—"see that guy who's up in the third-floor window, yelling and screaming? He's the other guy that was shooting."

Now the guy up in the window has no clothes on. He's telling the police the man they are looking for went to Riverside Drive, and he's pointing down to Riverside Drive.

So we go up and we have a conversation with him. We tell him, "Hey, we know you're the other guy, so get dressed." He takes us to a common bathroom, and we find a loaded .9 mm pistol.

But now I have to come back to the precinct and tell Lieutenant McBride this story about what actually happened.

He gets all upset. He goes, "Now you did it! You know, this is unbelievable; every night it's unbelievable with you. It's an adventure all the time."

He goes outside and checks the hole. Then he tells the captain. Then I have to explain to Captain Lakeman what happened. What transpired was these two Colombians were shooting at each other. The one Colombian that was going to shoot us had killed an individual four hours before with this same weapon on 155th Street and Broadway, in a garage. So it worked out very, very well for us.

Later I had to testify in front of the grand jury. I testified after every shooting I was involved in, and I didn't do anything wrong. I followed procedure every time my life was in danger. Although it's really not a nice feeling to have to shoot somebody, it's part of the job, and it's something you have to live with.

•

You dream about it, and in a sense you relive it. I mean, you'll wake up in a cold sweat. Then you sit and you think about it for a while. You got to convince yourself that this is what you had to do, and you're here and they're not, unfortunately.

You'll always find that when you have to go to the grand jury you remember a lot more facts the next day, and the next day after that. Because you're so hyper at the scene you're just focusing on that one part of him pointing the gun at you, or him shooting at you. And, unfortunately, a lot of people don't realize the psychological stress that you're under at that particular point.

Afterwards, you get the shakes. You'll be sitting down and something will trigger it. Most of the time it's not at work because your mind's preoccupied with what you're doing at work. But you'll be home, maybe reading a mystery—and something will trigger it off—like a similar incident happening in a cop novel. And you just have to stop and get a hold of yourself and put it out of your mind.

I always wanted to do homicides, and the DA's office doesn't do homicides. So I left the DA's office and went to the 113th squad in March of 1982.

We handled everything from missing persons to homicide.

In 1982, we had two separate homicides in Rochdale Village, a middle class, black and Hispanic apartment complex. One of the victims was Dunne Lewis, a senior citizen. The other was a seventeen-year-old girl by the name of Laura Evelyn.

Dunne Lewis had a domestic who helped her get around. Usually the domestic would take her down to sit on a bench on the grounds of the complex, and then bring her back upstairs when she was ready, but it happened to be a nice day, Dunne wanted to stay out, and the domestic had somewhere to go.

Dunne would wear a lot of costume jewelry, including

•

two big rings on her fingers. And these two·individuals happened to see her on the one day when the domestic left early.

Dunne eventually went up to her apartment, and as she was opening the door these two pushed her in. They tied her up and they ransacked the apartment. They got a TV, a couple of small items, and the costume jewelry. They thought they had a big score because of her rings. They stuffed a stocking in her mouth and tied a ligature to hold it in place. She gagged on the ligature and died. This was on a Friday afternoon.

I got the case on a Saturday afternoon. A few days later Laura Evelyn was raped and thrown nude off the thirteen-story roof.

Myself and several detectives, Bobby Houlihan and Larry Andrews from the 113th squad, worked on the Dunne Lewis case. Two other detectives, Ray Diaz and Jack McNicholas, worked on Laura Evelyn. And both cases meshed because of the neighborhood people that we interviewed were basically the same people.

Anthony Riggins was the first suspect that we came up with. Someone had seen him around the complex on the afternoon that Dunne Lewis was killed. He had lived in Rochdale, but was kicked out by his mother, and although she subsequently moved away he continually frequented the complex—hiding throughout the buildings. We had given a picture of him to the Rochdale police. And the Rochdale police had snapped him up.

We spoke to Anthony for a long time. Then we took him down to the polygraph unit. Detective Justin Peters determined that he was deceptive. But he finally told the detective that was giving the polygraph test, "I want to talk to Sundance and I'll tell him."

Sundance was a nickname that was given to me by a detective by the name of Mike Falciano. And it just stuck.

•

There are still people in the street that really don't know my name; they just refer to me as Sundance.

Anthony Riggins gave me a confession that led us to an individual by the name of Ellis Walker.

Ellis Walker lived in Far Rockaway with his grandparents. Ellis was brought to the 113th squad by Detective Jerry Shevlin and several detectives from the Homicide Squad. Jerry was one of the best detectives I ever worked with. Ellis eventually told us basically the same story that Riggins had told us. But he had little knowledge about the murder of Laura Evelyn.

We wound up looking for an individual by the name of Barry Coka. Barry was well-known to the 113th squad. He came in and talked to us on several occasions, and eventually confessed that he did it along with three others who we already had a good idea about from the investigation.

Laura, probably knowing she had few choices, had made a deal with one of her assailants just before she died. "If I let you do me once I can go and I don't have to do everybody else." But then what happened was after the first individual had finished raping her, the other individuals decided that they were going to rape her and she wouldn't stand for that. So she said, "I'm going to tell." And they picked her up and threw her thirteen floors to her death.

Laura came from a very nice family. She was a very nice little girl. A very pleasant individual, who was very well liked throughout the community.

We were able to solve those cases with the cooperation of the people from the Rochdale community. And we were all honored at an awards ceremony by the Rochdale community council.

One of Laura Evelyn's killers was prosecuted. We're still pursuing the other three. We know who they are, but with what we have so far we could never prove it in court. Unfortunately, they're still out there. They've been arrested a number of times since then for other crimes, but nobody's

•

come forward to place them where we could actually prosecute them and win the case. So we'll wait it out.

There are four things that solve homicides: crime scene, interviews, records, and surveillance. And those four things show up in practically every homicide. You're almost always going to have a crime scene. You have to start somewhere where the body was found: that's a crime scene. This was taught to me by the best detective supervisor in the police department, Lieutenant Dan Kelly.

At the crime scene we basically look at the body and where the body is located. You recover spent shells, you recover weapons, you recover blood, and all kinds of forensic evidence that will come into play down the road once you got a suspect.

When I say interviews, it means that you basically do a canvass of the area to see if anybody saw it, or anybody knows the individual. You can get background information. Also the interviews are conducted once you get the suspect in. And you try and pin down his alibis.

Records, of course, help when you are doing background checks on individuals, the victim, and any suspects.

Surveillance is basically the observation and apprehension of the individual who did this murder. Surveillances go on for varying lengths of time. For example, when police officer Scott Gadell was murdered in Rockaway, Queens, we worked almost sixty days on the case before we were able to apprehend the individual who did it. It involved numerous surveillances, and we pretty much knew who it was, going into the second or third day.

Scott Gadell was a young police officer in the 101st precinct. He responded to a radio run to—"meet a complainant." And when he met the complainant the complainant informed him that he was shot at by a man by the name of Robert "Darby" Ralston. But Ralston had taken off and went to another location. Scott Gadell, with his partner, went to this other location, and when they got there some-

•

one pointed Ralston out. Ralston ran to the back of a two-family house. Officer Gadell pursued him. And that was when it happened.

When we arrested Darby Ralston, two months later, he gave us a video confession, and he explained to me and the other detectives why he shot Scott Gadell. What had happened was when Gadell ran after him there was an exchange of fire. But Scott had run out of ammunition and was reloading. Now Ralston, from watching TV, thought that the other policeman had a fully loaded gun and would be on the other side of the building waiting for him to come that way, and he'd rather face the officer that was reloading. So there was only one way out for him. In reality he could have gone out the other side, and Scott Gadell would probably be alive today, since the other policeman stayed with the complainant out in front. While Scott was reloading his gun, Ralston went by him shooting his .9 mm automatic. The wounds were fatal to Scott. When Ralston came out front the other policeman shot at him. But Ralston ran and got away.

I didn't get in until the next day, and at that time I was assigned to Queens Sex Crimes. Chief Borelli, who is now the chief of detectives, was the chief of Queens detectives, and he formed a task force. I was assigned to it under Lieutenant Dan Kelly. We worked that investigation pursuing this guy from borough to borough. We knew who he was from the original complainant. Well, we pursued him through his haunts, through his family, through a car that he had.

We developed other informants along the way—people that wanted to give him up. We were on top of them. We were constantly hindering them in their drug business and knocking on their door, and nobody wants the police every hour knocking on your door. They wanted to get the pressure off of themselves, so they were anxious to get him off the street.

•

You can't take it as a personal affront. But you have to be realistic about it. It's not just another case. You will take a little bit more chance in trying to make the apprehension.

In the end we had received a tip, and detectives had gone to a location and spoke to a couple of people. They said he was there but he had left. The next day, the detectives went back to that location—it was a refurbished building. A detective noticed something different about the particular floor that he was supposed to be on. The window was open and the curtains were flying out. Apparently this individual that we wanted looked out the window, saw the detectives, and then ran out onto the fire escape. They ran up after him and he was apprehended.

A good percentage of the crimes are solved by speaking to people. If you interview people, and you get their trust and they're looking for help in their own case, you'll get the information needed to solve cases.

You get most of your information from street people. You're not going to get it from a priest or a minister. And you have to build your reputation with them that you're an honest guy, you're trustworthy. I get a great deal of information on the street because of the fact that my reputation is, "If he locks you up he doesn't go to court and lie on you."

If you are a detective that looks down on these people you will get nothing. But as long as you treat them with a certain amount of respect, you'll get that respect back. And they'll tell each other. Everybody knows everybody else in the street. And if a guy's down on his luck maybe you'll give him five or ten dollars. I've put people in drug-rehab programs and it's come back to me tenfold.

The worst thing you can do in the street is be macho. If you come off as a hardass in the street, you're never going to get the respect that you need to be successful.

In the fall of 1987 I was working in the Queens Homicide Squad and I had a case involving a woman named Mildred

Green. She was giving background information to the grand jury as to a shoot-out between drug dealers. But some individual who was testifying on his own behalf to the grand jury saw her there. He knew her from the neighborhood, and he told these drug dealers that she was the one that was testifying against them. She was consequently killed.

I knew Mildred Green. She was a very nice woman. She always was a help to the police. She was a taxi dispatcher. And taxi drivers would have fender benders and leave the scene, but we would get their license-plate number, and we'd call up Mildred and ask her to tell the guy to come in, and we'd give him a summons for leaving the scene. And you'd see her in the street on Sunday going to church or wherever, and she'd always wave to you.

Detective Ronnie Waddel and myself had an informant, early on in the investigations, who was privy to a conversation. This informant was originally brought in on the drug warrant, and he gave it up.

We learned that several possible suspects in Mildred's murder had stayed at a hotel in Nassau County. Detectives went to the hotel. They got the phone records, and we learned that a call was made from their room. Once we had a phone number we had an address. We went to that address to find out why they called there.

We knocked on the front door and we announced ourselves as the police. A young lady opened both doors and there's a house full of little kids. I told her I was a sergeant from Queens Homicide and could we come in. She said "yes."

I was going to show her a picture of one of the individuals we were looking for, a man by the name of Wadell Winston, when he steps forward from the dining area. He sees us and now the chase is on. Winston runs down a darkened staircase into a room. And as we're just about catching up to

•

18

him, he's reaching for a .9 mm machine pistol, though we didn't know it was there at the time.

We knock him down onto a mattress on the floor. We're fighting with him now, and it's really a fierce struggle. Winston is very well built, he's six-two, 190 pounds, and he's fighting. I just happen to look up and I'm yelling, "There's a gun, Ronnie! There's a gun, there's a gun!" This guy's putting up some struggle. We're on the floor with him in suits and ties with no vests on because we weren't prepared. We got caught with our pants down in the sense that we were only doing a canvass to check out a lead.

We had other detectives in the area who had seen us go into the house but hadn't seen us come out. So they came in, thank god.

I'm yelling, "There's a gun, there's a gun!" Eventually a detective by the name of Tom Healy comes down the stairs and I tell him, "Tommy, Tommy there's a gun! There's a gun on the TV!" There was also a clip in the bed for the gun, with thirty-some odd rounds in it. Tommy secured the gun, and we were able to secure Winston.

What we didn't know was that there was another individual in the shower. But by this time we had three or four detectives in the house. They take him out of the shower, and as they're getting him dressed there's a shotgun on the bed under his clothes. Underneath the bed there's a .45 caliber machine gun.

The other detectives look around upstairs and they find a loaded .357 Magnum and another loaded .9 mm pistol by a window facing the street. Apparently Winston had taught the girls in the house how to use these weapons if the police came.

What had happened was we had relaxed because there were so many kids in the house and we didn't know who was in there at the time. That's why we weren't looking for any gun plays.

Another .9 mm was in a pocketbook that we recovered

•

much later on during a search. Thank god there wasn't shooting, because there were three little children ranging from a year to about four years old in the residence.

Wadell Winston and several others were eventually convicted for Mildred Green's murder.

The apprehension is the most critical part of any investigation. And if you don't have a plan you're going to mess up and you're going to get hurt, or you're going to get somebody hurt, or the individual that you are trying to apprehend is going to get away, and you don't want to see any of that.

You want as many people as possible to cut off escape routes and as a show of force.

We are the homicide squad for the entire borough of Queens. We assist the PDUs with the investigation of murders. Whatever they need, that's what we do, including the provision of extra manpower. We're like the chief's army. We do a lot of canvasses and apprehensions.

The guys in the PDUs get a little disgruntled with us, because a good part of the time we're going to be the ones apprehending people. Hopefully, somebody in the PDU who has the case will be with us. But you can't always have a detective that's working in a Queens PDU go to Brooklyn, because if something else happens in Queens, then there's nobody there to investigate that particular crime. So a lot of the time, we will go to Brooklyn, the Bronx, Nassau or even somewhere in Queens itself. We'll do a surveillance for eight, ten, twelve hours. The PDU detective can't sit in that van with us for all that time while he's still catching cases, but we can be dedicated to one investigation.

When an apprehension is going down, what I try to do is get that suspect more or less confined to one area. When I say *confined* I mean that if he's in the street I'll wait until he walks into a store, or until he sits in a car, rather than just have a foot chase.

A good percentage of the people that are in my unit are a

little bit older; we can't run anymore. It's very similar to that episode of "Miami Vice" when Don Johnson finally catches up to this guy and pukes all over him. Well, I don't think any of us can run that far, but we'd probably be puking anyway. That chase was so realistic, and that's exactly what happens ninety percent of the time, if you're fortunate enough to catch the individual when he stumbles, or falls, or runs into a car, or something.

I just won't take anybody who's in a moving car due to the fact that innocent people can really get hurt in that situation. We try to limit the risk, although there's going to be situations where you have to do it. But, my rule of thumb is I don't want it done that way.

I've done a lot of apprehensions, that's my forte. I have a thing I call the five P's: proper planning prevents poor performance. I've worked a lot of big cases taking people down and nobody's gotten hurt, thank god. I'm very careful and meticulous in planning what I do. And it's my responsibility as a supervisor to make sure that nobody gets hurt. I don't want to live with that for the rest of my life, that somebody got hurt because I made a stupid, or silly mistake. I'll back off before I risk anybody getting hurt.

What I'm looking for is the advantage that I'm going to have over the individual I'm trying to apprehend, whether it be through confinement or a situation where I'm in control and he's not. He's at a loss.

I'll give you an example. We had a notorious case about two years ago, where a guy ran over someone called the "Balloon Man." He was an old-timer who sold balloons on Crossbay Boulevard. And what happened was an individual, I think his name was Prince Shabazz, had shot a man in the Rockaway section of Queens, then stole a car. He went through a roadblock on the Rockaway Bridge, then he ran into a car at a light, which in turn struck the balloon man and killed him. Prince got out of that vehicle and ran into a creek. He then swam across the creek. This guy was in top

•

shape. When he got on the other side of the creek he assaulted two or three police officers.

They finally got him cuffed. Then they took him to the 106th precinct. However, he didn't make court, so he went to the 110th precinct, where he was lodged for the night. He fagazead a desk officer into having him taken to the hospital because he had chest pains. And the desk officer, not knowing what had transpired before, sent him with only one police officer.

The doctor in Elmhurst General told the cop to take his cuffs off. The officer got one cuff off. Then Prince clocked him and knocked him down. Prince runs out of the hospital, leaps a ten-foot fence with barbed wire, breaks into a residence, and terrorizes the poor guy who lives there. Eventually he makes his way back to the 105th area in Queens over on Merrick Boulevard.

Now we have an escaped prisoner. So we go out and look for him. We do a little bit of investigation and go over to his mother's house. He calls his mother's house while we are there. He also calls his girlfriend. Then he calls some other people. Finally we pinpoint where he's making the phone calls from. He's at 228th Street and Merrick Boulevard.

We shoot up there. But he made us right away. Now the chase is on. This is why I say you have to be able to use the advantage. If we didn't go straight at him we might have gotten him right then and there.

He ran to a backyard. Then he turned on one of our officers. The officer thought he had a gun and fired two rounds at him. But he got away again.

We get emergency service and we search for two or three hours. The chief of patrol tells us, "You stay out there until you get him." So we situate the cars and we do a little bit of planning. Myself and another detective go to a 7-Eleven. I get a Slurpee and he gets a coffee. We're just riding around. It's 5:00 in the morning. He'd been missing since 2:00 P.M. So we go down the street where we last saw him, and here

•

he comes walking out of an alleyway. The detective says, "There he is! There he is!"

I said, "Okay, calm down."

I'm driving the car. The detective wants to get out. I said, "Don't get out of the car, because we're going to have another chase." This is where experience comes in. So I roll up on Prince. When he's no more than three feet away from us I roll down the window. I say, "Hey Prince. You know, you're really breaking my balls here tonight. For Christ's sake I could have been home in bed. I could have had a cocktail or two with the guys. Hey, stop fucking around and get in the car, all right?"

So he opens the back door. Now the detective again wants to get out of the car. I said to him, "Don't get out of the car."

Prince says, "Officer, there's a jacket in the backseat."

"It's my jacket." I reach back and pull it to the front.

Prince then gets in; and I say to him, "boy, you must be fucking tired. You look like a drenched rat." He had been lying in the grass, and in the mud. I said, "Here, you better drink some of this Slurpee." He drinks the Slurpee, and we talked for a little while. "You know, no one's going to bother you." I'm trying to gain his confidence. I tell him, "listen, you caused us a lot of problems here. The chief is pissed off, and I'm a little disturbed. You know, we got to bring you to the precinct."

"Yeah, I know."

"Now don't get overly upset about this. But we have got to handcuff you." Then the detective gets out, gets in the backseat and handcuffs him.

We get into the precinct. I'm very brash. That's the way I am, I don't give a fuck, I'm so happy this is over. I walk in and I always have a cigar in my mouth. It's 5:00 in the morning and I've got sunglasses on.

I walk into the squad, and I sit down. The detective then

•

brings our prisoner into the room. The detective captain asks me, "Who's that?"

"That's Prince."

But he says, "bullshit."

"That's him." Then I go through the whole story of how we got him.

The captain again says, "bullshit." Then he goes and tells the story to this old-time Irish inspector, who probably didn't like detectives too much anyway.

I'm sitting outside. I've got my feet up on the desk, and I'm smoking my cigar, when the captain calls me in. I go back into his office and there's the captain and this inspector who's got a real Irish brogue. He tells me to tell him the story. So I tell him the whole story.

"How the hell are you going to make me believe this bullshit story?"

"It's not bullshit, Inspector, this is what actually happened."

"Get out!" Then he calls the detective in.

The detective tells him, "The sergeant told me 'don't get out of the car. Because he's going to run again, and I can't catch him and you can't catch him.' He just pulled up and told him to get in the fucking car and stop the bullshit."

"You're full of shit. You're as full of shit as the goddamn sergeant out there smoking that goddamn cigar. Get out!"

The captain says to the inspector, "This is one of my most experienced sergeants. He's made a lot of apprehensions. He knows how to do this."

The inspector says, "Get me the perp."

So the perp goes in. We've already given him a shower and a change of clothes, and he's now feeling relaxed. He sits down and starts telling the inspector the story. He finishes the story and he's waiting for us to take him out. I'm sitting outside by the window.

The inspector then starts yelling and screaming at the captain. "That goddamn sergeant comes in here bullshit-

•

ting me. Then the detective comes in and he verifies that bullshit story the sergeant made up. And not only that, but the goddamn perp comes in here and now he tells me the same bullshit. They're all full of shit. It couldn't happen. The man committed eight crimes in twenty-four fucking hours, and you people expect me to believe that this asshole outside with the cigar told him to get in the goddamn car and he just got in? They were shooting at him. They chased him. He ran over a man. He shot another man. He stole a car. He beat up policemen, and you expect me to believe this—this bullshit."

This went on for days. And every day they'd call me up and say, "Listen Phillie, is this what really happened?"

"Why would I make up a story like this?"

Finally they accepted my story, although they couldn't believe that this would actually transpire because of the multitude of crimes that this guy committed. But the guy was dragging. He was worn out, and he had nowhere to go.

You have to get a feel for each situation, and it only comes with experience. Because each situation is different. Detectives have been taking people off the streets for years, without getting hurt, only because they're smarter than the individuals they apprehend. If you plan it right and you play the cards, it is to your advantage. You don't take that chance of getting hurt, or go with the notion that we've got to get him right now. You can always come back tomorrow. If he's there today, chances are that he'll be there tomorrow. Also, if you can't take him alone, get help and you'll be successful. Nobody gets hurt and everybody goes home.

There are guys who try to macho it. You'll see that quite often. They don't want help, and those are the guys that fail. Those are the guys that people get away on. And you can get hurt chasing a guy through the backyards. You can rip your suit, or damage your shoes, or whatever. And the city's not going to give you money to replace them.

Edward Byrne was a young police officer who was exe-

•

cuted in South Jamaica, Queens, in the 103rd precinct, in February 1988. He was guarding the house of a man by the name of Arjune, who had made complaints about drug dealers in the neighborhood. They had firebombed his house on two separate occasions, so the department put a radio car there.

The drug dealers were going to retaliate for the interference in their business, and as a result they had a plan to kill a police officer in uniform. They picked that location because the incidents at Arjune's house started the pressure on them. They snuck up on Eddie Byrne and shot him.

In our investigation we received a lot of help from the community in South Jamaica. Basically we had people calling us an hour later with tips; it could be this guy, it could be that guy, I saw this, I saw that. Through the phone calls and everything else, we were able to piece things together. We went to the house of an individual by the name of Scott Cobb.

Scott Cobb's mother was cooperative, in that she wanted her son to turn himself in. Scott called her, and we were able to trace the call to a house in Queens Village.

I was dispatched by Lt. Dan Kelly, who was my boss at the time in Queens Homicide, to survey the area and to see what kind of house it was.

The key to apprehending somebody in a residence is to be allowed in. Once you get in then you can control the situation and it's your house now. If the guy's there, he's yours, but you don't let your guard down in case he decides to take a shot at you. Somebody innocent could get hurt.

When I got to the street where the house was, I only had two detectives with me, Eddie Granshaw and Richie Sica. In my opinion I couldn't do a good surveillance with only two people, so I called Lt. Kelly and asked him to send me more manpower. He sent me Nick Rodelli and Joey Cialione from the Robbery Squad.

I was giving them instruction on how to surveil the block,

•

and what I wanted them to do, and I wanted everybody to have a vest on.

All of a sudden, Scott Cobb walks out of the house. We roll up on him. This is a cop killer, so we have to take him now. We don't have a choice in letting him go. He puts up a struggle. He's a big kid. We knock him down and handcuff him. As we start to put him in the radio car, Todd Scott, who is one of the three other people we were looking to apprehend, opened the side door, where Cobb had just exited.

I didn't know who it was. All I saw was a black male in a Refrigerator Perry football jersey. But one of the detectives yells, "That's him! That's Todd, that's Todd!"

Todd closes the door.

I said, "Well, get him."

They ran to the door and forced it open. They go down into the basement. They find him hiding in a closet and take him out. At this time, other detectives had arrived, and we cordoned off the area.

We took them both back to the 105th precinct in Queens. They were questioned and they confessed.

The next morning, another individual surrendered with his grandmother, and the fourth individual was already under arrest for another crime on a warrant.

But there was somebody else involved in this case, a man by the name of Pappy Mason, who was the drug kingpin of that area. He was in jail at the time Byrne was murdered. But he was the cause of police officer Byrne being killed—it was done on his orders. He was convicted in federal court for his involvement in Byrne's homicide.

It just shows that sometimes you get caught off guard. I didn't have time to plan, because we had just gotten out there to do a surveillance. We were just going to see who was going in and out of the house. We would make a later decision with the bosses to see what we were going to do about it. But that's how that went down. Thank god, it went down smooth.

•

One of the most difficult cases for us to solve involved bodies found in black garbage bags, which we did not long ago. A drug faction rubbed out six or seven Colombians, bagged them up and spread them out all through South Jamaica.

Normally when you have a homicide you have somewhere to go. You have someplace to canvass. If there's a shooting in the street and there's a building there, you can go and ask people in the building, and a good percentage of the time they'll know who the victim is. When you don't have a victim's identity, you don't have anyplace to start. You have a bag with a body, and that's it. You have to identify the individual first before you can go anywhere with it, and sometimes we don't identify people for months, if ever. There are other cases I know of where we still haven't identified the individual because of lack of fingerprints on file, or they were so badly decomposed we couldn't get prints. Your crime scene produces absolutely nothing for you on what we call a "dump job" where they'll kill somebody, say in the Bronx, and they'll dump them in Queens or another borough. And, without somebody helping you along the way, telling you, hey, I know that this body was dumped here, you're at a standstill. And most of the time the case goes unsolved.

We set up a joint investigation with the housing police and a special task force that I was in charge of. It was a five-man task force, and it emanated out of the Basily projects in the 113th precinct in Queens. The 113 detectives had worked on it, and we had incorporated them into the task force.

An informant we had spoken to gave us direction. And all you ask for is some kind of direction to go in.

The informant had been arrested for attempted murder of a police officer. I had arrested him in 1982, on attempted murder of a store owner, when I was a detective in the 113th, and I knew his whole family. He'd been convicted and sentenced and he got out of jail several years later. But when he was arrested this time, he reached out for me through the housing police, and I went and interviewed him. And I got the district attorney to formulate a package for him, so that he would go to jail, but if he helped us he would serve less time. Another reason he helped us was the fact that during the four or five months I was originally pursuing him I would go to his mother's house, and I never ripped her house apart. I knew his sisters and I always spoke nice to them. I always told them I have to come in and look around. And they would let me in and we became friends. And when I subsequently arrested him, even though I testified against him and put him in jail, he still trusted me. Like I explained earlier, it's your reputation in the street, who can I talk to, who can I trust.

Through his information and other investigative tactics that we use, we were able to apprehend the drug faction for the plastic bag murders.

Ultimately, we cleared forty-seven homicides throughout four boroughs in the last nineteen months. These all involved drug people.

Through my informant, we just kept leapfrogging into different crime factions. They were people that needed help, that wanted to talk to us, that felt they were wronged by their organization, or they were doing too much time and the other people were out in the street, and their families weren't being taken care of, or they just had a disagreement with the overall person who was running it and they were cut out of the money. And we were able to establish a network throughout the correctional system so that if people in jail wanted to talk to us we would go upstate and talk to them. We started on November fourth of 1989, and we have been quite successful.

In the drug world it's a here today, gone tomorrow-type thing. You're on top of the heap, but if you step on the wrong toes you could be gone tomorrow. The more money

•

29

that they make, the more money they want. It becomes a territorial thing like in the jungle. And that's basically what it is, survival of the fittest. Who's got the most guns to kill the other. And if you're doing good on one side of the street and I'm not doing good on my side, I take you out; now I have that side of the street to work, plus my side.

The money goes for showing off: Cars, gold jewelry, sneakers, eight-hundred dollar leather jackets, clothes for their family. They live high off the hog for a certain amount of time. A new faction comes in, or if you're smart enough and somebody tells you, "hey, it's over, I want this corner or I'm going to kill you," you leave. If you don't leave they shoot you. And now it's their corner and they live high off the hog for a certain amount of time. Then either they go to jail, get killed, or get crippled. And that's the way it works.

A good detective wants to accept the challenge of making this case work. Of saying, "Hey, I had a part in this case and I solved it." It's becoming part of a team. No one detective solves a homicide. And unless you work with a team as a team, you won't be successful. Yeah, you'll get the one or two cases where a detective will persevere and he will solve that case by himself. But he wasn't the first officer on the scene. He didn't do the crime scene. He didn't do the canvass. He didn't do every interview in the case. Okay, he may run with it for a length of time by himself and be successful, but no one is successful in homicide unless you work as a team. You have to have a partner to interview somebody, you have to have a partner to pick the guy up. There are no supermen. There are no Kojaks, there are no Columbos, although a lot of stuff that we do they copy for television.

Yeah, we do cases Columbo-style. All of Columbo's cases involve circumstantial evidence; very rarely does he get a case that is solid enough on probable cause to make an arrest and prosecute it.

A lot of people were under the impression that because a

•

detective makes an arrest in the homicide case it stops there. That's just the beginning of the investigation in reality, because you have to prepare this case to go to a grand jury, then to a hearing, and finally to go to a trial and convict him. It's no good arresting somebody just to arrest him and clear the case—you have to convict him. If you don't convict him, you lost the case. You solved it but you didn't solve it. And that's where the satisfaction comes in—you went to court, you testified and you got him off the street. A guy who did hurt somebody, whether it be a drug homicide or an innocent-victim homicide.

Several times during my years of experience we have had a murder suspect in the interview room, and a young police officer will come up and say, "let me see the murderer."

"Why do you want to see?"

"I want to see what a murderer looks like."

I say, "It could be you, me, your father, your mother, your brother, your sister, any one of us could be a murderer at any time. It has to do with triggering a person into a rage to do something like this. Or boxing a person in a corner where there's no out for him."

A lot of times you'll find murder-suicides in families where either a wife's been cheating or a husband has been cheating, or you'll find a young person who is using drugs will kill his mother and father and blame it on satanic cults or whatever, when in reality he's just pissed off because he didn't get a brand new car, or they cut his allowance down to the bare minimum because they know he's using drugs and squandering the money, or where an individual kills another individual based on the fact that the victim can identify him. For example, a male will have sex with an underage girl and she says, "I'm going to tell on you," or he's been "playing doctor" with her for a number of years and now she's a little bit older, and he's scared that she's going to tell mommy and daddy. And in order to prevent this he'll kill her. These cases can involve an uncle, or a stepbrother,

•

or even a brother. And you get these type of homicides in what you call affluent neighborhoods. They're treated like any other homicide. They're probably a little bit easier to solve than the street homicides, in that you have a direction to go in because most of the time they involve people that are known to each other over a number of years.

Yeah, in reality there are homicides and there are homicides. And you do work harder on victim homicides. Not that the drug-dealing homicides are worked on any less. But you put a little bit more heart into it, and you drive a little harder for the family. You want to get this guy that killed this poor store owner, or did a drive-by shooting where an innocent person gets shot or a kid is killed. It's similar to sharks' feeding frenzies. That's what happens with detectives. They get into a frenzy and they don't want to stop. You could work them for days and they won't go home. If you tell them "go home," they'll say, "I'll go in the back and sleep for two hours; I'll be right back up." That's what makes a good detective. He gets into it and he doesn't want to let go. He's like a pit bull. It's important to him. Even though he's not the case officer, he wants to be there when it goes down. He wants to be there every step of the way. He wants to make this case work. And that's the only satisfaction he has. You'll see that detectives are unique in a sense that they drive themselves to the point of exhaustion. We've gotten to the point now where we've learned a little bit about personalities. We have to send people home. We have to call fresh people in that are alert. And it bothers the detective that he's got to go home, but at this particular point he's exhausted, and we don't want him to make a mistake in the street and hurt somebody, or get himself hurt. So, we try to minimize how long people can stay up. I mean I saw guys in the Byrne homicide go for thirty hours straight, myself included, and come right back four hours or five hours later. I know detectives that worked on the

•

Eddie Byrne case and if they got twenty hours' sleep for the whole week it was a lot.

Sometimes you become disappointed. There's a case right now that we've been working on—we worked on before Eddie Byrne's case—the Christine Defenback case. She was a young little girl, I think thirteen or fourteen years old, went out for a newspaper on a Sunday and they found her body on the railroad tracks in the 102nd precinct in Queens. And I think it was like the third car there.

She left home like 6:30 in the morning and I think her body was found at 11:00 or 12:00. Her mother and father were driving around looking for her and saw the radio car at the staircase where her body was. A police officer came up and told me that there was a man downstairs that said his daughter was missing. So I went down and I spoke to him. The father wanted to go up and look at the body, but I told him that he couldn't go up there. He gave me a description of the girl's clothing and I went up and looked at her. I was pretty sure it was her. I went back downstairs and told him, "Listen, go back home and I'll be in touch with you in a little while." It was her. We worked that case for I guess about a month straight. We did nothing else.

She was a very, very nice little girl. Very much into drawing. She was a very good drawer. The thing was that we got taken off Christine's case to go on Eddie Byrne's case, but we went back to it and we're still working it. Hopefully, we'll get that one little piece of the puzzle that will break it. But it was a very emotional type of thing because she was a nice little girl. After you speak to the family, and speak to her friends, you get annoyed that this happened to her. Because it didn't have to happen to her. She had no money, she wasn't robbed. It was a case of what I call a "fixed crime scene"; it was made to look like something else. Which happens quite often when somebody close to you or somebody who knows you murders you. They make it look like another crime—which I doubt it really was. And the thing that

•

annoyed us was the fact that every lead we'd pursue went down a dead end. And we couldn't get a good grasp on it. And, we put a lot of time in and a lot of hard work, but we just couldn't get it. We couldn't get it because it was 6:30 in the morning on one of the coldest days of the year. And there was nobody in the street that saw it, or that saw anything suspicious that we could put our teeth into.

I still feel bad, right now. But, now it's about four years later and we have a few good suspects. Whether we'll ever prove it or not, I don't know. But, hopefully, with god's help, we'll get who did it.

•

2

•

DETECTIVE

SECOND GRADE

ANNE SOWINSKI

I became a police officer on November 7, 1979. It was a dream that I had for a very long time. My grandfather and my father were New York City police officers, and I have a brother and a cousin currently "on the job," but I'm the first female in my family to pursue this career. In the early seventies, when I was in high school, women pursuing male-oriented careers were uncommon. As a matter of fact, they told me, you should be a nurse or a teacher; the implication was that girls don't become cops. Well, I didn't let that discourage me.

As a kid my favorite shows were "Adam-12" and "Car 54, Where Are You?" It has always interested me. I liked the aspect of helping people: You're there when they really, really need you and you can possibly make a difference in somebody's life.

I was an avid reader of police novels, and many of them took place in New York City. And a lot of the shows on TV were about New York City cops. It was always said, "If you can make it in New York you can make it anywhere." And the big city just

•

seemed to have a lot of excitement and big challenges, and I liked that.

I took tests for state trooper, border patrol, court officer, city corrections, and state corrections officer. I even took the fire department test, although I really wanted to be a New York City police officer. That was my real dream.

I was pursuing my master's degree in criminal justice at C.W. Post College full-time before I came on the police department. I was a graduate assistant, but when they found out that I was studying for the police test they said, "Are you crazy? Why join such a bureaucratic department, you're only going to get lost. Why don't you get your Ph.D. and become a professor here?" But as much as I enjoyed teaching and reading about the theories of crime and the different aspects of criminal justice, I still wanted to get out in the streets.

When I came on the police department I lived in Suffolk County, and it's a different world out there. At the academy we were referred to as coming from "East Cupcake, Long Island." They would ask me, "What do you know about the city? What do you know about living or working in the ghetto?"

I would say, "Well, I'm willing to learn, and I am here to give it the best that I have."

I was at the police academy for five months when we had the transit strike in 1980. So they took us out to direct traffic because the whole transit system had shut down. I was put on Park and Fifty-fifth by myself, and at this intersection it was mass gridlock. So, here is this girl from "East Cupcake, Long Island" stuck in the center of traffic with no radio, no instructions, no nothing. And I'm saying to myself, "What am I doing here? I made a tremendous mistake." All of a sudden C.W. Post looked so much better to me. But I made the best of it. You look silly out there for a while, but eventually you learn how to do it right by simple trial and error.

When I graduated from the police academy I was hoping

•

to work in Manhattan because that's where it's at. But as it happened, I went out to Bayside, Queens, to the 111th precinct. When I walked in there I started talking to this old officer. I said to him, "My grandfather worked here in the 1950s." The officer then pulled out my grandfather's "ten-card," which is a record of all the different commands where he worked. This guy came on the job when my grandfather was retiring, but they had briefly worked together. It was a funny thing. He thought it was great that he had worked with my grandfather, then he became sad when he realized how very fast time flies.

I worked there for ten months in a neighborhood stabilization unit with a senior officer. We had a sector in the precinct. We responded on radio runs and walked foot posts.

When I came on in 1979 there were only five hundred policewomen in the whole police department. Now I believe the number is well over three thousand. I was in the first probationary police-officer class hired since the layoffs in 1975. And women only went on patrol for the first time in 1971 or 1972. The command I worked in when I was in training didn't have a locker room for women. That's one of the reasons why I didn't stay within the zone that I trained in. Even though most of the guys I trained with stayed in northeast Queens, which are relatively nice commands, I went down to the 101st precinct in Far Rockaway, Queens, because it had facilities for females.

It was like starting all over again: A new precinct, new neighborhood, new people. Far Rockaway is down by the water. In the eastern end of Rockaway there are a lot of housing projects, so the precinct can be busy. In the summertime it's very active, but in the wintertime it's just you out there with the seagulls on the boardwalk—everything shuts down.

We had mostly family dispute after family dispute after family dispute. But there were also some burglaries in stores. And a few of the incidents that I was involved in

•

were pretty rough. One of them was a near-shooting; another was a knife fight, and I almost fell off a rooftop.

I was down there about a year when I got a call from the sergeant who was the commanding officer of the Senior Citizens Robbery Unit asking me to work in a decoy operation.

They had a pattern of robberies and assaults against the elderly throughout the Queens area that had gotten out of control, and they wanted to employ a decoy operation. They usually do that only as a last resort, because decoy operations can be dangerous—putting somebody right in the middle of things and hoping to scoop up the bad guys.

What the Senior Citizens Robbery Unit normally did was investigate robberies, assaults, and burglaries against senior citizens in their home. It was detective work, though it was still considered a patrol function. If you did that for two or three years then you could possibly get into the Detective Bureau and get the coveted gold shield. It was a lot of people's dream.

But the sergeant said "no promises. There's no openings. I just need you for thirty days, then it's back to your command."

I said to him, "Sure, I'll do it. Especially if I can work the assignment from December to January, because in the wintertime Rockaway is like a graveyard."

Other people, however, were telling me. "You're crazy, it's dangerous."

I said to myself, "As much as I love patrol, there's got to be other parts of this job that I haven't seen, and I'm not going to turn this down. This is great."

There were a lot of bad cases. The victims were either mugged on the street or pushed into elevators and forced to go down to the basement. Sometimes the perpetrators would have the elevator pressed for the basement, or the subbasement. And when the victims got down there they'd get yanked out, robbed, and beaten up very badly. We had

•

attempted-murder charges on some of the individuals we were looking for.

I was twenty-three years old trying to look like seventy-five. Let me tell you—it was quite a challenge. The police department didn't have money for this. It was up to me, and I wanted to make it as good as I possibly could. I gave it my best shot, because all of these poor old people were getting attacked right and left. I went to a Salvation Army and got the ugliest, most hideous old clothing that I could find. I bought a cane and I got those old-fashioned eyeglasses the elderly people wear. I got a gray wig and powder to put on my face. It was twelve years ago. I didn't have wrinkles back then. But at that time I was saying, "Geez, why can't I have a few more wrinkles?"

When I went out as a decoy I was wired so that I could communicate with my backups. I was going in and out of banks like I was going to make a withdrawal, because many of the elderly were getting hit after they had gone to the bank. They were being watched by these punks who were figuring they're going in to cash checks or make withdrawals. While I played that role, we let the banks know what we were doing.

I was also going in and out of apartment buildings, but I'd try to stay out of the elevators because they're a real danger. I could be out of communication range if I went below ground.

My backup would radio me, "Annie, there's somebody coming from behind you on the right. He's wearing a red sweatshirt." Or, "There's somebody across the street to your left." So I would be on guard.

We employed that operation for about thirty days in all of the places where they were hitting on the elderly: The Lefrak City area, the Wavecrest housing project, and the neighborhood around the Jamaica bus terminal.

It turned out to be a pretty successful operation. We picked up a few people that way. But some criminals are

•

not dumb, although you might think they are. Some of them are pretty sharp. They could see that I was a decoy. One guy even said to me, "Either you're a cop or you're a crazy lady for walking around like that," because my pocketbook was partially opened. Some of them got spooked as they got close, because how much can you disguise yourself without putting a mask on?

I did the thirty days. Then I went back to the 101st precinct, back to my sector with my partner. The busy summertime came and went.

The commanding officer of the Senior Citizens Robbery Unit called me again. This time he said, "We have an opening and I'd like to pick you up."

I said, "Wow, this is great." Getting into investigations with only two years on the job is the opportunity of a lifetime.

So, in December of 1981, I started working in the Senior Citizens Robbery Unit.

I had so many cases in senior citizens. The oldest complainant that I had was one hundred years old. He lived in Flushing. He walked down the street and into his lobby, where he was approached from behind by an individual who pushed him down and started to assault him. Then this individual took his wallet, which had his social security card and all his identification in it.

He was pretty good for his age. He was still able to walk and talk, and he wasn't senile. He just kept saying, "I'm a hundred. I never thought this would happen."

He couldn't identify the person who mugged him. One of the reasons senior citizens are preyed upon so much is because the cowards who attack them know that most of the elderly can't see too well.

I just did the best I could to help him get all his identification back. But it was the saddest thing to see this man brutally beaten and robbed. You can be as hard, or as tough, as you feel you need to be to deal with this, but deep down you still have sympathy for these people.

The most interesting case for me in the Senior Citizens Unit was a pattern that I investigated in 1983. A pattern is anything more than three cases where the M.O., the modus operandi, is similar. For example, a perp goes out and repeatedly does the same thing over and over again. Then we have a problem: This person is going to continue to do that because he knows he's successful.

Joe Fazuzzi was my partner, and we were assigned to a pattern investigation of these two really brutal, brutal people. They operated in Kew Garden Hills where a lot of doctors and lawyers live, right off the Grand Central Parkway. It is a small community, about five square blocks.

In the beginning we didn't know what we had. All we knew was that people would be in bed sleeping, they'd be woken up, and two guys would force them, at knife point or at gunpoint, to open up their safes, take all their money, all their jewelry, everything that they had. I mean clean these people out.

Some of them were also physically assaulted, and some of them were sexually assaulted. And some of the people had cancer or heart conditions.

These two perps got more brutal as they were going along. We were really fearful that before we knew it we were going to have a murder on our hands.

And it was our job to try and find these guys. However, at one point they started wearing hoods so no one would be able to identify them. The break-ins were all at night. The lights were out, and people couldn't see them very well anyway. We were not really working with a lot.

It went on for several months. And in one case they'd become so brazen that they went in through the front door. Most of these homes had sophisticated alarms. But they were able to get over the alarm systems. They would pry off security gates like you open an aluminum can—almost

•

right before our eyes. We'd hear the alarms go off while we were sitting in the neighborhood, but when we'd get to the house they'd be in and out before you knew it. I mean these guys were really good.

We didn't know how they were getting into the neighborhood. It was an all-white area, but these two people were black. We called them "Mutt and Jeff." One was six-two, the other was five-six. This neighborhood had its own security people who were also keeping an eye out for them.

The burglaries usually occurred between 11:00 and 12:00 at night. It would be about a half an hour after the people turned their lights out. And just as they're falling asleep, the next thing they know there's a hand over their mouth, or a rope around their neck, or they're being tied up, and it's pitch-black. They didn't even know what hit them.

So what we did was change our tours. We started working steady six-to-twos—literally sitting in the neighborhood. Some of us hid in cars in driveways, and some of us sat on the roofs of buildings. My partner and I were actually sitting in a car in the back of driveways, laying low, hoping that if we were lucky enough they might walk right past us. Or that we would be right in the vicinity when something came over the radio and we'd be able to get them that way.

We also worked very closely with the Anti-Crime Unit in the precinct. We would check everybody coming in and out of the neighborhood. We even checked taxicabs to see who they were dropping off. But these two guys were smart.

In one case they got so brazen that on one of the main streets they overcame the alarm system and went right through a front-bay window. Then they tied up an elderly woman and brutally raped and sodomized her daughter in front of her.

We ended up getting some partial prints that we worked with. And we kept sitting in the backyard and stopping everybody. We were just waiting, waiting, and waiting. But one after another the residents kept getting knocked off.

•

I said, "this is really bad, really bad." So I made these posters up from the best composite that we could get, and we put them in all the precincts. We also went to every precinct's roll call to alert them to be on the lookout for these two guys.

But this was a case I started taking home with me. It was like these guys just had to get caught, because somebody is going to die here. But they were one step ahead of us. It was extremely frustrating.

A couple of times we got onto a scene where there was a burglary, and the witnesses would say, "Oh, they just went through the neighbor's yard." We would shut off the street, and start searching for them. We would even get aviation involved. We would do everything. It was amazing, because we just kept missing them. They were that good.

Then one day, I got a phone call at home about 3:00 in the morning that an Anti-Crime Unit had picked up two guys that fit the description. They had them in central booking in Queens. They just got them for trespass, because they walked across somebody's lawn. But it was only a violation; there was nothing that they could really hold them on. The Anti-Crime guys got their pedigree, and they were going to cut them loose.

I said, "Hang on to them, don't let them go. I'll be right there."

At the time I was still living at home with my parents, so my mother asked me, "where you going?"

"I've got to get to work. I just got to get there. I'll explain it to you tomorrow."

I headed into central booking. When I got there they were just cutting them loose. I said, "No, let me just take them back to my office. Let me debrief them."

Then I conferred with the ADA. I said, "I think we really got something here, we just can't let these people go."

So before we cut them loose I was able to put them in lineups. We worked literally day and night, twenty-four hours

•

a day for two or three days doing lineups. I don't even re-member how many lineups we did. We tried to get all the people involved to come in.

A lineup is done very, very carefully, because you have to go to hearings on it later on that could make or break your case. A lineup has to be as fair as it possibly can to the per-son that you're placing in it. You want to put six people in there that, as best as you can, have similar features. For ex-ample, you're not going to put somebody who is bald in there with somebody who's got hair. But you don't want them to be twins either. They should be close as you can get, but still have them a little distinct.

Now I had two individuals. They obviously couldn't be put in the same lineup. So I had to do two lineups each time we got a witness to come in. That means I have to get ten fillers or "extras" to stand in the lineup.

Again, you were on your own. As a detective you have to go out on the street and find people who are willing to be part of a lineup. Who in their right mind would want to be in a police lineup? Most of them think, "Hey, what if I get nailed?" Some of them you couldn't convince that if they get identified they're not going to go away for it. Especially when you told them that it was a sex crime case, forget it, they'd want nothing to do with it.

You have to use a little tact. I never really had a hard time getting fillers. I would be nice to them. The other detectives always said that they wanted to send me out to get the fill-ers because "you're a girl and you can charm them." I even had guys that I gave summonses to or guys that I locked up say "you can arrest me anytime, no problem. Somebody as nice as you." But I always thought they were crazy.

Five dollars for a half an hour or an hour was all the de-partment would give you to pay each of these people. I'm embarrassed giving them five dollars. So I'd say, "Oh, it's going to take two hours or so; I need ten bucks."

I used to go to a Jack La Lanne gym where guys would be

•

working out—although it depends on what you were looking for. What I did most of the time was go to the men's shelters in Brooklyn, or in case I needed a female I would go to the women's shelter in Flushing. A lot of these people wanted the money, and they'll do anything for a couple of bucks. We deal with a lot of dirtbags, and in the shelters you have a lot of people who are just what we're looking for.

When you are conducting a lineup you first have to put your suspect in the holding pen, then you bring these five other people in. Although in this case it was ten other people that we had to coordinate. So you really rely on your partners to assist you.

I think we probably had about forty-five complainants in this case. But we couldn't get them all to come down to the precinct. That was a very frustrating part of working in senior citizens—once they reported it to the police, they wanted nothing more to do with the case. They couldn't handle it. It was too stressful. It shook them up. It was the same way when I went to sex crimes. And understandably so. The victims don't want to keep reliving this. They want to put it behind them. It was a bad thing that happened. "Let me get on with my life." And a lot of times you work really, really hard to make a case, and a lot of times when you finally got it into the grand jury, to go to trial, you would lose the victim, even at that point, because they just didn't want to testify and have to relive this terrible thing that happened to them.

For senior citizens and sex crime victims the lineup is another traumatizing part of the whole thing—to have to go in to see this person again. Look at each face, study it, stare at it, keep looking at it. And usually the guys in the lineup, the real dirtbags, know what's going on and they'll give a real threatening look at the one-way mirror, and even though they cannot see the witness, they will still try to intimidate them.

But it is up to you, as a detective, to use tact and really

•

calm the witness down. You tell them, "this is just another step. We're going to take them off the street, so god forbid it doesn't happen to somebody else." In the end we only got about eighteen or nineteen people to come in and look at these guys, and out of that we got about eight or nine hits.

We had enough to go to court with these two guys. I was in seventh heaven. It was the greatest.

The two guys were Eddie Shaw and Woodrow Collins. They lived down in the 101st precinct in Far Rockaway. They would take a cab or get dropped off in the daytime, before we even started our tour of duty. And they would just somehow filter into the neighborhood, and wait in a backyard for hours, until the time was right for them to jump on their prey. Then they would make their quick getaway.

We had to go through all of the pretrial hearings, and all of these elderly, senior citizens had to come in and testify about their identification of these two guys.

One of the victims died of cancer before the case went to trial. Some of the people were so traumatized that they moved out of the state. Unfortunately, that's what happens when you're dealing with senior citizens and sex crimes. In the end you have so little to work with. But in this case it worked out really good.

We got convictions on both of them. It was a record in the courts. They each got 33⅓ to 100 years. We had them on the rape and sodomy of a young female, real brutal assaults and robberies on all these senior citizens. And they had gotten a lot of money and jewelry that was never recovered. They also had past records of robberies.

Collins was also wanted on a warrant in North Carolina for some things that he had done out there, so when we finished with him in New York he was going to be extradited to North Carolina to face those charges.

They fit the particular profile of the kind of people that attack the elderly. They really are cowards to begin with,

•

because they know they're going to win before they even play the game. They know they're going to overpower their victims right away. They know they're dealing with defenseless people who either can't hear or can hardly see. People who can't fight back. It's not like they're in a fair fight here.

For the most part, those we did arrest, in Senior Citizens—when we finally got them into our office and interrogated them, they would break down crying. I mean they were nothing, but in their own minds, I'm sure, they proved the strength of their ego or their manliness by overpowering defenseless people. The majority of them were second-, third-, or fourth-generation welfare recipients. And a lot of them were uneducated.

I really loved working with the senior citizens. It was very challenging. But I felt like I was helping my grandparents, because not only did we investigate the crimes, we assisted them socially. We were like Victim Services. If they needed counseling, or if they needed a driver's license, or when I got into their home and I saw they didn't have enough food, or they were financially strained, we were able to get them whatever they needed. You really could do so much for these people.

In that pattern case with Shaw and Collins, we had one rape, and that case went to Sex Crimes, because we only dealt with robberies and assaults. But because it was part of the pattern investigation, I started working with the Sex Crimes detectives. They came out with me once or twice, and the captain who was the supervisor of Sex Crimes got to know me.

He said, "Annie, why don't you come to Sex Crimes? You're young, you're a female, you're a good detective. You would be very good in Sex Crimes work. Cover sex crimes and you can get the gold shield in no time."

I said, "thank you very much. Thank you for the compliments. And the shield is something that I really want, but

•

not through Sex Crimes. I'll wait until my time comes. I just like the work that I'm doing and I want to stay here." And the two things I didn't want to do when I came on the job was sex crimes and narcotics.

He said, "fine."

So I stayed in Senior Citizens. However, in July of 1984 the Senior Citizens Robbery Unit was transferred into the Detective Bureau, which was good for us. We did the canvasses, the lineups, the catching of cases, all the detective work. Why shouldn't we be in the bureau?

It became the Detective Borough Queens Crimes Against Senior Citizens Squad, and they gave everybody that was in there credit for retroactive investigative time. And you needed at least eighteen months of investigative time before you could get the gold shield. It was also decided that you could get the gold shield and stay there, without having to go into a precinct detective squad. So I said, "wow, it worked out great. I didn't go to Sex Crimes, and I'm going to get the shield anyway." I was very happy. I can stay doing the job that I really love. I did get the credit for having 2½ years of investigative time, and then I got notified that I was being promoted to detective in August.

So on August 24, 1984, I made detective third grade. I was twenty-seven years old, and they remarked how young I was to make detective. I actually had only five years on the job, and I was so proud of myself. It was the greatest thing.

The promotion was held on a Friday at police headquarters at One Police Plaza. It was great. My family, my boss, my partners—everybody was there for the ceremony.

The next morning, I got a call at home from my boss, who said, "Anne, they transferred you to Sex Crimes." Sex Crimes had called up my boss earlier to try and get me and he told them, "I have eleven other detectives. If you want a detective we'll give you somebody else." My boss didn't want to give me up, which made me feel good. But then there weren't a lot of females out there, and they just had

•

their sights set on me. The Sex Crimes Unit was going to get me no matter what.

We're players in a game here, that's what it's all about. This is a paramilitary organization; you do what you're told. You take orders. I have no problem with that. But at the time I was thinking, what do I know about sex crimes investigations? I don't know anything.

I go to the Sex Crimes Unit, which was located in the 112th precinct in Forest Hills and, like Senior Citizens, they cover the whole borough of Queens.

I'll never forget that first day. I went out with a female detective by the name of Janet Guardino. She took me down to the 113th precinct in Jamaica. It was a case where a girl was raped. I said to Janet, "Let me just sit back. I mean I don't even know where to start in sex crimes; it's just so different from robbery." So she did the whole interview of the victim.

She started by introducing herself to the victim. "I'm Detective Janet Guardino. I'm with the Sex Crimes Unit. I received your case from the police officer that took the report, and I'm going to investigate the case. We're going to do everything that we can to try and solve this. But we need your help. The questions I'm going to ask you are very, very important, very critical. Think about everything I'm going to ask you, and try to remember as much as you possibly can, because this will help us that much more to apprehend this individual."

To me it was like, wow, now what is this girl from "East Cupcake" doing in the Big City. You have to talk about these personal things to people that you don't even know. They're sexually abused and you have to get the facts of the case. You have to really go into specifics about what happened—A, B, C, D—from how the girl was approached by the guy, to what he did and what he said—and I mean to the *tee*. But again, I said to myself, I'll learn. So I just listened to Janet and then *boom*, I started catching cases right away.

•

In that first case it turned out that the girl knew the guy. They were boyfriend and girlfriend. It was a date rape kind of thing. In a lot of the cases in sex crimes the perps are known to the complainants. Some were even their husband.

Many of them are intrafamily child sex abuse cases; for example, uncles abusing nieces or grandfathers sexually abusing granddaughters. But in most of those cases the family did not want to pursue it. They didn't want a family member going to jail, or they would turn around and not believe the child. "She doesn't know what she's talking about." But they were the easy cases because you knew all the facts. It was just a matter of putting it together, trying to get them to cooperate in order to prepare a solid case to take to court.

There were also the cases where the victim didn't know the rapist. That was a challenge, because these perpetrators were bad people. And it would only get more serious if the person was not apprehended, because they would do it more frequently and they can become more violent. I mean, no one's going to go out and rape one time and then just forget that they ever did it. It's a crime committed by real inadequate individuals.

After doing the initial interview we would have the victim view photos at Miraquic, in the 112th precinct, which is where all photos of people who have been arrested before are kept on file, and see if they can identify anybody. But if it's a first-time rapist, or he hasn't been arrested before, then we're not going to have a picture of him. So then you try to have a composite picture of the suspect made with the help of a police artist.

Also in trying to put a case together you want to see if it's part of a pattern, because, I would say, in at least half of the cases it wasn't the perp's first time.

I had a real vicious pattern with a guy by the name of Jeffrey Heath. He pretended to be a gypsy cabdriver in the Jamaica area. It was a black neighborhood and he was black. Late at night he would pull up to where taxicabs would stand, and these girls would get in his cab and ask to go to their destination. He would first head in the direction of the destination that they wanted to go to, but as soon as he would get on the Van Wyck Expressway he'd take a knife out and put it to the girl's neck. Most of them, unfortunately, got in the front seat with him. Then he'd unzip his pants and force them to give him oral sex as he was driving the car on the Expressway. Saying to them, "If you don't do what I tell you to do I'm going to kill you." He cut some of them. After he did whatever he wanted to do with them he would just open the door and throw them out.

I ended up working on that case for a couple of months. What happened was he picked up a whole range of girls from teenagers to women in their fifties and sixties. He would pull up, and take whoever was there, so long as there was only one.

But what led me to apprehend him was that he picked up a girl that was going to work in the morning. And he did the same thing to her on the Van Wyck Expressway: He took the knife out and put it to her throat. He was really forcing it to her. Then he unzips his pants, and put her head right between his legs. Then he put the knife behind her neck so that she's either going to do it or she's going to get stabbed in the neck. But she resisted. This was the first one that resisted.

She fought with him. She got cut up pretty bad. She got slashed on the hands, and got cut once or twice on the neck. She also got cut all over her arms. But she was able to get the knife away from him and turn it around and plunged it right into his chest. She was one tough girl. She didn't know how bad she stabbed him, but it was enough to where he pulled over, opened up the door, and threw her out. Then he took off.

She was picked up on the highway and brought to an emergency room. We got a call from a cop in the emergency

•

room that a girl was just stabbed on the Van Wyck during a fight with some guy, and they were sewing her up.

So I went and interviewed her at the hospital. She gave me a description. I said, "this is it."

But then she started saying, "now that I think of it, I don't think I really got the guy, I just scared him, because I was fighting a lot with this guy and he didn't expect it. I think I just nicked him on the neck."

My partners and I started calling every hospital in Queens, figuring that if he did get some type of an injury he's going to go to an emergency room. We told them if they get any type of a stab victim, or anybody bleeding from any type of a cut, to notify us forthwith.

I was notified that Jamaica Hospital had a possible stabbing victim, so I called them up. They said, "No, we just have one guy, but he said he was just robbed. He's a cabdriver who was dropping somebody off, and they robbed him and cut him."

I said, "Whatever you do, tell him he needs X rays, tell him he needs whatever, just hold him until we get there."

We went there forthwith. When we got to the emergency room entrance I said, "Before I go in there, and even see this guy, let me look around the parking lot to see if I can find a car that has any type of evidence in it. The girl said she left her pocketbook in the car."

So I canvassed the parking lot up and down looking at every car. Sure enough, there's a car with blood all over the front seat. And there was a pocketbook in the backseat. But I can't go opening the car door. I need a warrant. But this gives me reason to believe that this is the guy.

I go into the hospital. They're working on him. They say he might have to go into surgery. They won't let me talk to him. Then they put him in the operating room. We had one detective stay there to make sure that he didn't get out.

I hightailed my butt over to the D.A.'s office with my case folder and I got the warrant. Then I went back to the hospi-

•

tal and opened up his car. It was the girl's pocketbook, and there was also one of her earrings in the front seat.

I get the Crime Scene Unit down there. They did a job on the car. They took scrapings of the blood and vouchered everything.

Then I went into the hospital and interrogated him. I was trying to get anything that I could from him. But he just kept changing his story: He said first that it was a fare that robbed him; then he said yeah, there was a girl but he just dropped her off at her destination, he didn't do anything. Then he denied everything.

He ended up being admitted to the hospital. She punctured his lung. But in two days he was fine, and he was discharged. I got another warrant, and put him in lineups. I got anybody that had any type of case that resembled this M.O. and I had them all view the lineups. This was the guy.

In that case we lost a couple of the girls. They moved away because it was really brutal and they just didn't want to go to court and testify. They didn't want to see him again, or they were afraid of retribution—that this guy's going to come back out and get them. This guy even threatened me. He said, "I'm going to come out and I'm going to find you. I'm going to get you someday."

Now, I start thinking about my family and maybe I should have stayed out in "East Cupcake." But then I took my own precautions: I got an unlisted phone number.

But I was happy that we got this guy. We went to trial and it turned out well—he got a lot of time. He's still doing time. And it made a lot of the girls happy that he was off the street.

A lot of the cases were really sad because there were children involved. I caught a case where a baby, several months old, was anally sodomized by her father. This occurred in their home.

The father brought the baby to an emergency room because it had a fever from an ear infection. The emergency

•

room doctor, for whatever reason he had, started to do a whole examination of this child. He saw that the child had severe injuries around her anus, and there was also rectal damage. So he started questioning the father about this. The father ran out of the hospital, but left the child there.

I interviewed the mother. She denied everything, "no, no, no, he never did anything. Everything's fine."

There was also a five-year-old daughter at home. And I said to my partner, "if he's starting out with this baby that's several months old, what's he doing to the five year old?" So I thoroughly interviewed the five-year-old girl. She denied that anything happened.

At that point, I had investigated so many sex crime cases that you get a feeling for it. You know if you're being lied to. With child cases a lot of the parents would say, "they're making it up." But there are certain things that a child just can't make up. There are things that they'll describe to you that there's no way they would know about them unless they had firsthand knowledge.

In this case I became convinced nothing happened with the five year old. However, the wife eventually said, "Yeah, yeah, I kind of suspected, but I wasn't really sure. But if he goes to jail that means there's less money coming into the house." Then she became very uncooperative. She wouldn't tell me where he hung out. And anytime I went to the house he was just in the wind.

Then one day, I was reading the *Daily News* and I see the father's name. He had been treated for something in the emergency room at Bellevue and he stabbed a nurse. So he was locked up for the assault on a nurse. I said, "holy shit, this is the guy." Then I called the Manhattan detectives who had the case, and said, "I want this guy. He sodomized his little baby."

I got all the information about the guy and went to see the D.A. We drew up a case on it, but they eventually said, "just

•

forget it. Drop it. It's not going to go anywhere. The guy is insane. He's got all kinds of psychiatrists to testify to that."

I said, "This is baloney. This guy's not insane. This is just another game that's being played by him to avoid going to jail and doing time for stabbing this nurse and for sodomizing his baby daughter."

But that was it, I just couldn't do anything with this case. I was mad at the injustice of it. It's not fair. We know this guy did it, but there's nothing we can do about it. He pled the insanity defense and he won. We lost. Society lost.

A lot of cases in sex crimes are with children under the age of seven, the age of reason, where all you have is the child's testimony and there's no physical evidence. So, you're not going to get corroboration and he's not going to admit to it. It's frustrating, because you're not going to get anywhere in court.

Although I was successful with one five-year-old girl, which they said was a record because it never happened before in Queens County. The girl was sexually abused by her uncle. All I had was her statement. The district attorney's office didn't want to put a child under seven on the stand to testify to the grand jury. But I literally jumped up and down with the A.D.A. I said, "You just have to listen to her. She is so convincing. If she doesn't convince the grand jury I'll just give it all up. Just give me a chance, just listen."

Sure enough, we got her to testify to the grand jury through closed-circuit TV. We didn't put her right in there because children are just so delicate, especially after they've been sexually and physically abused. You can see in them a spirit that has been crushed and that will never heal. They will never be the same.

We had cases, all the time, of kids from two months to eight months of age with syphilis, or gonorrhea in the throat. But these cases were just so stomach turning, so sickening, and so sad.

The perpetrators of these crimes are severely inadequate

•

people. They were just like the people that I arrested in senior citizens.

When I first got to Sex Crimes, in the 104th precinct, which is in the Glendale-Maspeth area, an elderly man was grabbing little boys and sodomizing them in a park. In all we had about six or seven little boys who were grabbed by this man. And he was distinct. I knew when I saw this guy I was going to know who he was. The description was of an old, partially bald with white hair white guy. I went out and I found him.

I just felt so bad for these little boys; they won't forget this. I didn't know if this would have a long-term effect on them. You just know it's not natural, it's not the way it's supposed to be.

That was the one and only time with somebody that I was arresting that I lost control for a little while. I remember standing up behind my desk and saying, "you know, you are a sick motherfucker." I remember I was using all kinds of profanity, because I couldn't deal with this. I lost my usual ladylike cool head. "How could you do this to these little boys? Don't you know they'll never be the same? You know, you're sick and you should get help. You're really a piece of garbage—society's lowlife." I really railed into this guy. I couldn't believe somebody could do these kinds of things, especially the way I grew up, I just didn't know that these things really happened. He just looked at me and began to cry uncontrollably. At that moment, I realized that there are many sick people in this world, and my losing my cool with him was a waste of time. From that point on, I did my job the very best that I could.

But the number of times in which child sexual abuse does occur astounded me. I never realized how prevalent child sex crimes and physical abuse really are. I was told by Sex Crimes in Queens that for the first quarter, January, February, and March of 1991, they received over one thousand BCW (Bureau of Child Welfare) referrals. A lot of them

•

were unfounded, but even if you cut the number in half, you still have five hundred abused little kids, many with VD, bruises, burns, spiral fractures of their limbs, and sub-dural hematomas. And what's reported is only a fraction of the actual number of incidents.

I had a case of a baby with a spiral fracture of her leg. I asked the baby-sitter, "How did that happen?"

"Oh, she fell off the changing table."

Some of these cases were simple to solve. You just talk to a doctor, and you find out that if a child falls from a changing table to a floor it can break a leg, but you're not going to get a spiral fracture because that comes from a twist.

But in that case the child was too young to testify; it was one year old. So here's a baby that had a leg twisted, and you can't make an arrest on the case.

I had another case with a baby that had been in the care of a baby-sitter and had a subdural hematoma, which is a blood clot on the brain. It was the result of what's called "the shaken baby syndrome." It's common, when a baby is crying and you get so frustrated that you shake the baby so much that it causes blood clots on the brain. That baby was brain damaged. It would never be normal.

We had a lot of cases with baby-sitters and day care centers, more in the lower-class neighborhoods, but some of them were high-class ones.

I remember a case where a gynecologist raped a woman that was on the table being examined. I mean she goes for a regular GYN examination and the guy ends up getting on the table on top of her. He was arrested.

We really believed that girl for many reasons. This woman had never gone to him before. Along with other fac-tors, there would be no reason to think that she's going to make this up, but the grand jury did not believe her. They didn't believe that a gynecologist would rape a woman in his office. So he walked.

There were eighteen detectives in sex crimes; five were

•

female. I worked in my team with five guys. I was the only female. And you always wanted to have females on a team, because sometimes a woman wouldn't talk to a man. So in my squad, being the only female, I had to go out more than necessary with the guys because they would deal with girls that wanted to have a girl present. But, I believe that the job can be done and done well by either a female or a male. There's no difference. And when it comes to being a detective, whether you're a female or a male, it's irrelevant.

Some of the guys I worked with, at first, I would never have thought that they could be a Sex Crimes detective. I mean they were joking all the time, talking about crass locker room stuff. We get used to that right away—it comes with the territory. But you would wonder how is this guy going to interview a young girl that's been abused. But they were the best. They really were—they had tact, sensitivity, and patience. I loved working with them.

Working in Sex Crimes was the worst, but, at times, it was the best place that I ever worked. Because you saw the worst, and it was very frustrating and heartbreaking, but at the same time when you got a conviction you got the bad guy. The feeling was just unbelievable. It's a real high. I mean, I changed society. I made it better by something that I did out there. And as much as I was dragged down into the gutter while I was doing it, and I fell down emotionally maybe once or twice, it was very, very gratifying when you did put a guy away. To me it was a challenge to get a case, make it solid, make it strong, make it stick, and send this guy away where he'll never see daylight again. That was always my goal. And also to help the girl or the child as best that I could.

I still have sex crimes victims that keep in touch with me today. Some of them have moved away, but they call me up, or they send me birthday cards. It's moving—I made a difference in their life.

I had one lady who was seventy some-odd years old. She

•

was brutally raped and stabbed in the neck with a screwdriver by her granddaughter's husband, in the basement of the house where they all lived. It was really vicious.

I interviewed her at Queens General Hospital. I thought she was dead when I walked in there. I said, "Is she still alive?" She was semiconscious and it was really, really bad.

It was on the Fourth of July. It was my birthday. I was supposed to be at a barbecue, but I couldn't get the day off. Another holiday where you're just stuck having to do everything. I had hoped it was going to be a quiet day so I could get out of work early and just go home. But I had her the first thing in the morning.

She still keeps in touch with me. She's doing very well.

I think about her because she was at death's door, but she was such a strong person. To this day, I'm still there for her. If she ever needed anything I would help her as best I could.

Her granddaughter's husband hit the road. I went looking for him. I went back to the house, time after time. The granddaughter said, "I don't know where he is." Uncooperative again.

So I put a "want card" out on him. When you can't find somebody you put a "want card" out in case they are arrested on another charge. This will hold him until we can take him and follow through with the case. Eventually the card popped. They picked him up for jumping a subway turnstile in Manhattan, but in the meantime I had been transferred to the Hostage Team. However, I got a phone call that the transit police had arrested him and I was ecstatic. I called Sex Crimes. But at that time the victim had just moved out of state and they couldn't get hold of her. So, unfortunately, that case did not go as far as it could have.

I just said to myself, "I wish I would have stayed in Sex Crimes, I would have really followed through and made this guy go away for it." When I get on a case I stick to it to the bitter end, until I know that I gave my 110 percent. And

•

I sleep real good because of that. The case was still active, but after I left the unit I had no control over it.

I was in Sex Crimes almost three years. I liked doing the work. It was the best and the worst of times. It was challenging. I achieved my goals and it was great. But I was ready for a change. I loved making the arrests, doing the patterns, and the investigations. But to try to get some normalcy back into my life, aside from the burnout that I felt coming on from being so deep in it, I said, "let me see what else is out there."

I heard there was an opening down at headquarters in the Special Projects Unit. So I called up my boss in Sex Crimes and told him, "I just got to make a quick trip into Manhattan." I didn't tell anybody what I was doing. I wasn't even dressed like I was going for an interview.

After the interview they said, "well, what do you think? Do you want it?"

I said to myself, "if I spend the weekend thinking about this I'm going to get cold feet or something's going to happen, but I know I want a change. I know I want to broaden my horizons even more." So I gave them the answer right then and there. I said, "Yes, I'll take it."

A short time later they transferred me out of Sex Crimes and into Special Projects. At that time Bob Louden was in charge of the Hostage Negotiating Team. I'll never forget the day he said, "Anne, would you like to be a hostage negotiator?" I lost my breath. "You really think I would make a good hostage negotiator?"

"I know you'd make a great hostage negotiator. I'd like to put you on the team."

I was ecstatic. This was like another dream come true. And so I went to the next class he trained. He trained very small classes, because it's a lot of one-on-one intense training. And from that point on I worked strictly hostage. I just loved it.

The class was two weeks long and included three days at

•

the outdoor range with the heavy weapons that Emergency Service uses. You get acquainted with shooting them, but you didn't have to qualify with them. We have since changed that. We now qualify them with some of the heavy weapons that are used in a hostage situation, because, god forbid, if an emergency service officer gets shot and goes down, and he has a pump shotgun or a mini-14 or an MP5 and he drops it, I'm standing there as a negotiator and I look at this gun. I mean an MP5, what the hell would I know what to do with it if I never handled it or fired it before? I may as well just take it and throw it someplace, because it's not going to do me any good. So we used that rationale to say that we want to train our negotiators just in case. It may come to this. With hostage situations you just don't know what's going to happen minute by minute. They change in a heartbeat.

After the first few days of weapons training we got trained in short-term crisis intervention, and that's what we're all about, because we're dealing with people who are in intense emotional states.

We also develop active listening skills. When people are in these intense emotional states, an important part of communicating with them is listening. And that's what a lot of people don't understand about communication in their own relationships—people just don't listen to what other people are saying. They hear them, but they're not really listening on the inside. We learn to listen for the feelings and what their message really is. What they want to get out to us.

We do a lot of role-playing of barricade and hostage situations with suicidal, or emotionally disturbed people. It's not the real thing, but when you go in front of your peers and you have somebody you don't know too well really acting out that they want to kill themselves, believe me, the stress that's put on you is like the real thing. We also

•

include training on how to cope when a job goes bad. We're people too.

We also train with Emergency Service, because we work so closely with them. With hostage situations we set up an inner and outer perimeter. And in the inner perimeter it is just Emergency Service and the hostage negotiators. If there's an alleged bomb device, we'll have a bomb squad technician in there. But in the inner perimeter there is only a select number of people because it's dangerous. You're in the line of fire. So we keep it real tight and small.

After you pass this two-week course you're on the hostage team.

What we like to do, after you've been on a few hostage or barricade situations, is to send you to the FBI hostage negotiators school, which is another two-week school.

After that we go with Emergency Service for training at John Jay College for five days to become an emergency psychological technician. They have people from the college and from the New York City Department of Mental Health come in to teach us how to deal with people who are drug abusers or alcoholics, or emotionally disturbed or suicidal. You're only as good as your training. So we really try and stay up on it.

We also have two training days a year, where we get the entire team together and we'll have guest lecturers come in the mornings. And in the afternoons we'll go through some jobs that we've handled that were good or that were bad. We also invite Emergency Service to be there.

We have a newsletter, *Inner Perimeter,* that we send out every other month, in which we talk about different jobs that have occurred. We give the negotiators a pat on the back. We try to make them feel good—because it's strictly a volunteer program. We also try and make it a fraternal type thing—by writing about who's on the team, whose wife just had a baby, who's been promoted, who's been transferred.

The job that really stands out in my mind occurred on

•

Seaman Avenue, two days before Thanksgiving, 1989. My boss and my partner were on vacation. I was at John Jay College giving a lecture to new detectives, when I got beeped by my inspector. I called him immediately and he said, "Annie, we have a hostage situation going on. I need you to go up there just to check on it, and let me know what's happening." So I went up there.

When I got there everything was set up. It was an ideal hostage situation, if there could be one. Of course there is no such thing, but if you could handpick the players they were there, including some great supervisors, like Kenney Bowen, who had been around awhile.

I called the inspector back and said, "We have an excellent team working here, trained negotiators, and emergency personnel."

I then called my boss, Lt. McGowan, the commanding officer of the Hostage Team, at home. I said, "We have a hostage situation up here in the thirty-fourth precinct, but don't worry about it, everything's under control. We're in conversation with the individual. His name is Timothy White. He is a Vietnam vet. He's holding his elderly father hostage. The father is senile and really doesn't even know what is going on. The son isn't threatening to kill him. But in every sense of the term the father is a hostage, since he is in there."

After some initial conversation with this guy, I really thought that it was just going to be a matter of time before we break him down and drive home to him the message that, as dark as it may seem, there's light at the end of the tunnel. And that's what we try and bring to these people.

So we continue talking with him, and we're thinking he's going to come out. But we had a video camera in there, and we can see him sitting on a chair right on the other side of the door that we're negotiating through.

The initial negotiator had been on a barricade situation with a potentially suicidal individual a couple of weeks ear-

•

lier—and they lost him, right when this negotiator got there—so he really had nothing to do with it, but a supervisor went over to him and said, "All right, you just back up, and start doing some canvassing. We'll handle it."

We use the canvasses to help us through the negotiation process, because we're trying to gain a rapport with this individual who's barricaded, and may be emotionally disturbed, and who we don't know. Often, we don't even know what he looks like. So we try to talk to people that live around him, including family members, friends, employer, priest, or doctor, to get as much information as we can about him that will assist us in dealing with this guy. For example, where is he coming from or how bad is his situation. You have to really try to find something positive in this picture of black, negative ugliness. The canvass is also done to find out what he likes, or what he's interested in, or something that he cares about. The first officer on the scene maybe had a conversation with him that could help us, so it is very important that we try and get as much information as we can from him.

We also have detectives from the squad there doing some of the canvassing and running BCI checks, background checks, on him. We found out that he was a former drug addict and he was in Vietnam, and he was unemployed, and his girlfriend had just broken up with him. These are some common factors in hostage situations.

After a while, a decision was made that I was going to switch from backup to primary negotiator.

The backup basically guides the primary negotiator in case the primary draws a blank and doesn't know what to say, or runs out of ideas. You're also trying to give the primary support; while also making sure that he doesn't get too involved, or too close physically. You hold him back. Because a "creeping up" effect takes place when you're negotiating with somebody. You try and gain the barricade's confidence, and it's only human nature that when

•

you talk to somebody, the closer you get to them emotionally the closer your bodies get. And as a negotiator you don't really realize this is happening. You'll be talking far away and then you'll take a step closer, and then another step, etc. And you'll feel like you're really gaining ground and you have good rapport. He's starting to trust you, but now you're starting to trust him, and that can become very dangerous. Because it could change in an instant. You're putting yourself in a very dangerous situation.

As I was talking with him he wasn't really threatening or anything. But through the camera I could see him sitting there—he had a knife and he had a gun.

It's my job to like this guy and to want him to like me so we can both come out of this a winner. But we have to always be on guard. He wanted me to open up the door to give him a cigarette, and I figured okay, give him a cigarette, that's nothing. But as the door opened up he came up with the gun. So now I know this guy was just looking for a confrontation. I knew it wasn't anything against me. I wasn't taking it personal, because we were having a good conversation. He was just looking to start something here.

At one point he wanted me to come in, but at the same time I knew I can't go in there. I would like to, it's easier to talk to someone face-to-face, but it's also the most dangerous way. We train to avoid face-to-face negotiations, especially with a weapon present.

But I really believed that we were going to get to him. It was a matter of time that we would break him down. I sort of kept his emotions down, talking about different kinds of things. But again he wanted me in the apartment, and he wanted that door open. Also, he kept saying, "the cigarettes, where are the cigarettes?"

I said, "Go to the back window." Emergency Service dropped them down in a bucket. "The cigarettes are there, go get them." Now the cigarettes suddenly were unimpor-

•

tant. So the cigarettes were not the issue. He used them as an excuse.

Again, he wanted the door fully open. He wanted a confrontation, although at the time I'm not understanding this. Instead I'm wondering why can't we gain an inch with this guy.

Eventually he started a fire in the kitchen. It started to get smoky. Now we're on the first floor of an apartment building. The door's chocked open a crack because we have a small, discreet surveillance camera at the top of it. The flames are going up the wall. Now we gotta call the fire department.

The fire department arrives and they're ready to come in, but, at the same time, the guy is still sitting there with the gun. Then he says to me, "Annie, if you're not going to come in, the firemen will come in. I'll get somebody in here."

I just kept trying to keep him calm. "John, we'll stay here as long as you want us to stay here, and we'll talk about whatever you want. But you're putting us all in danger, and you know we're not going to come in there. We're not going to do it."

He just kept fanning the fire, making it bigger and bigger and bigger, until several of us were overcome by smoke from trying to stay there and talk to him. Someone said, "come on, we gotta get out. We gotta get out. Anne, you can't talk anymore."

I'm still talking and they're trying to pull me away; the smoke has become too much for us.

It's not our job to make tactical entries, that's Emergency's job. Also inside the apartment were two German shepherds and two Dobermans roaming around, which was another reason why we couldn't really have the firemen go right in. So I stepped back, and all I remember doing was just saying a prayer. "Just let nobody get hurt here."

•

Now Emergency Service went in. I just ducked down, and the next thing I knew about eight or nine shots went off. It was like *pow, bang, bang, bang, bang, bang, bang,* it seemed like it was going on forever. At this point the smoke was really coming out, we couldn't see, and all you could hear is gunshots. Shots flying everywhere, *ping, ping.* I'm thinking about ricochets and saying "holy shit, this is bad." I don't want to get hit by a ricochet, even though I'm out of the direct line of fire; I was crouched down to the side. Then I said to myself, "I hope no cop got hurt because of this." You can only help people so much, but if they want to die, they're going to die. Hopefully they don't take innocent people with them.

I was thinking, we had a jumper the other day. A woman, with two kids, was going to jump. She went out the window. Thank god she didn't take the two kids with her.

It was just crazy—it was dark. And I'm thinking about these poor firemen, how do they put out fires when they can't even see?

Then they drag out one body. At first we didn't know who he was. It turned out to be the old man, the father. We thought he was shot, but miraculously he wasn't hit. Also none of us were hit. But John was hit twice in his shoulder area. They said that he came through the smoke like Freddy Krueger with a look on his face of death, and with the gun leveled at them.

When they took him out they were pulling knives out of all his pockets. He really, really wanted a confrontation; we just didn't see it at this time. What it comes down to is this: I believed in the hostage negotiation process, I believed that we could do it. And I was going to stay there as long as it took. But this guy just didn't want to live. And he was going to do anything in his means to bring on this confrontation.

EMS was there to give first aid right away. They stripped him down to find out where the blood was coming from, and there's blood everywhere. It's dark and I'm holding a

•

flashlight on him so we could see what we're doing. We see the two holes in his shoulder and his eyes are rolling around. And I'm still talking to him, "John, I'm still with you. How are you doing?" And he's still talking a little bit.

We all had to go to Columbia Presbyterian Hospital. He went for the bullet wounds, and we went for smoke inhalation.

They did the test to see how much carbon monoxide we had in our blood. It hurts. As a matter of fact, when Tony, who is a big, strapping, tough guy detective and hostage negotiator, saw the needle they use for this test I thought he was going to pass out.

They were working on John in another room. They had completely opened up his chest, but even then I didn't think he was going to die. But it ended up that he died on the operating table.

Afterwards, the doctors came by and said to us, "Did you know he had AIDS?"

"No, I didn't know." Nobody knew that.

They asked, "Did you get close to him? Was there any type of contact or anything like that?"

I said, "No. I saw the blood, but I just never thought he had AIDS." I should have really put two and two together with him being a former heroin addict. I guess the guy really felt like he had nothing to live for, his girlfriend left him, he had no job, he was behind in rent, and he was dying of AIDS. And I think he just wanted to go out in a blaze of glory. And he did.

I don't believe there was any discharge in his weapon, but it's not for us to stand there and wait for that. And again, we're not in this to die, we're in this to live.

I second-guessed myself for two or three days afterwards. Maybe there was something else that I could have said or done where I could have reached him. But with the debriefing and talking with other negotiators, I realized the guy had nothing to live for, and he more or less set the stage

●

and there was nothing that we could really do about it. We call it "suicide by cop." We try to identify it and we do everything in our power to prevent it, but sometimes we can't.

Going back to Sex Crimes and Senior Citizens, dealing with life and death is what a detective's job is all about.

3

•

LIEUTENANT

HUGH

MCGOWAN

I left patrol to go into the Bomb Squad in 1977. Actually, what happened was in September 1976 there was a terrorist incident in New York. A bomb was left in Grand Central Station by a Croatian group that was seeking independence from Yugoslavia. The Bomb Squad responded to the station, and they removed this device. At the same time there was a plane being hijacked to Paris by these people who wanted freedom for Croatia.

In the late sixties into the mid seventies a lot of these movements were going on. There was a Cuban liberation movement, a Puerto Rican independence group, a Turkish freedom group, and I'm probably leaving out four or five other groups.

But this particular group hijacking the plane communicated through the pilot, and their message was we have a bomb on board, and if you doubt us look at the device that we left in Grand Central Station in locker-number so and so.

The device in the locker was in a big, iron kettle. The Bomb Squad took it up to the demolition range

•

at Rodman's Neck in the Bronx. They wanted to see if they could dismantle it, because when that hijacked plane landed in Paris the French police would have to handle it, and we might be able to tell them how to disarm it. Well, when our squad tried to "render it safe" the device detonated with police officer Brian Murray and Sergeant Terry McTigue beside it.

Terry was very seriously hurt. There were no doctors or nurses standing by, but the Emergency Service officers were able to cut an airway in his throat. He survived because of that airway.

Brian was killed. Consequently, there was an opening in the Bomb Squad for a sergeant.

I always tell people that I was very conscious of how I got into the Bomb Squad, and I was always very conscious of how I could leave the Squad.

When the airliner landed in Paris, the French police arrested a Croatian by the name of Busic and his American wife. The bomb they were carrying was a phony; they had used putty instead of plastic explosive. The French put them on a plane back to New York, where they were turned over to the federal authorities.

Busic and his wife were also suspected of planting a bomb in a locker at La Guardia Airport during the 1975 Christmas holiday season. It killed seven or eight people. However, there wasn't enough evidence to charge them on this.

I got into the Bomb Squad at a time when it was very difficult. They had an investigation going on as to what actually happened with Murray and McTigue. There was some question about whether they had made a mistake. I think the squad felt they didn't do anything wrong, and I believed this as well. The Bomb Squad was in existence for at least sixty years when I came into it, and over the years they handled thousands of devices. However, it would be like driving in a police car with your lights and sirens on for

•

every assignment you go on. Sooner or later, you're going to have an accident. The numbers are against you. And that's what really happened with Murray and McTigue.

The good thing that came out of this tragedy was that we received increased funding, which enabled us to get bomb suits similar to ones that the British had developed for use in Northern Ireland, but previously hadn't been used here in New York because of financial reasons. At that time, the suits cost 20,000 dollars apiece, but each one has proven its worth.

In 1982, when bombs were put down all over the city by the FALN Puerto Rican terrorist group, two officers from the Bomb Squad, Detectives Richie Pastorella and Tony Senft, tried to remove a device that was left at the federal courthouse, but the bomb detonated on them.

They didn't have on the helmet that came with the suit. The reason that they chose not to wear their helmets was in order to have better visibility. But the fact that they just had the suits on enabled them to survive their very serious injuries.

The British really developed these suits out of necessity. In Northern Ireland a lot of the devices they were encountering were in cars that were seemingly abandoned. When they would go up to check out the suspicious car, often there was another device planted nearby. Sometimes the first device had already gone off, so this was also an attempt to lure the policemen to the scene, after which the second device would go off. Because of that tactic they lost quite a few of their officers.

The suit is made out of the same material that you find in a ballistic vest: Kevlar. But the material is much thicker than in a vest. If you have ten layers of this Kevlar in a vest, then the bomb suit has about forty or fifty layers of it. The suit is like a pair of pants that you put on backwards. The back of the pants open up to enable you to get in. The bottom of the pants cover your shoes. The pants have suspenders to hold

•

them up. Then you have an army-type of field jacket, also made of Kevlar, that you put on backwards. You actually need someone to help you get into the suit, and they would zip you up from the back. On the front of the suit they also have a ceramic type of chest protector, and there is a ceramic groin protector that fits into these slots. The ceramic material is the same kind of material that you'd find in a missile's nose cone.

Even though there's a shock wave that comes from an explosion and certainly the noise and the heat, many of the officers were killed by either the material that was part of the device, like a pipe, or material that was purposely put into it. For example, sometimes they would put nails in it that would make it an antipersonnel type of device. While the Kevlar would protect you somewhat, it couldn't fully stop that kind of shrapnel, so they added the ceramic material.

The helmet is very similar to what a tank operator would use. It is a big, full, covering helmet. But in the front it has a piece of Plexiglas about an inch thick that would come down over your face.

The one thing that they didn't have was gloves. They couldn't come up with any you could effectively use when working on a device. The feeling was that they'd be too cumbersome, and you'd probably blow yourself up trying to do anything with them on. So the decision was made that you wouldn't have gloves, but the sleeves would be a little bit longer and if you perceived that something was going to happen, hopefully, you'd have time to pull your hands back into the sleeves.

Not only do you have a problem with shrapnel, but you also have flames when a bomb explodes. So, it had a Nomex-type of coating on it. And it was a very, very heavy thing to wear.

One of the things that I found when I worked in that first-generation suit, at a bomb factory that was discovered in

•

Elmhurst, Queens, was that in wearing it for eight or nine hours you build up a lot of body heat because the suit couldn't breathe. I lost about five pounds at that operation.

When I first came into the Bomb Squad, a lot of the old-timers felt that you really shouldn't wear the suit because it would actually hinder you. My feeling was that if you gave up some maneuverability for the safety it was a good judgement call. Now it's standard operating procedure to wear a suit on approaching everything. I think the Bomb Squad is now using a second- or third-generation suit.

The British felt that the suit really couldn't protect you if you were actually on a device when it went off, but if you were approaching or walking away from it, the suit would save you. That's the kind of disclaimer they gave us. However, we actually had people subjected to an explosion right next to them and survived because the suit exceeded its expectations.

I was home. I had worked a day tour. It was New Year's eve. I guess it was about a little bit after 10:30 when I got the call from Tony Senft telling me that bombs were going off all over the city. There had been a device placed at the federal building at 26 Federal Plaza, and two across the street at the federal courthouse. There was also one at the federal courthouse in Brooklyn, and another one was just discovered at police headquarters.

Tony was letting me know what was going on because the procedure was to call in the supervisor and get additional help to handle the device. I can remember my words to him, even to this day. I said, "Okay, just take it easy. I'll be right in." Because both Tony and his partner Richie Pastorella were fairly new members of the Bomb Squad. And as seniority works, those are the people that often have to catch the weekend duty. Not that we had any reason to think anything would happen, otherwise we would have had more people on duty.

•

I asked for a Highway Patrol car to bring me in because of all the traffic going into Manhattan.

It was really quite effective to take this night to strike in New York. A police officer at headquarters discovered a device while he was doing a security sweep. Before he had a chance to do anything it exploded and took his leg off.

Monsignor Kowsky, the police department chaplain, had responded to the scene, and was tending to him before they removed him to Bellevue Hospital. They didn't know if he was going to survive or not.

My sense was that once I got in there and surveyed the scene I'd probably end up calling in most of the people from the Bomb Squad. That's the time when you start getting all of your people in and decide how to handle this thing.

Tony and Richie were attempting to remove these devices, which were out in the open, and place them in the bomb truck. They weren't going to disassemble them. Our sense was let's get them safe as can be, and the feeling always was that the safest place for a detonation was at the demolition area of the outdoor range at Rodman's Neck. That's the place designed to have a bomb go off. If you couldn't have a device go off there, then the only other safe place was in the bomb truck, which was designed to handle a blast from twenty-five sticks of dynamite. So Tony and Richie's thinking was good.

I was still on my way in when I heard a call over the air for the Bomb Squad supervisor to respond forthwith to the federal courthouse in Manhattan. And without any more knowledge than that, I believed that at least two of my guys had been blown up and killed.

Tony and Richie were both taken to Bellevue Hospital.

When I got to the scene, however, I realized that there was still another device that hadn't detonated. So I decided to get two other technicians to come in from home as soon as possible.

I explained to them what had happened. One of them,

Charlie Wells, was a junior sergeant in the Bomb Squad at the time. I said to him, "I think that you know the best thing we can do is just take this nice and easy. Why don't you get some more people here and, in the meantime, I'm going to go up to the hospital and see what happened to Tony and Richie."

That probably was the toughest device the Bomb Squad worked on, because you're working on a device while you're kneeling in the blood of two of your brother officers, who you think are dead, and you don't know if this bomb, like the ones in Northern Ireland, is set to go off later to kill the police who have rushed to the scene of the first explosion.

When I got to the hospital I found that they were both alive. It was unbelievable that they had survived. Richie was very, very seriously hurt. He had been blinded. He also lost a piece of his hand and had terrible injuries to his ears— he was deaf in one ear.

I'm convinced that they wouldn't have survived the detonation if they didn't have their bomb suits on. And the bomb suits only came into use because of Brian Murray and Terry McTigue.

Just an aside on Richie and Tony—they are both still with the Bomb Squad, but they're on sick leave. Richie was in a master's of social work program at Hunter College. He has done an awful lot of counseling of officers who have been seriously hurt, not only for this department, but for other departments as well. And he has written quite a lot. He can't see, but he still has the ability to speak into a recorder and have somebody transcribe it.

Richie was instrumental in forming the police self-help group, which is under the auspices of the police department, but is run entirely by officers who have either been shot or hurt badly in automobile or other accidents. When cops have been crippled or paralyzed, they just want to crawl into a corner. They are down on the world and down

•

on the police department. But this program is an attempt to really let them know that their life goes on and they can still make something of it.

Tony Senft is now the president of the police self-help group, and he will continue to help many police officers pick up the pieces of their lives and go about the business of living.

I know these two guys, along with Terry McTigue, have been tremendously important to the other people in the Bomb Squad who had to go on after this accident. After looking at a brother officer who has been so seriously hurt, you ask yourself if you really want to continue on in this line of work. We all have families and they worry, and certainly wives of the Bomb Squad worry as much as any police wife. But the message that Richie and Tony gave us was that you really can't live in fear. You can't just curl up and turn the lights out and say I'm not going to go on with my life.

After that accident, we really put a full court press on for robotics. The first robot that we looked at was a bucket of bolts. It was assembled by a man up in Canada using spare parts like windshield-wiper motors from a Volkswagen to power the arm, and tires from a lawn tractor. But it was absolutely perfect for what we needed, because it was a pretty tough little device. It was small enough to get through doors, but able to handle the bouncing around from the potholes you hit riding in a department vehicle.

The Bomb Squad now has a second-generation robot that they bring to every scene. They use a robot almost every time they can, rather than having a human go up and touch any of these devices, because there is always an extra element of risk that's involved with terrorist bombings. Terrorists are not only looking to have the device go off, but if they can take out some police officers while they're trying to disarm it, that adds to their headlines.

The robot has been used many, many times in New York

•

City, and we haven't lost one yet. However, in Nassau County they sent the robot in to pick up an explosive device, and it detonated. There was their 20,000 dollar or 30,000 dollar bucket of bolts all blown up, but it was a very, very good investment because that was not a human being blown up.

One of the tools we had before the robot was an explosive-detection canine. A lot of people think that's the be-all and end-all. If you had the dog why would you need anything else? But the thing is the dog only finds the explosive device for us. Once he does that, his job is over.

Many times we already know where the package is. Now the problem is, what are we going to do with it? We have to get it from point X to point Y. Many times you would have the human go over to this package, dressed up in this bomb suit, and they would physically pick it up and put it into the bomb truck. Well, one of the things that came about in addition to the new robots was a total containment vessel. You only have to move the bomb a short distance to get it into this vessel, and then the whole thing can be carried out of a building in relative safety. The containment vessel is actually based on the design of a diving bell, which has to withstand great pressures under the sea. And if it withstands great pressure from without, it probably can withstand great pressures from within. They also designed into this container little ports that would allow the gases to vent.

From the time of Alfred Nobel, who invented dynamite, up to the present day, an explosion is really something burning very, very fast and displacing a great amount of gas. But for terrorists, over the years, it's not enough just to have the explosive go off. You can actually encase the explosive in something, such as a pipe, and now you've made a hand grenade, only it's a very, very big hand grenade that has a very effective killing range. That's why pipe bombs came into their own. Also, depending on the amount of explosive, you could secrete the charge, for example, in a car,

•

and if the car blew up you have made a huge device, because all the parts flying off the car will act as shrapnel.

When I first came into the Bomb Squad I attended a four-week long course run by the FBI down at the Redstone Arsenal in Huntsville, Alabama. It's kind of a basic course. But one thing that they told us was that if you know what a bomb looks like, hold that idea off to the side, because when most people think of bombs they think about the things that fall out of airplanes. But in fact a bomb's design is limited only by the imagination of the bomb maker. You can put one in a lunch bag, or in a briefcase, or you can put it in a locker in Grand Central Station, and everything that you put between yourself and the explosive device becomes part of that device when it detonates.

The thing we would always find in New York is that somebody would say, "that attaché case doesn't belong there." Now it becomes a suspicious package. Fortunately, in many, many cases, it's just somebody's attaché case that had been left behind. But with our portable X ray machine we can often look inside these cases without the risk of engaging a possible booby trap.

The first job in the Bomb Squad that I actually handled occurred when I was in the squad for only a very short time. I don't think I had even gone to bomb school yet, when a Mr. Frosty ice-cream truck exploded. It knocked a mounted policeman off his horse. And it got a lot of media attention. I don't want to call it a slow news day, but it was the only thing that made the headlines. Why would this truck explode? Who put this bomb in this truck around lunch hour? There were a lot of people on the street, but fortunately, other than the policeman, only a couple of people had injuries to their ears.

This was a big investigation. We called in all of our best people. But where do you start? Here's this ice-cream truck that blew up, and somebody had whispered into the chief's ear, "oh, this explosion must be equal to four sticks of dyna-

•

mite." So the chief wants to know everything, and he wants to know it by tomorrow. I remember working the whole night on it.

We took the ice-cream truck from where it blew up, somewhere in the Wall Street area, on a flatbed and moved it over to a vacant lot on the East Side, where we figured we could work on it and go through all of the debris. However, we found out that was not a good location, because the lot was filled with rats and it was their neighborhood. They were giving us a hard time. So I said, "this is not really going to work. We're going to have to move this thing to somewhere else." We ended up moving it to a pier on the West Side.

The way the Bomb Squad works is very similar to an archeologist: We get wire screens out and we start sifting through all of the material to try and see what the device was made of.

In the meantime I had two detectives go out to the plant from where this truck had turned out. And they looked at all of the engineering on a similar truck. They also tried to find out why somebody would do this. Maybe it was a revenge type of thing. Maybe Mr. Frosty worked in an area he shouldn't have. But these lead nowhere.

What we did discover, though, was that the Mr. Frosty truck was a step-in vehicle with a large door on each side, but only the driver's door was used to get in and out. He had a freezer pushed against the door on the passenger's side. And he smoked.

It turns out he was selling fireworks from the truck, which was illegal, but it was another way of getting a little more business. He kept the fireworks in the freezer, so if the police came by they wouldn't see them. However, he knocked over a coffee cup that he used as an ashtray, and it fell into the freezer and set the fireworks on fire.

Well, he took one look at that and bailed out of the truck. And all anybody knew was that this guy jumped out of his

•

truck and ran away and just disappeared. And the truck blew up.

Now our job was to tell the chief of detectives that it wasn't four sticks of dynamite that caused this blast, but it was "Super M-80's" and "Blockbuster" fireworks that had started on fire and caused the truck to explode.

I remember that was the first time that I saw my name in print. I guess everybody was a little suspicious of our conclusion. They must have said, let's put McGowan's name in the paper and if it all blows up later on we can blame him.

That was my first job, which turned out not to be a bombing, but in some ways told me about the type of people that we had in the Bomb Squad. Here is a squad that has a deadline. We have got to get the answer. It was a Friday night in the summer, when most of the civilian employees of the police department were off. I had to get Emergency Service officers to find a flatbed and somebody else to get a tow truck.

Other detectives were able to get back out to the factory, where they found the driver, who figured he was going to be arrested. It was like, "come over here. I want to talk to you. What's the story now? Why did the truck . . . ?" The guy opened up and told them the whole story.

Detectives get people to do things they don't normally want to do. They get them to tell the truth when they really want to tell a lie. I don't know how legitimate the ice-cream truck industry is, but my understanding was that there were some unsavory characters involved in this. However, they understood it was better to cooperate with these detectives, because they really weren't looking to put them out of business. They were just trying to find out the facts.

The hard part was putting it all down on paper. We had all these loose ends. It was an amazing exercise, watching them all work together on the report.

"Sergeant, why don't you try this?" And one of the detectives would write out a line.

"Now, we can start it this way."

•

"Oh yeah, I like that."

Somebody else would say, "No . . . no . . . we used that adjective before. Let's try this one."

So the whole thing was a team effort from beginning to end. And in the end, everybody in our squad was satisfied that we had done our work, even though some people said, "yeah, but are you really sure it wasn't a bomb?"

"Yeah, we're absolutely sure."

The Bomb Squad's line of demarcation in a case would be to determine what type of device it was, how it was manufactured, and certainly trace back to see if the explosives were stolen. The actual apprehending of the people who planted the bomb would be done by either the detectives from the squad in the precinct where the bomb was found, or by the Joint Terrorist Task Force if it was a terrorist bombing. When the case came to court, we would provide the expert testimonies on the construction of the device.

In 1978 I had been in the Bomb Squad about a year. On this particular summer evening we got a call that there had been an explosion in an apartment building in East Elmhurst, not far from La Guardia Airport. The fire department had responded, and at first they assumed that it was a gas explosion. But as they started to go through the apartment, they found a man severely injured. They rushed him to the hospital, fortunately under police escort. The fire department also found in the apartment things that looked like pipe bombs. So they called for the Bomb Squad. It was one of those times when they're calling for you and you know you better get there quickly.

When we got to the location, we donned bomb suits and went in and looked at the apartment. The firemen were very, very lucky when they first went in there because, as they will, they move things around to see what the extent of the fire is. They pulled the stove out, and that's when they found these pipe bombs that hadn't detonated, even though

•

one pipe bomb had detonated when this fellow, William Morales, was assembling it.

In the bathroom we found instructions on making an incendiary chemical mixture. On one wall there were other instructions laid out, step-by-step, on how to take a wristwatch apart and make it so that it could be used as a timing device for these pipe bombs. So we started to very carefully go through the apartment. We found fifty-seven sticks of dynamite in a closet that had survived this explosion. On seeing this, my reaction was one that has been used in police work since the time of Julius Caesar. I said, "oh, shit!"

It was 5:00 when we got the call, and people were home making supper. There must have been two hundred or three hundred people in that and the adjacent buildings. The death toll would have been horrendous.

We later learned that the apartment was basically a safe house for terrorists. Nobody really lived there. William Morales had been seen going in and out of this apartment along with some other people.

We also found literature attributed to the FALN, along with a couple of hundred pounds of explosive chemicals that was being used to make incendiary devices.

At that time there was a wave of these incendiary devices going off in department stores. The terrorists would place these devices in the pocket of a garment. They were the size of a Marlboro box. They contained two incendiary chemicals, and after a period of time one of the chemicals would melt through its outer wrapping and join up with the other one, and they would burst into flames, setting the garment on fire, which in turn would cause the whole section to go on fire. I guess their hope was to burn down the entire store. And that particular night we had a dozen of these calls about these incendiary devices going off. So apparently some of the incendiary devices had been given to whoever was the mule, and they had been placed in the stores in the

•

area of Thirty-fourth Street, such as Macy's, Korvettes, and Gimbels.

We had a really huge undertaking. For all intent and purposes it was a bomb factory. I had to call in additional manpower to help us to handle this thing.

Starting at about 8:00, we had both of the big La Guardia bomb trucks set up in front of this location.

The red bomb trucks look a bit like Conestoga wagons. They are known as the "La Guardia bomb trucks" because they were built when Fiorello La Guardia was mayor of the city. They have a basket of bridge cable woven together inside a cylindrical type of an arrangement of more woven bridge cables.

The trucks were made in 1940, after two officers from the Bomb Squad, detectives Sochia and Lynch, had tried to remove a device found at the 1939 World's Fair. It was in a suitcase left in the British pavilion. At that time, there was no vehicle to transport this thing. So they took it off to the side of what is now the service road for the Grand Central Parkway, and were attempting to examine it, when it detonated. Both of the officers were killed. These were the first two fatalities in the Bomb Squad.

The vehicles were designed as a WPA project. I was told that they made three of them, two very large ones placed on the chassis of old garbage trucks, and a third one that was a miniature version, about the size of my desk—maybe three feet wide and five feet long.

The miniature one was taken down to Washington and used by the Secret Service in the event that a device would be found in the White House. I don't know whether it's in the Smithsonian Museum now, or if it's still in the White House basement.

The three of them were made by the company that was building the Triborough Bridge at the time. And that's where the bridge cables came from.

We evacuated the entire block with the fire department

•

standing by, and we had to have the route cleared by the highway units from East Elmhurst all the way up to Rodman's Neck in the Bronx.

The FBI, the NYPD Intelligence Unit, and the Arson Explosion Squad were called in to handle the other materials that were found here. Finding written material, such as the communiqués they would distribute and other writings, along with their personal effects, was a major break. It was really the beginning of the end for the FALN when we started to come up with this material. It also developed that there were fingerprints that we were able to follow-up with, along with other investigative leads in this apartment.

I knew what they were looking for, but at the same time my primary obligation was to make this apartment house as safe as I could, as quickly as I could. The pressure was on us, and I was constantly asked, "well, can you get us some more of the material?" or "when can we go in there?" I had not only our own people from the NYPD but we had the federal people as well, and they couldn't wait to get in there. Plus we had other federal people being flown in from Washington who were going to help us with the explosive wrappers that we found in the apartment. The FBI had been waiting for a big break—and this was it.

It turned out that the dynamite was part of a theft from somewhere in the Midwest.

Most of the time the explosives that we find have detonated so we don't have the advantage of knowing the exact type of explosives used. The only time you'd find anything like this would be when something didn't detonate because of faulty assembly of the device, or that we got to it before it was scheduled to go off.

A similar type of apartment was later found in Chicago, by some junkie who broke in thinking he was going to score by cleaning out this apartment, but what he found was dynamite. I guess his conscience got the better of him, and he

•

told the police about it. They found explosives from the same shipment that we had uncovered in New York.

The thing that we were very leery of was that explosives that have undergone an explosion can become very unstable. There's a list of things that make explosives unstable, including shock, heat, exposure to the elements, and failure to be properly maintained.

Nitroglycerin is the basic component of dynamite. The nitroglycerin is put in the filler material, much like sawdust, and that filler basically keeps it stable by keeping it from being subject to effects of heat or shock. They put the wrapper on it to enable you to handle it.

Dynamite, however, has to be turned when it's in storage because the nitroglycerin ends up sinking to the bottom and, if you don't turn it on a regular basis, will actually leak through the paper. What we found was that it had leaked on to the floor of the closet that it was kept in.

Now the closet becomes explosive. The nitroglycerin is in the wood, and you have to take the wood out unless you can treat it in such a way that it will be rendered safe. In the meantime, the nitroglycerin can be set off by almost anything, including dropping something out of your pocket.

So we were dealing with something that, at the time, only god knew where it had come from, but we knew it had been very poorly treated—stored in a closet with no ventilation. Now we were required to go in and take it out. Our goal was to make smaller bombs out of this one apartment, which itself was one big bomb.

The first thing that we put into the bomb truck were the incendiary devices and the pipe bombs. A pipe bomb is a pipe with two nipples on each end and a watch with explosives inside. In this case, the explosive was dynamite. The additional problem with them was that you didn't know when they were set to go off. When Morales was blown up, he was loading one of these pipe bombs. Now were the other pipe bombs also loaded? The only way we would

•

know this was if we x-rayed them and saw what the components were. But even if the X ray showed a watch in there, it still couldn't tell what time it was set to go off. Our sense was that they were probably set to go off within twelve hours, which was the maximum amount of time that you can get on a wristwatch. So our biggest problem was to get the pipe bombs out of there as quick as possible. The pipe bombs were the most dangerous part of the operation.

We took each one and wrapped it in a bomb blanket. By wrapping the bombs in the blankets we weren't trying to protect ourselves, we were just trying to safely move them away from the building. Then we carried them out, one at a time, and put them in a bomb truck. We decided to put all the pipe bombs in one truck so we could get that truck out of there as soon as possible. But we ended up keeping that truck in the block for about another hour until we were sure we had all of them out of the apartment. And we couldn't be 100 percent sure until we had searched the entire place.

Now the dynamite was the next thing to be moved. Not only was it dangerous, but it had probably had the most information as far as the investigation was concerned.

We very gingerly took each stick out and wrapped them individually with a bomb blanket, and carried them to the street. It took us many trips to bring all the explosives down because we could only carry them down, very gently, by hand. We didn't have the robots at the time, and we didn't want to take them and just throw them all in a bag.

But we couldn't put all of the dynamite in one truck, so we took half of it and put it in the truck that was still in front of the apartment house. When we finished loading that truck the first truck was back from the range. I had other Bomb Squad people called in from home and sent to the range to receive the explosives.

There was a lot of pressure put on us, not only from the enormity of the job that we were handling, but from our own people to get into the apartment. However, we

•

couldn't let them in until we were really finished with our job. The intelligence people wanted photographs, but I was afraid to take photos inside the apartment because of the unstable chemicals that were still in there. So we had to feed the information to our people who were out in the street as best we could.

We worked all through the night emptying the apartment. Afterwards, I think we had all of ten minutes to brush our teeth with our fingers and get down to police headquarters, because this big press conference was going to be held. Well, I know after I've been wearing the same clothes and sweating for these number of hours the last thing that I want to do is appear on camera, because I feel like a grimeball. I remember the chief saying "make sure you look presentable." Well, somebody came up with a razor, and we were able to shave the stubble off our faces. But the chief was certainly great in making sure that we were there rather than just the spokesman.

It is a fun thing to look back on, but at the time I said "my god, we really worked hard on this job." It was great satisfaction to know that these bombs were not going to be set off in New York, and that we were able to get a start on apprehending the terrorists.

We were intimately involved with this event, but we didn't realize the enormity of it until it was over. It was really bigger than the Bomb Squad, because so many different people were involved. We had people from Highway Patrol helping us get to the various locations, and the people from Emergency Service, who have always been the backbone of the Bomb Squad, really came through for us.

Whenever you work in an environment involving dynamite, the nitroglycerin can permeate your skin, and you'll normally find anybody who works around explosives chewing aspirin because the nitro can give you a raging migraine headache. The tension of the situation was another factor that was going to add to your headache. And because

•

of that one-inch piece of Plexiglas right in front of your face when you are wearing the bomb-suit helmet, you really aren't getting a good supply of oxygen.

A couple of the fellows in Emergency Service set up this first-aid station for us to give us a whiff of oxygen, which would kind of clear our heads and enable us to continue working in that particular environment.

I remember that the fire department was very cooperative. They did things like set up the hydrants so we could get a drink of water. That was the most wonderful-tasting water that I ever had in my life, because you were just sweating so much in that bomb suit.

After the pipe bombs came up to the range, they were unloaded from the bomb truck and put into a magazine. But before a detective by the name of Dan Buckley, who was assigned to the range, had a chance to close up the magazine, the pipe bombs exploded.

We got a call at the temporary headquarters, out in the street, that the magazine exploded, and they were calling for the fire department. We had a chief with us from the fire department, and I said to him, "Don't let the fire department come into the range. Have them fight the fire from outside."

He replied, "Why are you saying that, Sergeant?"

"Chief, I don't know how many of the pipe bombs exploded, and the last thing in the world I want is for a fireman to go into the range and have one go off on him while he's trying to fight the fire. There's nothing there that the fire can hurt. That's the place where bombs were meant to explode."

Right away he picked up on what I was saying, and he said "no problem. I agree with you one hundred percent." Then he got on his radio and sent a message up there.

The fire department came around to the side of the range and just poured water on the magazine and put the fire out.

I talked to the chief later on. "I hope you didn't think I

•

was saying the fire department is not allowed in a police department facility."

He said, "Initially I took offense at what you were saying, but then I realized it was good advice when you told me why you were doing it."

"Chief, that's why everybody's going to walk away from this job in one piece." He agreed.

I wasn't paid to take bombs apart. I was paid to make sure that everything went well.

I remember meeting the Lieutenant, Frank McGee, who was in charge of the range. I figured this guy's going to be really annoyed at me—I blew up his range.

He said, "That's what it was meant for. All these years that we're working up there, and this is the first time we had an accidental detonation." It was accidental in the sense that normally we went downrange to an area that was very sandy, and we would blow devices up when we were ready. These magazines were kind of a safety factor.

Then the lieutenant said, "You did a good job."

My sense was that we had all done it. It wasn't me as the sergeant, it was the team. The thing that helped me in this assignment was the idea that if you have the right team you can handle anything.

The other thing that made it go so well was the fact that when I made demands on people, whether it was "get me some sodas" or "reach out and get me these three guys"— who we haven't called in yet, and have them respond to the office, get some tools, and go up to those jobs at Korvettes and Gimbels,—they did it without hesitation.

When we were doing the write-up on this job, somebody higher up in the chain of command said "well, you can't have too many people involved in it, because it looks like you're trying to get a medal for everyone in the Bomb Squad."

I said, "but all these people were involved in this job. I

•

mean we all had an equal hand in it, although some had more dangerous assignments than others."

"Just keep it to a minimum."

It was so terribly frustrating to have to do that. But that's the "fun" of police work: Handling the aftermath of these things.

I was very proud of myself for coordinating this operation, because my boss was down at the FBI national academy. And we were all kidding about this after the job was over. Someone said, "We'll have to do a suicide watch on him to make sure he doesn't slash his wrists, because this was the major break that we've been looking for."

As a postscript to this story, Morales didn't die from his injuries. He lost both of his hands. He was being held in the Bellevue Hospital medical prison ward, on the second floor of the old C and D building, and somehow he was able to make his escape.

Another prisoner, who was escaping with him, went out the window on a rope made of sheets tied together, but he fell down an airshaft that ran along the side of the building to his death. I'm not even sure to this day if they know whether there were people who got into the prison ward who enabled Morales to make his escape, or if he got out on his own. I find it very difficult to believe that somebody with no hands could make that escape by himself, especially when his partner, who had full use of his hands, didn't make it. Yet other than a few correction officers, who were disciplined for whatever lapse in their behavior was thought to have contributed to the escape, no one else was ever apprehended.

We were told there were fifty or sixty people actually involved in the FALN, and they had any number of other people that would support them in their cause. I think that somebody had to be waiting for Morales outside to drive him away. I mean somebody coming out with a hospital gown on and no hands couldn't be walking on First Avenue

•

very long. He made good his escape. He reappeared in Cuba and then later in Mexico.

Morales was eventually apprehended in a shootout in Mexico. Mexico held him in jail for a number of years, but I believe they refused to extradite him back to the United States. I believe he's not even in jail anymore. He's probably back in Cuba.

Those of us in the Bomb Squad never thought highly of any of these so-called liberation groups. I remember this British detective coming over from Scotland Yard, and I know initially his sense was that because there were more than a couple of men in the squad that had Irish names that maybe we would be sympathetic to the IRA. But it wasn't true in my case, and it wasn't true in the case of anybody else, and there was a couple of fellows who had actually been born in Ireland who were part of the Bomb Squad. We viewed the setting off bombs as a cowardly way of fighting a battle. You can almost admire a stickup man who goes into the bank and at least presents himself there, because he's taking his chances that he's going to get away with this thing. But the bomber puts the bomb down and just floats away into the night, and minutes or hours later the device goes off, without him knowing or caring who the target is going to be.

Sometimes being in the Bomb Squad can have its lighter side. For example, we'd be asked to do VIP security when the president or some other head of state was in town. We would go ahead of time to where they were scheduled to stay or speak, and sweep the place with the bomb dog to make sure that it was secure. We would also stand by in the event that something was discovered later on. I remember one time we were at a gathering in the Waldorf-Astoria Hotel. We were a little bit off to the side and we were blending in as well as we could even though we had the dog there, when a man comes up to us and starts to question the dog handler about why is this dog here in the hotel.

•

The handler said, "well, we're part of the security."

The guy said, "Yeah, but why would you have an attack dog here in the Waldorf? That doesn't make any sense to me."

Now this dog he was looking at was no more an attack dog than Snoopy. It was a Labrador retriever, and it was a very nice dog. The handler, Detective Ron McLean, says, "well, you look like a pretty patriotic American, so maybe I can tell you the real story of why we're here."

"Yeah, okay, what's the secret?"

"If, god forbid, the president was struck blind—this is a Seeing Eye dog—we would just put the leash in his hand and he'd be able to walk out of here without any problems at all."

The guy said, "god, you Secret Service people think of everything, don't you?"

Another time we were sweeping a ballroom—I think Jimmy Carter was going to be there—when this man tries to come into the room. It turns out it's Charlton Heston. But this detective from the Bomb Squad, Neil Monaco, says to him, "Sorry, you can't come in here, sir."

Charlton Heston looks at him and says, "Do you know who I am?"

And Neil says, "I'm sorry, you just can't come in here—we're security."

Heston then says he was part of the event—the master of ceremonies—and he wanted to get in there to prepare himself before the other people arrived.

Neil says, "I'm sorry, but you can't come in here yet."

Again Heston says, "Do you know who I am?"

"Yes, you're Moses, but you still can't come in here until we're finished." Heston, of course, had played that role in *The Ten Commandments*.

With that Charlton Heston went "oh, okay," and walked away. Great place for one-liners.

I knew I was getting promoted, and one of the units that I

•

had wanted to go to as a sergeant if I hadn't gotten into the Bomb Squad was the Emergency Service Unit. In Emergency Service you could do anything from climbing a bridge for someone who was threatening to jump, to extricating someone who fell under a subway train, to vesting up and going into buildings after bad guys. Also, I really wanted to go there because the lieutenants in Emergency Service were field supervisors, and most lieutenants, other than being in the Detective Bureau, would normally be desk officers assigned to a station house. That didn't appeal to me.

I was interviewed by Captain Hanratty of Emergency Service, and I got the assignment. But I really couldn't handle any of the heavy weapons that Emergency Service uses until a training course came along. The first course that came along was the course that they ran for hostage negotiators. So I went through the heavy-weapons course with them. It was run by Lieutenant Bobby Louden, who was in charge of the team. I knew him from having been in the Bomb Squad, and we were very good friends. The second week of the training was how they handled the hostage situations from the negotiators' side, which is also important for the Emergency Service supervisors to know. "Well," I said to Bobby, "do you mind if I sit in for the whole course?"

He said, "no problem." So at the end of the two weeks' training, Bob Louden presented me with a certificate that I was a hostage negotiator. I really wouldn't use it because I was not in the Detective Bureau anymore. It was one of those things that I said, "gee, isn't that nice," and I never really gave it another thought, until a couple of years later when I was applying for the job of the commanding officer of the Hostage Team. Not only was I in the Detective Bureau before, but I could say, quite honestly, to the chief of detectives, "I'm also a hostage negotiator."

He said, "oh, is that so?"

•

I showed him my certificate and said "trained by Bob Louden." It's very interesting how things turn out.

What happened was in September 1988 there was an incident down on the Lower East Side, on Clinton Street, that involved a Chinese man who barricaded himself in his apartment after firing shots out the window at passersby. It turned out the police were some of the passersby. After some time they were able to locate where the shots came from.

From neighbors they discovered that this man lived in the apartment with his wife and two children. The initial sense was that the wife and the children were in there with him. The incident started between 5:00 and 6:00 in the morning. As the morning went on they were able to find out that the wife wasn't in the house anymore, but they felt the children were.

Since he spoke very little English, they had to use a security guard who was also Oriental. However, eventually they were able to locate a Chinese-speaking detective, Doug Lee, who was not a negotiator at the time, but was assigned to what's known as the Jade Squad. He was acting as a negotiator to get through to this guy barricaded in the apartment, but they never really had an effective negotiation going on with him.

The guy would talk incoherently about things that they really just couldn't understand. And they were trying to talk to him through a locked door. He had furniture up against it, so it was very difficult to communicate with him.

They saw him quite a few times from behind the ballistic shield, but they never saw the children, with the exception of one time—they had a camera lowered down to the window and they saw the little girl go by. So they knew that at some time she was alive in the house. They knew they had to do something with this guy to try to get the children out.

So, one of the things that they decided they were going to do was to try and knock the door off its hinges, but because of the barricade situation they weren't able to really get the door down.

Well, after they attempted to take the door down, at approximately 12:00 or 1:00 in the afternoon, he came up with a shotgun, pointed it at the door where the police officers were trying to talk to him, fires, and hits this ballistic shield. He was firing birdshot. But the birdshot didn't get absorbed into the shield because it's very light shot. Instead, it ended up ricocheting off the shield, and it hit about nine or ten of the Emergency Service officers that were out in the hallway. Fortunately, none too seriously, but nevertheless they were hit. After he fired a second time, one of the Emergency Service officers fired back and killed him.

When they got into the apartment they found that the man had killed his two children. This was the first time that we had lost a hostage during a hostage situation.

Not too long after that incident there was an opening for a commanding officer of the Hostage Team, and having the tactical background from Emergency Service, and having the training from the Detective Bureau, I really think that I had the inside track on the job.

Although I didn't know all of the negotiators, I had worked with many of them during my time as an Emergency Service supervisor. I was the one who would call them to these types of jobs.

The other thing that I think helped me to get the job was that I believed in the hostage negotiating process. I believed it was not only very important to rescue the people who were trapped in these circumstances, but it was also important to get the hostage taker out without having to use deadly physical force. It was a method that the department had adopted about twenty years ago, and it has saved a lot of police lives. We don't have to kick the door down and do a John Wayne-rush down the hall with guns firing, and this means that all these police officers are going to leave this job without even a hangnail.

•

If the job of the Hostage Negotiation Team is to get the people who were being held against their will out, and also get the bad guy out, we do that not only with our talking but with our listening.

Many times I'll have people tell me, "oh, I got a great guy for you. He's a great talker."

I tell them, "I got about twenty-nine thousand good talkers in this department. What I really need is some good listeners." Because sometimes the big secret is just letting this person ventilate. I know great detectives, and the best of them know when to talk and when to listen. That's the art in this business.

The way that we approach the situation is also important. Being calm was one thing the Bomb Squad taught me. These hostage situations are pretty volatile, especially within the first hour or so that they're going on, but usually by being calm you lower the anxieties of the bad guys, and you also lower the anxieties of the good guys—the police—because I'm sure that if I was a high-ranking chief in this department, and I saw a guy coming up to me who's all upset, I don't think I'd have a lot of confidence in him.

I have to say that one reason I'm calm is because I know the caliber of the people that I have for negotiators. I mean they're guys from Homicide and Robbery Squads, and precinct detective units. In order to get into the Hostage Negotiation Team they have to have at least three years in the Detective Bureau, and usually they have more than that. Which also means they probably have about eleven years or twelve years on the police department. They're recommended by their supervisors, but I tell the supervisors, "I want a person who's above standards among all the detectives that you have, and is able to not only handle their work, but is able to be called away to do this assignment and still keep current with their caseload."

The Hostage Negotiation Team is made up of one hundred, part-time, trained negotiators, plus Dominick Masio

•

and Rafaela Valdez, who are assigned to me full-time. Rafaela is a second-grade detective, and Dominick's a third-grade detective.

The basic training course for new negotiators consists of three days of weapons training, and then seven days of other training that involves some exposure to psychology and to the different types of mental illness, and different terrorist activities that have gone on in the past and could go on in the future. And where potential hostage takers come from: There are three types that the literature talks about. The first is the terrorist who will hold hostages for his political purposes. The second is the criminal who is caught in the act committing a crime. The police will arrive on the scene and actually trap him in the location, so he holds the people that are there hostage and says, if you don't let me go I'm going to do such and such a thing to them. The third type is the emotionally disturbed person.

Many times the best way of teaching new negotiators is to talk about previous incidents that we've had. First of all, who was involved and why they were involved. We start with the bank robbery in Brooklyn—which was made into the movie *Dog Day Afternoon*. We'll show a little clip from that film, and talk about how there was no hostage team at that time, and that it is an example of how there was a lack of cooperation between the NYPD and other agencies, in particular the FBI.

It turns out that I recently found some photos, and Al Pacino is a dead ringer for the guy whose role he played. I don't know if that's art imitating life or life imitating art.

I also ask some of the negotiators presently on the team to come and talk about their incidents, and how they were used in these situations.

The other thing that I do is to tell them that all of the skills that I'm looking for they already have. They just don't know them in the same way that I know them. In hostage situations we're dealing with people who are either lying to

•

us, are upset, or don't want to reveal certain information, and don't want to go along with what we want them to do. But these are the same type of people they deal with in their everyday assignments—people who may or may not be a suspect, so the detectives need to interview them. But not just talk to them, since there will be a real direction to the conversation they have with them. Sometimes they're dealing with somebody who's under arrest for another crime and he's going to give them information, but he's not telling them out of his sense of good citizenship. He's really looking to get something out of this.

These people that we're dealing with in hostage situations feel they have the upper hand, but there are things that enable us to negotiate with them. We have a certain leverage. We have them contained, so they can't get away. We can talk to them for as long as we want. They're going to get tired. We're not going to get tired, because if you get tired as my negotiator Jones, I'm going to bring negotiator Smith in. I can bring relays of people in. He's got nobody to replace him.

We let the hostage taker know in the beginning that we're not alone. We also make it clear that he's in a situation that wasn't of his making, and we understand that, and we're here to help him get out of this situation. Sometimes it involves a lot of time, and sometimes not. Sometimes it involves concessions. When they start off with, "I want an airplane and a million dollars." Well . . . yeah, me too. But we never say no, we just don't always say yes to them. A lot of times I think that they are aware of how the situation is going to be played out.

What do they look for? The bottom line is, don't hurt me, promise you won't hurt me.

"I'll be there to make sure that nobody hurts you."

"Will you tell the D.A. that I let the person go?"

"Absolutely, we'll tell the D.A. you let the person go." All

•

the promises that we make we can live up to. They're not really hard.

The negotiator becomes very, very important for them as far as their way of saving face, keeping their dignity and not coming out like an animal. What we want to do is enable this person to come out of this situation, especially if they're emotionally disturbed and really haven't done a criminal act, and get them to somebody who can start helping them with their cure. We're not going to cure anybody. That's not our job.

Many of the situations we get involved in are domestic in nature. For example, we had this job in Brooklyn where a woman had gone to court and gotten an order of protection from her husband. But he violated the order of protection and punched her around. He was arrested and sent to Riker's. He did about six months in Riker's. But he's no sooner out than he comes back to the house with a gun and pushes his way in.

Her mother was able to escape before he got into the apartment, and she calls 911.

Uniformed officers respond to the situation. They go up to the door and knock on it. They hear from inside, "don't try to come in or I'll kill you and I'll kill her."

The uniformed officers then call for the Emergency Service Unit. And the Emergency Service Unit's first task is to contain the situation and make sure it doesn't get any bigger than it is, otherwise this guy would be holding the whole apartment house hostage. They locked him into the location, and they in turn started to set up certain tactical things. They bring a ballistic shield up there. It's a big shield, probably the size of a door—approximately eight feet tall, four feet wide, and about two inches thick, and is on wheels. It's made of not only ballistic material, but it's also that ceramic material I was talking about that is in the bomb suit, which enables you to take any kind of rifle round. It's a real great help because the most dangerous

•

place you can be in these situations is standing in front of a door. If this guy decides to fire through it, we have some protection other than just hiding behind each other.

They try and talk to this individual. In this case, they knew they clearly had a hostage situation, because they could look in from the windows and see him holding the gun to the woman's head.

So a request was put in for the Hostage Team to respond. It went to the Chief of Detectives Office, who in turn notify me and I in turn make sure the Detective Bureau, in this case, Brooklyn, is notified. Every week we have a schedule made up of who's available on what tour. And they drop whatever they're doing and respond to the situation. Sometimes they can't because they're working on a very important case, but I can also reach out to any of the other boroughs. And I have Ralphy and Dominick who I can call in from home, and I also have some of the TARU people that I can use if I have to. I can always get a negotiator.

I guess it took about five hours to convince him that he wasn't advancing his cause, which was to see his child, by doing what he was doing. In fact, he already knew it from having been in jail for his previous bad conduct. We convinced him that even though he didn't like his wife, and he was very, very angry at her, that depriving a child of its mother would be the wrong thing. We helped him to make his own decisions. We didn't tell him what he should be doing. He saw this as clearly as we saw it.

"Now, why don't we get rid of the gun. We really don't need it. I mean nobody's going to go charging in there. You're in control of the situation." Well, how could he do that safely was his question to us. Sometimes this becomes a big area of discussion, but in this case we decided to lower down a basket to him.

He decided he wanted to unload the gun. I don't like them to do that. But in this case it was a revolver, and it opened up easily, and he didn't really want to give the

•

loaded gun to his wife. But he didn't want to go to the window either because, from watching television, he was afraid a sniper was going to shoot him. So we said, "All right, well, as long as it's unloaded now, there's no reason why you can't give it to her and let her reach out to the window." So she put the gun in the basket. Then he gave her the bullets, and she put them in the basket and we took the basket back up. Now he had no gun—maybe. We're not going to bet our lives on it.

Now the big thing is, "Why don't you let her come out?" So he decides okay, he's going to do that. He lets her go out in the hall. As soon as she's behind that shield, she is taken into custody by Emergency Service and searched, because there's no guarantee that she is who she says she is. I mean supposing she changed her mind inside and she has a gun on her. We search everybody that comes out. That's the standard operating procedure.

Sometimes we handcuff hostages, because you have a lot of them coming out and you don't know who's who, especially when you have multiple hostage takers. I've seen it in robbery situations where they try to blend in with the victims, and they'll say to them, "if you tell the cops that I'm one of the bad guys I'll kill you."

So you separate them and get their pedigrees. You explain to them, "listen, this is the way we have to do it. It's for your own safety. This way if you put your hands up or you went to your pockets, nobody would think you're going for a gun." And if anybody's upset by it, we make sure that we smooth out their ruffled feathers later on.

Just before the hostage taker comes out we basically tell him the same thing. "There's going to be an officer out here who's going to want to see your hands and take you into custody." And as quickly as possible you put handcuffs on them.

The beginning and the end of the job are the most critical times. The first forty-five minutes is the time when the FBI

•

says 75 or 85 percent of the incidents that have gone bad have done so. That's when everybody's adrenaline level is probably at the highest. But once you have it all set up and let some time go by, it helps everybody calm down.

The end of the situation is where we'll negotiate the guy out. I first talk to the tactical force. "How do you want this guy to come out?"

"I want him to come out with his hands up." "I want him to come out backwards." Whatever they're comfortable with, that's what we tell this guy to do. And sometimes we'll tell it to him almost like we're imbeciles. We'll say it so slow and make him repeat it back so he knows exactly what we want. Sometimes we talk them out with the telephone right to their ear, because if he's got a telephone in his hand he can't have a gun in his hand. But that's the time that I'm the most nervous. Because sometimes these guys come to the door, open the door, see this big shield in front of them, and all these cops with guns, and then they slam the door and go back inside. And you'll have to start all over again, because you didn't paint the picture for him of what he was going to see when he comes out.

If all of a sudden a guy says, "I want to come out right now," we tell him, "you can't come out right now. It's going to take me a couple of minutes. You did things inside to protect you. Well, we did things out here to protect us. We got a big shield out here, and we have to move it out of the way, and that's going to take time."

Really what we're doing is alerting the ESU apprehension team who's actually going to take this guy into custody. The apprehension team will have somebody else covering them, so we don't have guys with shotguns in their hand trying to grab somebody. They'll also have the handcuffs all ready to physically take the guy into custody.

Hopefully, everything has been spelled out for the guy: "There are police officers outside. They're wearing big vests. They got a big helmet on. Don't be afraid when you

•

see them. My friend Bill (or whatever the leading apprehending officer's name is) will be right there."

When he comes out, the first thing the officer says is, "I am Bill. Hughie told you that you're going to talk to me, and I'm here right now."

The most difficult case I had came shortly after I took over the team in '89—it involved an ex-cop by the name of Angelo who was holding his daughter hostage, but in fact his daughter wasn't being held hostage. His daughter was in there willingly.

What we found out later on was that his ex-wife came home and found him in the house. He pistol-whipped her, and he tried to rape her. But she was able to make good her escape.

He started off with, "Don't give me any psychology bullshit. I know all about Frank Bolez." Frank Bolez was the first commanding officer of the Hostage Team.

I thought, "geez, why would my first big one have to involve an ex-cop? This is going to be a tough guy."

The guy was like the character in "Li'l Abner" that always has a cloud over his head. He had been wounded in Vietnam, came back to the world, and came on the police department. He invites his dad to go to a baseball game between the precinct and television news anchor Jim Jensen and the CBS news team. His dad comes to the game, gets hit by a line drive, and is killed. He's on restricted duty—they take his guns away. His marriage is falling apart for whatever reason. His wife throws him out of the house, but she feels some sympathy for him so she lets him sleep in his car in the driveway. It's a typical commuter car that he uses for going to work; it's not in the greatest shape. One night he's running the engine and the catalytic converter goes on fire and starts the car on fire. His sneaker is melted to the gas pedal, so he can't get out of the car. The fire department arrives and they get him out. Then they rush him up to the Hyperbaric Center on City Island in the Bronx because of all the noxious fumes he breathed in. They ended up transferring him to Jacobi Hospital to implant a cardiac pacemaker. He's still not allowed back in the house. But his ex-wife allows him to bring a newer car into the driveway and sleep in it.

I'm telling the chief this story. However, the chief is a little suspicious of me, because he's known me for years, and he never thought I could tell a straight story without there being a punch line to it. So he says, "I can't believe it."

I tell him, "This is a real black cloud, tough luck, Harry."

He says, "You gotta be pulling my leg." And he goes and asks somebody else. When he comes back he says, "I'm sorry. I did find out that in fact you're telling me the truth about this guy. He really is this kind of a hard-luck guy."

I said, "And he's got a three-legged dog named Lucky, chief."

"Now I know you're bullshitting."

Angelo ends up throwing his dog out after he physically throws his daughter out of the house. But she fights to get back in. ESU ends up having to go up with portable shields and drag her away from the house.

She loves him and she's afraid he's going to kill himself. He says he's going to kill himself, or he wants us to kill him, and he comes to the window a couple of times. Then he says, "If you don't think I mean business," *ba boom*, he lets a shot go. We thought he meant business, because he has thrown the girl out, he's thrown the dog out, and he's thrown his wallet out, and there's a thing called the suicide scenario where you give away all of your valuables to the people that you want to take care of them. Well, these are all his valuables. His daughter, his dog, and his wallet that has some money in it. And, that's it. He's not going to talk to us anymore, and we hear another shot. Well, he did himself.

Ever cautious, we send a tactical team in there to see what happened. They get inside. They search the first floor. Then they get up to the second floor and they look in the bedroom. He is sitting there with a gun to his head. He gets up and he starts to follow them as they back out of the room. He's telling them he wants them to kill him.

I thought we lost the guy. Damn, my first big job and we couldn't get him out. But the next thing I hear he's not dead. The team backs out and we start all over again.

It snowed that day. It was probably the only snow that we had in '89. And the ESU officers are covered with snow. We knew he wasn't going to like the police department too much, but we were talking to him as cops: "Angelo, Angelo, you're a cop. Give us a break, why don't you? We're cops. If we were in trouble we know you'd come to our assistance. We're trying to help you when you need help. We're freezing out here. Give us a break, Angelo."

So Angelo thinks about that for a while, and he comes back to the window and he says, "you're right." He then takes his shirt off and throws it out in the street, and says, "If you guys are cold I'm going to be cold also."

I'm thinking, that's not exactly the kind of message that we were trying to give Angelo. So we go into the theme about his daughter. He actually has two daughters, but the one he threw out he is especially close to, and we tell him, "If you love your daughter, you won't do this. You won't kill yourself."

It was the thing that we were able to get him with. He said to us later on, "as much as I tried to block out what you were saying, and not hear you, I love my daughter, and you said I'd have to be here for my daughter." We said it a thousand times if we said it once.

Eventually, one of the Emergency Service officers, Lieutenant Al Baker, ends up talking to him, while taking cues from me. "Angelo, if you love your daughter, you don't need that gun. We all have guns. What's the big deal with the gun? Throw the gun away. It's only in the way."

Angelo come out on the steps, with no shirt on and barefoot, and he says, "I don't need this gun?"

•

"You don't need the gun, Angelo."

He then throws the gun away, and we walk up and take him into custody, and that was the end of it. I did not suspect that he was going to throw that gun away. I thought we were going to have another full crew come on, and we were going to go another twelve hours until we eventually got him out, or until he killed himself.

He was arrested for unlawful imprisonment, assault, attempted rape on his ex-wife, and illegal possession of the weapon. He's been in jail after taking a plea to cover all the charges, and he will be there for a long time. What a way for a cop and a Vietnam vet to end up. . . .

When it's over sometimes you're physically drained, and you really feel like you can't go any further. I say that an hour of negotiating is the equivalent to four hours of hard manual labor.

But even though we were exhausted at the end of the situation, one of the things that we do is make sure that we talk to all of the people who have been involved in the negotiation process. They're probably on a high now, and they have to come down from that high. You put so much of yourself into it. I've heard negotiators reveal things that they probably wouldn't have revealed to their best friend in an attempt to get close to a barricaded person. You want to have that positive transference and let them know you're there for them. "I care for you." And, as you go on, it's not playacting, it's real. And I'm not saying that we're going to take the guy home, but that sense of being committed to getting this person out is a tremendous thing.

I've been with the Hostage Team for five years, and I have to say it's one of the most rewarding positions in the NYPD. I get to work with some of the finest men and women in the department. The work we do always reflects postively on the NYPD, and we are always aware that our success is due to the team effort of the patrol officers, the ESU, and the hostage negotiators.

•

4

DETECTIVE

FIRST GRADE

AUGUSTUS PEANO

It was a beautiful sunny day on November 22, 1963. A month earlier I had taken the oath to become a police officer, and now I was in the academy. I was at the Rodman's Neck pistol range, firing at a bull's-eye target. They gave you several minutes to fire fifty rounds. I fired five or six rounds when the range instructor said, "cease fire. Holster all weapons."

We ceased firing and holstered our weapons. Then the range instructor turned up the volume of the radio in the control tower and played it over the loudspeaker. The announcer said, "The president of the United States has just been assassinated in Dallas."

We were held at the range, because our superiors thought that there would be massive rioting in the city when the people heard the news that Kennedy had been assassinated. But there wasn't any rioting that night.

That was my introduction to police work, and it made me quite aware that there was a lot of violence in this society, and that I would be involved

•

with violent individuals for at least the next twenty years. On May 20, 1968, after being promoted to detective third grade, I was transferred from the 25th precinct in Harlem to the 77th Detective Squad in Bedford-Stuyvesant. I reported to the squad commander, a Lieutenant William Machen. He was an old-time detective boss and a staunch disciplinarian. I was young and presumably inexperienced as a detective. So when he saw me walk into his squad, which had about sixteen seasoned detectives, he immediately assigned me to the fire marshals' office.

I had to work with fire marshal John Barracato. Our job was to work out of the fire department's 44th battalion on Watkins Avenue in Brooklyn. At that time, the Brownsville section of Brooklyn was burning to the ground, and firemen were being shot at and had objects hurled from rooftops at them, including bathtubs, and there was an unusual rise in arson fires.

I was a fledgling detective and knew nothing about investigations, but I was amazed when I realized that the fire marshals, in general, were great investigators even though their investigations pertain to one crime, arson.

This fellow Barracato was very, very thorough, and didn't work just his eight-hour tour. He was on call almost twenty-four hours a day. If something big happened, he would leave his residence and respond to it. I guess besides being a fire marshal, paid by the city, he was also a buff, and enjoyed interesting investigations.

We worked the Brownsville neighborhood for a period of about four or five months. I met other fire marshals there including Ernie Bauer, who was somewhat of a legend, and John Connell, who's father was the surgeon for the fire department. I have the utmost respect for them. And in working that detail I realized the great job that firemen do. I saw firemen from truck companies go into burning buildings, without the Scott airpack, making rescues. I also witnessed

•

times when they ran into problems and where there were civilians trapped, how the rescue company responded so quickly and seemed to be without any regard for their own safety. They raced into these buildings, saving infants, grown-ups, and other firemen. It amazed me how dedicated these men from the rescue companies were.

We handled several arson investigations, and I can't recall ever going to trial on an arson arrest. The fire marshals put together such an airtight case that there was usually plea bargaining involved. I consider it a very interesting and rewarding part of my career, and an honor, to work with the men of the fire marshals' office and to follow, at that time, the busiest truck or the busiest battalion in the world. The busiest truck happened to be 120 Truck. Buffs from all over the city and all over the country were honored just to ride with 120 Truck.

After putting in my time with the fire marshals, I went back to the squad to handle cases just like any other detective in the unit. On a winter's day, my partner, Gary Friedferteg, and I went to the projects to answer a 61, a complaint of a second-degree assault on a man and a woman by another man. The uniformed cops had prepared the 61 after interviewing the complainants in the hospital.

It seems that this acquaintance of theirs became enraged at them while in their apartment. He was a very big and powerful man. In his anger he broke off the leg of one of their chairs and beat them with it.

A friend of the couple called me up and said that the guy we were looking for was in a Mary Jane somebody's apartment in the projects.

When we got to the apartment I listened at the door and I could hear a guy shouting at a woman. I told Gary to go downstairs and get the housing cops for backup.

After Gary leaves, the apartment door suddenly opens, and this guy brushes by me and runs down the hall into the elevator. I run after him. I manage to push my way into the elevator. The door closes behind me and the elevator starts down. He reaches into the pocket of his raincoat. I immediately pull out my gun. I tell him, "don't move." But he kicks me squarely in the groin. It knocks the wind out of me, and I start to fall to the floor. He grabs my wrist and the gun and tries to wrestle it away from me. I manage to squeeze off a round. It hits him in the chest. He remains standing, but leans back against the door. When the elevator reaches the ground floor the door opens, and he falls out dead, much to the astonishment of Gary and the housing cops who were waiting to take the elevator back upstairs. I was taken to the hospital to be treated for the groin injury.

The 77th Detective Squad, by the way, happened to be the busiest detective squad in the city, with the highest homicide rate. But from there I went to the quietest, the 102nd Detective Squad in Richmond Hill, Queens.

I'll never forget when I walked into the 102nd's squad room. I noticed five detectives sitting around a desk chatting. It was unusual because in the 77th we were either conducting a canvas on a homicide case, or in court processing an arrest, or I was out with the fire marshals. There was very, very little time to just sit around and chat. But when I entered the office, one of the senior detectives asked if he could help me, thinking that I was a complainant. I identified myself, saying that I had just been transferred to the 102nd squad. The men sat there in amazement, and a few seconds later the room cleared out. I was the only one in the room. They all ran for telephones in other parts of the building. They called various people, for instance—my former command, the detective delegate in my former command, the people who they knew in Brooklyn North, and just about anybody they could, even in their own borough, to see what I was about.

•

Twenty minutes later they straggled back and welcomed me aboard. I had been the first detective transferred to that particular squad in several years. Every man in this squad at the time was a World War II veteran, and I was only a twenty-eight-year-old detective.

They explained to me that things were quite different in Richmond Hill as compared to the Bedford-Stuyvesant area, and that it was almost time for cocktails. I recall when I worked in Brooklyn we barely had time to grab a slice of pizza or a quick hamburger.

Even though the 102nd was the quietest precinct in the city, it had some of the most celebrated cases that the city has known. For instance, the Kitty Genovese case, where I believe thirty-five people heard her screaming for help as she was being stabbed to death in an alleyway, and nobody helped her either physically, or even calling the police.

Before I arrived in the 102nd precinct in Queens, there was a shooting of a police officer by the name of Graffia. He was killed in the adjoining precinct, the 106th, in a stickup. And they had absolutely no leads, or no physical evidence. The case was going nowhere.

But there was this old-time detective, Frankie Collins, in the 102nd. I'd say he stood about five-eight or five-nine. He was very gray. He was old beyond his years. Let's say he was fifty-five to sixty—he looked like he was eighty, and he didn't look like a cop at all.

At that point in time, when a police officer made an arrest he brought the arrestee up to the squad, and the detectives interrogated and fingerprinted the perpetrator. So Frankie had this burglar in the office, and Frankie was thinking about the unsolved murder of brother officer Graffia. The burglary, of course, occurred in an adjoining precinct. Frankie had a hunch, so he decided to question this fellow about the murder in a very unusual way. Frankie reached into his pocket, grabbed his rosary beads, and threw them

•

on the desk in front of the person who was arrested for the burglary, and screamed, "okay, why did you have to kill the cop? Why did you have to kill the cop? Don't you know that god will punish you for this?"

The guy broke down and said, "I didn't mean it. I didn't mean to kill him. He surprised me. I didn't mean to kill him. I did it. I'm sorry. I'm sorry. I did it."

And, of course, they called in the detectives from the 106th and the Homicide Squad, and the district attorney. This fellow made a complete confession and gave all the details on how he killed officer Graffia. If Frankie hadn't thrown down those rosary beads the case would probably still be open today.

There was a case that I handled that is known, to this day, as the Cheryl McCarthy case. It happened on December 23, 1969. When I was notified about this homicide I was in a restaurant called the Inn. It's on 114th Street and Jamaica Avenue in Queens. I had just finished my dinner and was having coffee and a piece of cake when Captain Nicastro's driver, Hank Rogers, who happened to be a member of our squad, came in and said, "The captain is up at one hundred and thirty-second and Jamaica Avenue in the train station. We have a bad one," which in detective terms means it's a homicide that would gain great publicity. So we left immediately and met with Nicastro up on the subway station, where we saw a young lady who was dead.

This was an elevated subway station. There was an entrance at 130th Street, and the station went all the way across to 132nd Street, where there was a second entrance. The 132nd Street entrance was closed, so you could only enter and exit from 130th Street.

Cheryl McCarthy's body was found at the 132nd Street entrance, by a transit cop, about 8:00 at night. It appeared that Cheryl had been sexually abused. She was naked from

•

the waist down, and we noticed a lot of blood coming from the anal-vaginal area.

The medical examiner determined that she died from strangulation, although the killer apparently penetrated the area between the vagina and the anus with a sharp object.

We immediately conducted a canvass of the area. It was night, and there were not many businesses open, so we went to the bars, which were located on either side of the subway on the 130th Street side and on the 132nd Street side. We interviewed everyone in the bars. We had a form with us. It was a simple form asking if they saw or heard anything unusual, and how long they were at the particular area, and how long they were present at the bar. We also interviewed people in the local pharmacy. There did come a time when we interviewed everyone who worked in the post office, which was located right beneath the 132nd Street entrance. Nobody reported anything unusual, and we went on with the investigation. Eventually everybody who lived within a five-block radius of the spot where she was killed was interviewed, and there were literally thousands of supplementary reports on this particular case.

Cheryl was going to a party in Woodhaven that particular night, and according to her girlfriend, who was traveling from Jamaica, Cheryl was to meet her at that particular station at 8:00. When the girlfriend arrived at that station at 8:00, she looked out of the train, but didn't see Cheryl. She assumed that Cheryl had taken the previous train down to Woodhaven, so she just continued on to the party. She had no idea, of course, that Cheryl was lying dead at the other end of that station.

We had several people call the squad or the precinct, saying they were responsible for the murder. Of course, they couldn't give any details as to how she was murdered. We had others actually turn themselves in, because of the great publicity that this case had. Cheryl's picture was on the front page of the *Daily News* for two days in a row, and

•

there were articles about her murder for at least a week or two after that.

The chief of detectives, Freddie Lussen, spent an entire week in the 102nd precinct. He took over the squad commander's office. It was unprecedented, because the old-timers told me that they recalled hundreds of homicides they worked on over their twenty and thirty years on the job, and they never recalled the chief of detectives coming to a squad and setting up his office.

We were determined to make an arrest. We knew that if we made an arrest we would be promoted to the next grade immediately due to the notoriety of this case. Several unusual things came up. For instance, there were arrests made on the fringes of this particular investigation.

We got every report of a rape or a homicide in the entire city. If there was a rape up in the 52nd precinct in the Bronx, we wanted to know about it, and wanted to see if we could match anything up with Cheryl's murder, even though Cheryl was not raped—she received a puncture wound. She was already dead, or near death, when this puncture occurred. So, we were very, very concerned about everything that went on in the city, because we were trying to get any information at all that might help us with this investigation.

In February of 1970, when we interviewed a bartender to see whether he had heard anything about it, he said, "well, how about Gloria, who lives up on the twenty-sixth floor of the Silver Towers." The Silver Towers is a large building, located across from the Queens criminal court which, at that time, housed over 250 flight attendants from various airlines.

I was with my lieutenant, Jack Cronen. He had a photographic memory and he said, "We definitely didn't interview a Gloria on the twenty-sixth floor about the Cheryl McCarthy murder." So we decided to go up to the twenty-sixth floor.

•

One of her roommates opened the door, and we identified ourselves and she invited us in. There were four very beautiful flight attendants lounging around watching TV. Gloria happened to be a very pretty blonde. She said that she was going to JFK Airport, and she was walking up Kew Gardens Road from the Silver Towers building in her uniform, in January, when she saw a man seated in a green Mustang with a black vinyl top, and the man called to her. She couldn't hear him too clearly. But as she got closer to his car this fellow, the sole occupant of the Mustang, said, "Take a look at what I have hanging out of my pants." She noticed that his penis was erect and exposed. She called him a bastard and walked in front of the car.

This fellow became enraged and said, "I'm going to kill you the same way I killed the girl up on the subway station," and revved up the engine and attempted to run her over. She dove to the sidewalk, tearing her stockings, jumped up and ran to the subway station. The man did not follow her.

We sat there in amazement. Then I asked if she would accompany me to the Bureau of Criminal Identification in the morning to try to identify this fellow by photo.

I came in the following morning—it was about 7:30—and I noticed a green Mustang with a black vinyl top parked right outside of the precinct in an area that's reserved for only police cars. I asked the officer at the door who owned that car, and he said it belonged to a perp that the detectives were printing. He had been arrested for vehicular homicide—he ran an old woman over and kept on going. When he was apprehended by officers he fought with them, so he was also charged with resisting arrest. I took a look at this fellow and noticed that his description fit the description that was given to me by Gloria the previous night. So instead of asking her down to the Bureau of Criminal Identification, I asked her to accompany me to the arraignment part of the Queens criminal court. I told her that she would see

•

several persons stand before the bench that morning, and that if this person was among them to let me know. I believe twenty cases or more were called before this fellow came out for arraignment, and as soon as she saw him she said, "That's the guy who said he was going to kill me the way he killed the girl on the subway station, and that's the guy who tried to run me over in a green Mustang."

Well, one of my partners, who happened to be a first-grade detective and an excellent investigator, Al Largo, who was also a very religious man, said, "Augie, it is so strange how you interviewed the bartender last night, and you were able to find the stewardess home. Normally, if you try to find a stewardess she's on a flight, and you can't catch up with her for a couple of weeks. And she agreed to go with you the next day. Then you saw that particular green Mustang with a black vinyl top happened to be parked in front of the precinct, even though there happens to be fifty-thousand green Mustangs with black vinyl tops in New York City alone. And she identified the fellow positively, today. Augie, it's the lord's will that the murderer of Cheryl McCarthy be apprehended and this is the guy. Congratulations—you got him."

I said, "well, I hope you're right."

We watched him—he was out on bail for the vehicular homicide. We learned that this fellow worked for TWA airlines, refueling aircraft at Kennedy Airport. By the way, Gloria also worked for TWA. But we determined later that they never saw each other before the incident. His behavior, otherwise, was quite normal for a thirty-year-old single man. He had no previous arrest record. Ultimately, we determined that he was not the killer of Cheryl McCarthy. So we continued with the investigation, supplementary reports piling up by the thousands.

A month later there was a homicide of a young lady in Forest Hills. Her name was Joyce Florida. She was coming out of her apartment building to go to work when she was

•

accosted by a robber—a man with a gun. She decided to struggle and he shot her in the throat. Somehow she acknowledged to the police on the scene that she had been robbed, but before she could identify this fellow in any way she died. The bullet was taken from her body by the medical examiner and was sent to ballistics. We were very interested in this particular case, but why more than any other case? Cheryl died of strangulation. This young lady was shot. No similarities at all, except that Forest Hills isn't that far from Richmond Hill.

Nothing further panned out until a couple of months later, when a young lady who happened to be black and lived in the 105th precinct in Cambria Heights was raped by a black man. The rapist told her, "baby, you were so good, I'm coming back for some more tonight." She notified the detectives in the 105th Detective Squad, and they staked out her apartment. Sure enough, the rapist came back. Only he came back with a gun in each pocket. They surprised him before he was able to reach for either gun. Both guns were sent to ballistics. They determined that one of them was the gun that was used in the killing of Joyce Florida in Forest Hills.

The man's name was Ernie Reynolds. His job was that of a postal worker, and he worked right beneath the spot where Cheryl McCarthy was killed. He worked in the post office at 132nd Street and Jamaica Avenue, and he happened to be working that night. I interviewed him the very night that Cheryl was killed, but the answers that he gave were quite standard.

We went back to the post office, and found out that Ernie would come to work about 7:30 every night even though he didn't start until 8:00. The night of McCarthy's murder he walked in at 8:05. We then felt that there was a good possibility that he killed Cheryl prior to going to work that night.

Ernie was convicted of the murder of Joyce Florida, and he was also convicted of the rape of the young lady in the

•

105th precinct. I believe he received a twenty-five-year sentence for both crimes.

We put somebody in the cell with him to try to get an admission of the murder of Cheryl McCarthy. He wouldn't even discuss the matter. We did determine that prior to coming to New York from Virginia, Ernie found his two next-door neighbors stabbed to death, and that case remains open today. No arrest was ever made for the murder of those two next-door neighbors. But Ernie Reynolds was never charged with the murder of Cheryl McCarthy, and the reason for this was that there was no physical evidence linking Ernie Reynolds to the murder. There were no witnesses, and he certainly didn't make any admissions, and without the three you have absolutely nothing. The case is still open. Some other detective in the 102nd Squad is carrying this particular case, just as a detective in the Missing Persons Squad is carrying the cases of Jimmy Hoffa and Judge Crater.

I recall another case that also happened in the 102nd precinct. This case involved the theft of 1500 dollars from a restaurant.

The theft occurred on a very hot August night. It was one of those nights that had to be like 105 degrees during the day and maybe 99 at night. We were sweating profusely.

We received a call from the owner of the restaurant, and he told us that after the place had been closed to the public twelve employees remained cleaning up and changing clothes. And that the assistant manager was supposed to deposit 1500 dollars in the night depository. Instead, he went across the street to see his girlfriend in a bar, and had thrown the money in a file cabinet. When the assistant manager came back he realized that the money was gone. So we had a Charlie Chan-type mystery—1500 dollars was missing and 12 employees were present. We interviewed every person who was working that night, all twelve people.

Well, at that time detectives always had informants.

•

Whether they were bartenders, or short-order cooks, or local hoodlums, the informants usually came to the detectives to give other people up—who did them dirty, so to speak. In the restaurant we had an informant who happened to be a 320-pound short-order cook named Zack*. Zack had given us information on several crimes in the area that we solved. So we go to Zack and he said, "yes, I'll tell you who did it. Angelo did it. Angelo quit the job the night of the theft and was going to Palermo, Sicily the following morning."

My partner, Bob Roessle, and I race over to Ozone Park where Angelo lives. His bags were packed, and he was definitely going to Palermo the following day.

In the detective teams you always had a good guy and a bad guy. I was always the good guy, Bob was the bad tough guy. I asked Angelo if he had taken the money. He said no, he did not. My partner told him, "If we should find out that you took the fifteen hundred dollars you will probably have to serve ninety-nine years in the Sicilian prison first, and then we will extradite you to answer the charges from the State of New York." Angelo swore that he didn't do it. He boarded the plane the next morning and took off to Palermo.

We go back to the restaurant, and Zack now recalls that a young man, who had just been hired, walked out of the restaurant that night apparently concealing something under his shirt.

We asked this fellow, "Did you take it?"

"Yes."

"Okay, where is it?"

"I ate it."

"What did you eat?"

"Food, a smoked pork tenderloin." He had walked out with a piece of meat under his shirt.

Well, there was an area of the restaurant, the manager's office, that the other employees were not permitted in, but

•

we had a report that one of the young men and a young lady were in the office. We determined that they were lovers and they were making love in that office at the time, while four others were having a whipped-cream fight with the large, silver whipped-cream canisters. We went on and on and on.

It took about two and a half weeks when I told my partner, "Bob, I'm convinced I know who took the money."

He said, "Well, who took it?"

I said, "Our man Zack."

"It's impossible. Zack would never do anything like that." But I had received information the day before that Zack had a very heavy gambling problem, and that Zack lived at the big A—Aqueduct racetrack. He spent all of his off-duty time at the racetrack, and had run up debts into the thousands of dollars.

Bob said, "Augie, I still insist Zack didn't do it."

I said, "Bob, since it's my case let me handle it." So I went back over to the restaurant and told Zack, "I think you're going to be delighted—we finally determined who took the fifteen hundred dollars."

Zack went off into a tirade, "lock the bastard up! Throw the key away! Throw the book at him! Who was it?"

I said, "Zack, it was you."

"What do you mean it was me, I didn't take any money."

"Zack, you didn't only take the money you gambled it away at the big A."

His reply was, "How did you know?"

I said, "Well, Zack, I found out that you had a very heavy gambling problem, and that you're in debt, and I also know that you're very jealous of the assistant manager, and that you felt that you should have been promoted to assistant manager instead of being left on the grill."

He said, "All right, I did it. I admit I did it, but I can't give you the money back. I gambled it away. I have no more money. What should we do?"

•

"Well, let's go right over to the station house now and we'll call the owner up." So the three of us went over to the 102nd precinct, where I called him and I informed him that I had the perpetrator in my office. He screamed, "lock him up! I'll be right down to court to sign the complaint. By the way, who is it?"

I said, "It happens to be Zack."

"Don't do anything. I'll be right down. Don't arrest him, I'll be right down." And he practically flew down to the precinct—he came from Westchester in about fifteen minutes.

He was in the office begging us not to arrest Zack, stating that "Zack was worth his weight in gold at the grill." He was the fastest short-order man he had ever seen, and he could not afford to lose him.

Well, the next step was to notify the squad commander, who was at home. The squad commander said, "Even though it's a felony case, and we don't have the right to close out a felony, we won't have much of a case with the complaining witness refusing to follow up. Call the assistant district attorney and see what he has to say."

So I call the assistant district attorney, and he responded to the 102nd precinct. The ADA said, "okay, I've interviewed the complainant, and since the complainant refuses to go any further, just use my name and close out the case." So that's what we did.

Well, the owner kept Zack on for quite some time until Zack found greener pastures, but this was after he paid back the entire 1500 dollars that he had stolen.

The Detective Bureau experimented for a while with disbanding the PDUs and putting everybody into specialty units. I was assigned to the 15th Robbery Squad.

My partner and I were on a stakeout in the back of a dry-cleaning store in Brooklyn. There had been frequent robberies here and at cleaning establishments nearby. It was a very hot day, so we had our bulletproof vests off, and our shot-

•

guns were resting on a shelf. There was a window between us and the front of the store that we covered with butcher paper, but we were able to look out through a pinhole in the paper.

Well, a guy runs into the store brandishing a gun. He announces "this is a stickup, give me all your money."

We run into the front of the store, and tell him "we're police officers!" Where upon he turns pointing the gun at us. *Boom! Boom!* I shot twice with my revolver. He runs out of the store with two bullets in him. But I was able to subdue him after running a block. I cuffed him and brought him back to the store. We called the ambulance and he was taken to the hospital. He survived. He was convicted. At the trial he threatened to kill me when he got out of prison. He would have to wait at least seven years before that would happen.

We had another rash of cleaning-store robberies. It was a one-man crime spree. This violent white, a known junkie with LOVE tattooed on his knuckles, had held up forty-four stores with either a knife or a gun.

We were working with another team of detectives. They were two young, gung-ho guys. So my partner and I decided to take the quieter of the two locations we were to stakeout, a store located on 80th Street and Jamaica Avenue.

Again, it was hot, as we sat in the back of the store that Good Friday morning, and we had our vests off. All of a sudden a white guy runs in with a hunting knife in his hand. The store clerk screams and runs through one of two spaced-apart swinging doors into the back, where we are. The perp runs after him. He sees us and runs out again. My partner goes after him. The perp turns. My partner tells him, "drop the knife." Instead, he lunges, and is about to stab my partner in the chest when I come through the other door. I get two shots off. I hit him in the heart and down he goes. We get on the radio and call for backup and an ambulance.

•

Well, the call goes out as if a detective was shot. The first person to show up was the Reverend Kalajian, a police department chaplain.

I was transferred to the 101st precinct in Far Rockaway, and one day I got a call to respond to either a suicide or homicide of a black man who jumped or was thrown out of a thirteen-story project, and now was splattered on the pavement.

The deceased was dressed in jeans and a shirt and sneakers. The uniformed sergeant had the officers search the body and found nothing.

We decided to interview the residents of the building to see if they heard or saw anything. And this reverend said, "yes, I did hear something unusual. I heard a very violent fight. He was arguing with a very nasty man, and every other word out of his mouth was a profanity. He was apparently a very big man."

I said, "well, how could you tell he was a big man?"

"Well, his voice was very big because the deceased had a sort of a high-pitched voice."

"Okay." I went on and interviewed other neighbors, and they all heard this violent fight, and then they were told that the guy was dead.

"Did anybody see this person leave the apartment?"

"No."

"Did the deceased live alone?"

"No, he had a wife."

"Where was the wife?"

"The wife was at work."

"How did the police get into the apartment?"

"They had to use a key; the door was locked from the outside."

"It wasn't chained, it was just locked from the outside?"

"Yes."

The wife said, "He was murdered."

"How do you know he was murdered?"

•

"Because he always kept his house key in his left-hand pocket. Someone took the key from him, threw him out the window, and then locked the door and left. Otherwise the key would still be in his pocket."

I called the medical examiner up. I said, "Doctor, it's very important. Was anything found on the person of the deceased?"

"Yeah, one house key in his left-hand pocket."

I thanked him and went back and interviewed the deceased's girlfriend. She said that the guy was crazy as a bedbug. "He's been acting very funny lately. He's been arguing with himself, and that's why I left him."

But the wife never reported anything about him acting strange or talking in different voices.

In that case, everybody responded, including the Homicide Squad, and they're making a big investigation of it. But I told them the case is over, the case is solved, he killed himself. I felt that the guy flipped out and threw himself out of the window because of the spurned relationship with his girlfriend, even though he was a married man.

In the 101st precinct Detective Squad, it was common to get a missing persons case. I'd say we had several missing persons cases a day. Most ended after an hour or two where there was a child involved. The child might not have told his or her mother where he or she was going, and the mother would come to the station house and report the child missing, and a couple of hours later the child would be reported home or staying with a relative or whatever.

I recall this day where I received a missing person case involving a seven-year-old girl, Adrien Reyes, from a building in Far Rockaway. The building was at 1450 Greenport Road, and we had at least one arrest a day from that building. It was a very large apartment house, and a pretty violent building. But we also had numerous missing persons cases from that building involving children.

Well, several hours had passed and we interviewed the

•

mother. The mother said that she went out shopping and Adrien was playing when she left, but when she returned Adrien wasn't in the house and the child wasn't downstairs, and she was concerned. So we asked her if they had any relatives in the area, or if Adrien knew how to travel on the train, perhaps to visit people who were from outside of the peninsula. She said no, there was only one person, an uncle in Brooklyn, and the kid couldn't contact him. We were just hoping that when the sector car arrived at the uncle's location in Brooklyn that they would tell us that they found the child, and that the case would be solved. But the uncle hadn't seen the child.

We were quite concerned, especially as nightfall came, and because of all the water that surrounds Far Rockaway and in the Bayswater section, which isn't too far from this child's residence, you have a lot of private swimming pools. So we did a very, very thorough canvass of the area: rooftops, basements, backyards, and swimming pools. The child didn't turn up.

I came back the next day, and the investigation got bigger. I don't think the public really is aware of this, but missing persons investigations are taken very, very seriously. Especially if it's a child, since most police officers have children themselves, and can identify with the horror of not knowing where your child is. Professionally and personally, these cases are handled very, very thoroughly. But another day passed and Adrien still wasn't around.

I went home late that night. We do four tours a set. The first two tours are from four in the afternoon until one in the morning. The third and fourth day you work 8:00 A.M. to 4:00 P.M. I was scheduled to come in at 8:00, but I got in about 7:30, and when I walked into the station house the desk officer said to get right over to 1450 Greenport Road. They had found the child dead in the courtyard.

When I got to the scene, the "night watch" squad was already there. I noticed the body of a seven-year-old child.

•

Her legs were sticking out of a green plastic garbage bag. I also noticed a lot of blood around the bag. They told me that the child had apparently been thrown from the roof. But I recall being on that roof the night before, and there certainly wasn't a bag on it, and several other detectives also went on that roof and nobody saw a bag. This led us to believe that the body had been kept in an apartment before it was thrown off the roof. We noticed a window ledge that had blood on it, and we theorized that the body bounced off the ledge and then into the courtyard. Even though the entire building had been canvassed previously, now that the body had been discovered we had to interview everyone in them again, especially the people whose apartments faced the courtyard. A senior detective from the Homicide Task Force, Patty Kelly, called me and said, "Augie, come up here, right away." I walked up to the apartment, which was right above the spot where the body was found. Kelly then said, "take a look at this," and he showed me blood on a mop. "This guy killed the girl."

The guy's name was Bruce Bostwick. At first he denied this, but when we told him that we would match up the blood from the mop with the blood of Adrien Reyes he admitted to killing her.

He used to let Adrien walk his dog. The little girl loved his dog, and she would come up to the apartment to play with it, but this particular day his wife was out working and he was alone with Adrien. He made sexual advances to her, but Adrien resisted. He grabbed a kitchen knife and stabbed this little girl fifty-one times. Afterwards he put Adrien's body into several plastic garbage bags and threw it into the closet. It happened to be a very hot night, and this apartment didn't have any air-conditioning, and his wife complained about a smell coming from the closet. Bruce told his wife that it was from a dead rat he had killed earlier that evening. He wasn't able to put it in a garbage bag and throw it out, but he would handle it in the morning. His

•

wife was deathly afraid of rats, so she wouldn't go into the closet. Bruce Bostwick then told us that at about 3:00 in the morning he got up out of bed and took Adrien's body in the bag from the closet and just threw it out the window. It was his window ledge that had the blood on it.

Several of the neighbors in this particular building, who had previous arrest records, had found out that Bostwick was the murderer, and they said that we were not going to take this fellow out alive, that they were going to kill him right on the premises. Reinforcements were called in, and we made two lines of uniformed police officers and detectives, and attempted to get this guy from the courtyard into the radio car. Several officers were punched and kicked in this melee of people trying to get at Bruce Bostwick. We finally got him into the car and brought him to the precinct. Whereupon the same crowd converged on the precinct and said they wouldn't let us take him out, that they were going to have street justice, they were going to kill him on the spot, a man like this didn't deserve to go to trial and they were going to take care of it themselves. Well, we were able to take Bostwick out of a window in the precinct into the garage, and on a given signal a couple of cops opened the garage door and we drove around the corner up to the borough headquarters in the 113th precinct, where we processed him.

He was convicted, and he received a long sentence for the murder of this little seven-year-old child.

It was a very sad case. It was a case that every father identified with. I was on the front page of the *Daily News* standing by her body. Somebody gave me the newspaper, but I had to throw it away because I didn't want to keep anything to remember this sad case. No matter how seasoned you are as a detective, no matter how many homicide cases you have handled, you really never get used to the death of a child.

I was in the 108th Squad. I was available to catch a case. I

●

got a call about 6:00 in the morning from one of my friends who was doing the night watch. He said, "Augie, you're up first and you got a homicide."

I said, "okay, what is it?"

"Male white found dead in a car, Orchard Street and Jackson Avenue, in Long Island City, in a factory's driveway. He had no wallet or identification on him. In the window of the car was a DEA card and a PBA card with a shield number on it. They checked the shield number, and it came back to a detective in the chief of department's office."

"Was it the detective who was lying dead in the car?"

"They checked the license plate. The plate came back to a fellow by the name of Bill Burke."

Well, after I received the phone call I got dressed and I went to the crime scene. The body was still there.

Bill Burke, as it was disclosed during the investigation, was the maître d' of the Old Homestead restaurant on Ninth Avenue and Fourteenth Street. Burke was a big man, about six-three, very well built. He used to work out in a gym three days a week, and was known as a tough fellow who could handle himself, and maybe two or three adversaries. So Bill Burke was no slouch.

He worked New Year's eve. After work, he decided to stop by P.J. Clarke's and have a few drinks before going home. Bill drank until about 4:00 in the morning. He was drinking Johnnie Walker Red and soda. Witnesses said that when Bill left P.J. Clarke's he was feeling no pain. Bill lived in Jackson Heights, and would normally take the Fifty-ninth Street Bridge onto Roosevelt Avenue and to his home. But that night Bill decided to make another stop. He made a stop on Jackson Avenue and Orchard Street in Long Island City. Well, that area was known for its prostitutes, transvestites, and pimps. It was a factory area and it was pretty desolate at night, and that's why they used it. As we reconstructed it, Bill picked up a prostitute for oral sex. During the oral sex he noticed that the prostitute was reach-

•

ing into his pants pocket, and had his wallet in her hand. He then attempted to grab the wallet and a scuffle ensued. Bill Burke carried an unlicensed .32 automatic under the armrest of the car. He grabbed his gun, but the gun was wrestled away from him by the prostitute. Bill was drunk. The prostitute turned out to be a transvestite who was quite strong. Bill was shot to death with his own gun, and the transvestite fled.

When I got back to the office that morning I called that detective in the commissioner's office. I informed him that a man by the name of Bill Burke had been murdered, and that we found his PBA card and the DEA card in the deceased's car. I asked him if he knew whether Bill had any family, because we had to have somebody identify the body. He said that Bill had been divorced, and that the only relatives were out of state. So he came in and went down to the medical examiner's office with me, and he positively identified the body as Bill Burke's. He offered to do anything possible to aid in this investigation. He indicated that Bill was a good friend of the commissioner, the deputy commissioners, and a lot of brass and district attorneys because of the nature of his job—the maître d' of a very famous restaurant. I thanked him and continued on with the investigation.

We put pressure on the pimps, prostitutes, and transvestites. We cleaned up the area. There was no illegal activity going on in that area for quite some time.

Word got to me through an informant, who also happened to be a transvestite, that the murderer was a fellow known as Black Nickie. Black Nickie had no permanent residence, but floated from "stroll to stroll."

We enlisted the help of a detective who had worked undercover in Manhattan as a pimp. He was a black man, about six-two, very slender, and while he was working undercover he wore very fine "threads." He wore a large "sky," meaning a hat, and actually had a stable of twelve prostitutes. He played the role so well while he was working undercover that the prostitutes never found out he was "the Man." But while he was in that capacity, he was able to solve several homicides, and was instrumental in the arrest of major drug dealers and robbery teams. This fellow was now out from undercover, and was working in a local detective squad, but because of his expertise he knew all the strolls and the crack houses and places that these people frequented.

I found myself going up to the Ravella Hotel on 116th Street and Eighth Avenue. We walked in one room, and there had to be twenty of these transvestites engaging in oral sex, anal sex, or shooting heroin. It was a sight that I had never seen before. But the word was that Black Nickie was nowhere to be found.

Several months went by, and we did find Black Nickie. But at the particular date and time of Burke's murder, Nickie was in police custody in a holding pen in the 25th precinct in East Harlem. He was not our man. And we had to start all over.

Well, investigations, as they get old, lose steam, because you might start out with five or ten detectives in certain cases, thirty detectives on a particularly newsworthy homicide, but as the time goes by they take more and more men away from you, because people are being killed every day. I think we have six or eight homicides in New York City every single day.

Nine months passed, ten months, eleven months; it was a year, almost to the day, when the squad-room door opened and in walks a six-four transvestite in drag, with a pocketbook over his arm, wearing specially made high-heeled shoes, because he had to take a size thirteen or fourteen shoe. And this transvestite spoke just like Pearl Bailey. It was a fellow who I knew from the stroll in Long Island City. His name was Barry Chambers, and he was known as Big B. When I approached Barry on a hundred previous occasions about where Black Nickie was, he was always cordial but he was giving me the runaround. But on this particular day, Big B asked if he could sit down and talk to me about the murder of Bill Burke. He said, "Augie, my mama told me come in and tell you who killed Bill."

I said, "Well, B, your mother told you the right thing. A man's life has been taken, and his murderer must come to justice. His murderer must be arrested and must go before the court. I want you to tell me who it is."

He gave me the name of the murderer: Jerry Collier. He said that his mother told him that he would be murdered just as Bill Burke was murdered when this fellow became angry. Jerry Collier was also a transvestite. He was living with Barry.

I said, "okay, will you work with us?"

He said, "yes."

Collier was at the Clinton Hotel on Thirty-first Street in Manhattan. The Clinton Hotel was another den of iniquity. We decided to wire Big B up with a Nagra and a Kell. He was recording what was going on in the hotel room, and we were hearing it while seated in a radio car in the vicinity.

B said, "Oh, by the way, Jerry, you know the night you killed that john down there on the stroll in Long Island City? You told me that you got eight hundred dollars, but the paper read nine hundred dollars was stolen from him," etc., etc.

"I killed him, but all he had was eight hundred dollars."

"What did you do with the eight hundred dollars? You didn't do anything by me. You didn't do anything for anybody else."

Jerry said that he blew it on drugs and it went fast. So now we had an admission. The following day I picked up Jerry Collier. I also called the assistant district attorney who was in charge of the Homicide Bureau. The ADA came in, and Collier made a full confession—after being advised of his rights, of course. This case did not go to trial. Collier copped a plea. But he went to jail.

•

On August 10, 1981 I went to the Intelligence Division, where I primarily handled motorcades for visiting dignitaries. We interacted with the State Department, the Secret Service, naval intelligence, and army CID. Then in October of 1989, I became one of Mayor Dinkins's bodyguards, and that's where I am presently assigned. Last week, I realized a dream I've had for thirty years. I was promoted to detective first grade, and it sure feels good.

●

5

•

DETECTIVE

SECOND GRADE

RAYMOND PIERCE

The 75th precinct in East New York, Brooklyn, where I worked had five hundred people assigned to it. In November of 1973, six of us were promoted to the rank of detective third grade, and given the title of "field training specialist." In this Brooklyn command our assignment was to continue to work in a radio car performing our normal duties, but with the additional salary and rank of detective. As recruits were graduated from the police academy and came to the precinct, rather than just being thrown out on the street with only a basic orientation, they were assigned to work with us for a period of time. The idea was to put them with an experienced person who was getting an extra incentive to actually do a good job of training them. I did that training on and off until 1979, when I was transferred into the Plainclothes Anti-Crime Unit within the same precinct.

There were five openings, because five police officers from this anticrime unit were transferred to Greenhaven Prison after being convicted of corrupt activities.

There was a cloud over the unit. We knew that we

•

were going to be scrutinized. So we went out and really scraped the streets for arrests. And that's what we did on a daily basis. I mean there was nothing but activity all day long.

The neighborhood was a mixture of blacks and Hispanics, with very few Asians or Caucasians. Over the last twenty years it almost always led the city in the homicide rate. And for the last several years it had well over a hundred homicides each year. It's a large precinct, over five square miles.

However, very few times would we actually be walking the streets unless we were closely following someone. Most of the time we'd be in an unmarked vehicle, which was a little bit of a game because everyone knows the look of an unmarked police car. So, frequently we would augment it with one of our own cars. We did not respond to radio runs unless there was an urgent need—but generally we'd go out on patrol in plainclothes and concentrate on an area that was having a problem.

Burglaries, while generally not violent, were a great problem in this precinct, because there was so much poverty, and many people were looking for a quick score for drugs. Particularly during the daylight hours, burglary was always in the back of our minds. We'd check out locations where we knew there was a burglar working. We would also concentrate on robberies and any other violent activity on the street.

You could generally spot someone on the street who you knew had a prior arrest record. And if he looked a little strung out, you knew that he was going to do something that day. Obviously you couldn't sit on him all day long, but you would keep coming back to the area to see what he was up to.

I can recall following two people, thinking that they were going to do a robbery in a store, but it turned out they did a dual purse snatch. Simultaneously they took two women—

•

one on the corner and the other across the street. We had been on them for about a good forty-five minutes to an hour. We had, of course, the benefit of working with radios, which they didn't have, and we caught them right away.

The arrests were frequent, but there weren't any John Dillingers, although there were some serious murderers. To us at that time almost every collar was just another statistic. There were no requirements that we make a certain number of arrests every month. But as one person I worked with explained it, although the majority of officers in this unit were white or Hispanic, and the area was predominantly black, he could stand out in the middle of a busy intersection, in a bathing suit and walking backwards, and still make an arrest. Because so many of the people there were preoccupied with other things you could actually blend into the community.

In late 1979 or early 1980, we started wearing vests every day, because the number of shooting incidents had increased in the area. The department vests that we have now are actually much more comfortable. The danger was always there, but that's part of being a police officer. It's part of the high or the enjoyment of being out there working.

I looked forward to going to work the next day even after spending hours and hours in court. There still isn't a day that I don't enjoy going to work. It is something that I've chosen to do, and I've been doing it since I became a police officer on April Fools' Day in 1970.

I made a lateral transfer from Anti-Crime to being a detective investigator in 1981. One difference was that as an investigator your daily attire is different. You're wearing a jacket and a tie. You're in an office. You're not going out as much as the radio motor patrol officers, who are out all day long circulating throughout the precinct, or the Anti-Crime officers, who are hitting the streets every day. You're balancing a caseload.

A uniform officer will take a report and refer it to the de-

•

tectives. The detective does the follow-up investigation. Well, if you're working in a very busy command, that investigation is followed with another and then another. Many times you'll feel like you're just a secretary answering the phone and typing. A secretary with a gun. And if you don't manage that caseload effectively, if you don't stay on top of your paperwork, you're not going to go out there and do police work that often. Realistically, to stay on top of it, you should have a course in case management before you become a detective.

A commander once told me that to be an effective investigator, a detective should have no more than fifteen cases a month to manage. The next day I went into work and caught thirteen cases, which is a little extreme. But in a city this large, with as many problems as we have, when you're balancing many cases it's very difficult to be an effective investigator and not just a paper manager. I worked with a very good team of people. We were able to manage our work, get out on the street, and we did interesting work.

We'd catch all types of cases: homicide, robbery, burglary, larceny, or perhaps a serious assault, anything other than sex crimes. At that time, there was a separate sex crimes unit.

If it was my turn to catch the next homicide, then I'd work exclusively on that case, either individually or with other members of the team, for as long as possible, but generally no more than four days.

In 1983, I had an interesting case. A young woman was killed in the precinct. She and her husband had only been married about five months. The case started on an October morning, a Tuesday morning, the same day we invaded the island of Grenada. The husband had gone to work about 7:00 in the morning. He was an intern in a hospital. She was an X-ray technician in the same hospital. She wasn't due in to work until 12:00 in the afternoon.

They lived in a garden apartment next to this hospital.

•

Underneath their garden apartment was a small clinic. Shortly after 10:00 a nurse came into the clinic, and she noticed water gushing from the ceiling. So she went up to the victim's apartment. The door was slightly ajar. She knocked on it, and the door opened. She saw the neighbor lying in a pool of her own blood on the kitchen floor. She had apparently been stabbed. The nurse retreated immediately and called the hospital security officers.

I probably got there about fifteen or twenty minutes after the nurse found the victim. When I arrived at the scene I evaluated everything as a good detective should. But I didn't have any solid suspects in the case. We had many possible suspects. They lived directly across the street in a city housing project. It was a low-income project with maybe eighty thousand residents who were never checked fully. The feeling was that this was a daytime burglary that went bad. The victim was probably not expected to be home at the time, and the individual wound up killing her. I felt that was possible, but I also felt it was very possible that it was someone who knew the victim that had killed her.

Already at that point this was a little more involved than most of the homicides that I had investigated. My specialty at that time was baseball-bat homicides. When somebody hit somebody over the head with a baseball bat, I either found the bat, or the body, or the blood, and occasionally the person that did it.

The water that was gushing from the ceiling was stopped by one of the hospital security officers. He went into the apartment, walked past the victim, and turned off the bathtub faucet. The killer had left the bathtub overflowing. Now, it was common knowledge in the garden apartments that at 10:00 this clinic downstairs was going to open. Could that person be anticipating this, or could they have another reason for leaving the water on? There was some property placed in the bathtub. Naturally, you can remove fingerprints with water. But I thought there was a little bit more to it than that. I just didn't know what. I didn't have that solid gut feeling that tells you, yes, this was someone who knew the victim. Maybe the other detectives were right, that it very well could be a kid from the city project across the street.

There wasn't any forced entry into the apartment. So she probably opened the door at some point. Could a kid from the project con her into opening the door? It was unlikely. She was from another part of Brooklyn, a very tough part of Brooklyn. She wouldn't have opened that door to just anyone, and there was a peephole in the door.

In the bathtub was a jewelry box taken from the bedroom, and a carving knife taken from the kitchen drawer. The next day I took that carving knife down to the autopsy, and I spoke with the medical examiner. We had a little bit of difficulty communicating; he was German, I believe, and he probably just landed a short while before.

There are certain things you want to see at an autopsy as an investigator. Once the wounds have been cleansed they look very different. And sometimes, particularly with chest wounds, from the entry point, with the direction and depth of the wound, you can approximate the size of the murderer if you can establish where they were in relation to the victim.

Once the medical examiner had cleansed the wounds, I saw that there were eight stab wounds in the throat. And as that doctor was continuing with his autopsy, the chief medical examiner of Brooklyn, Dr. Michael Baden, walked by and pointed at the victim and said, "aha, officer, we have rage here."

I said, "excuse me?"

He said, "We have rage here."

As he started to walk away, I grabbed his coat for a second and said, "At least we can communicate, doctor. Why don't you come back here for a second. And what do you mean that we have rage here?"

•

139

He said, "well, generally when we see stab wounds to the throat it's an indication that the attacker knew the victim. They may have known the victim very well, or only for a short period of time, but that's really intense rage when someone stabs someone in the throat like that." That was very interesting. It stuck in the back of my mind.

The other fact I learned at the autopsy was that she was manually strangled to death before she was stabbed. In all probability, she was lying on her back when the killer picked her head up by the hair and proceeded to stab her in the neck. If my skills were a little sharper, at the time, I would have realized that the blood-spatter pattern that was present when we found the body was not consistent with that coming from a person who was alive.

My feeling that it was someone who knew her now had something supporting it. When I returned to my command, the theory was still that it was someone from the projects. But because she was a doctor's wife, I got some assistance from a task force to work on the case.

We really did everything that we should have been doing on the case, but it was still going nowhere. About six to seven weeks into the investigation I was sitting in my office. I didn't have any leads, but I recalled that about two years earlier I had attended a seminar where a process called psychological profiling was mentioned. My feeling in an investigation is that if something's going to help the investigation and it's not going to cost me anything but time and effort, why not try it? We have an obligation to our victims to try everything. So I called the person who presented that portion of the seminar. His name is Harry O'Riley. He's a retired New York City investigator and supervisor of the original Sex Crimes Squad. At this time, he was an assistant professor at John Jay College of Criminal Justice. I gave him a rough idea of the case, and he said, "Why don't you come up and see me?"

So, my partner and I went up there with our crime scene

•

photographs and we showed the case to him. He said, "Probably the best advice I can give you is that this wasn't a typical homicide or sexual assault." Because not only was she stabbed in the throat eight times, she was strangled to death first.

He said, "What you may want to do is contact someone in the FBI, in the behavioral science unit in Quantico, Virginia. They've done a lot of research into violent sexual assault as well as homicide. Maybe they can help you." He then gave me the name of special agent Roy Hazelwood.

I called him, and he gave me a rundown of what he would need to assist me with the investigation—which simply came down to a summary of the case, some investigative information, crime scene photographs, and the autopsy protocol.

I had hit a deadlock in the case, and I really didn't have any direction, and what I was looking for was direction. Well, in three and a half weeks the FBI came back with a formal report, and not only did the FBI give me direction, but this profile provided a list of the physical characteristics of the individual, his educational background, his employment background, and where he would live in relation to where the crime scene was—in this case, where the victim lived also. And, the most important information that the FBI provided was that this person had been in the victim's home in the past. Well, that was the key. It narrowed the investigation to six people, whereas originally we had been looking at probably a kid from a project where there were eighty thousand residents. Only six people had been in the apartment in the past.

One minute after I received the report we were able to narrow it down to one person. Then we centered in on the one individual we ultimately identified as the killer. And the person that we centered in on was from the victim's immediate circle of friends.

Unfortunately, at that point we at best had only circum-

•

stantial evidence. We had already lost almost eleven weeks in the case. So, any evidence that we may have obtained earlier was gone. The apartment was clean as far as fingerprints, or even hair and fiber, were concerned. There was really nothing that we identified that first day from the apartment that was of forensic value. Consequently, an arrest was not made. The case is still active. But it was a most interesting experience for me.

I continued through the rest of 1983 and most of 1984 not needing that service again. Most of the cases were either readily solvable, or they were still in progress.

Then, in late 1984, my name was submitted to a program that the FBI had decided to start. They had worked on this process of psychological profiling for about ten years, and they decided to train several local detectives in it.

In late 1984 I was transferred to our Crime Scene Unit, to work with them for about a month, to really pick up some of the forensic identification procedures that generally squad detectives don't get too involved with, because we have the luxury in New York City of having a sixty-member crime scene unit that comes out and does the technical portion of our investigation. At the time of my transfer, I thought, "gee, why do I have to work with Crime Scene? I've seen enough homicide investigations." Well, I think had I not worked with our Crime Scene Unit for that month I would have definitely embarrassed myself and the department when I went down for this training. That's how good our Crime Scene Unit is. I mean, in one month I learned quite a bit about the recovery procedures for evidence, as well as forensic identification.

Then in late January of 1985 I went to the FBI academy in Quantico, where I remained for almost eleven months in this fellowship program.

Sometimes we'd sit in a conference room and for two days we'd go over a case that was already solved, such as the Dr. Jeffrey McDonald case. He was the Green Beret doc-

•

tor who killed his wife and two daughters. We'd go over the really fine points of the case. Then we wouldn't have an expert come in for, let's say, another week. But just as I had sent that case in for analysis from Brooklyn, other detectives from around the country and around the free world would send in unsolved investigations to this behavioral science unit, and we would observe the agents working on these cases as trained profilers to see what they looked for, and what keys they used. After about five or six months the light finally went on and I said, "Uh huh, now I see exactly what they're doing."

Then we worked for about another four to five months actually doing our own profiles, but still under the supervision of the experienced profilers.

Just to go back for a minute to the Jeffrey McDonald case: He said that three men and one woman came into his house, and they were dressed in a hippie style. This was in February of 1969. He said that he was at home with his wife and his two daughters, and his wife was pregnant at the time. The intruders came in through his rear door and attacked him, his wife, and the two children. One child never got out of her bed. Everyone was killed but Jeffrey. He received a wound that punctured his lung from an ice-pick type of weapon.

The story, at the time, was believed by just about everyone. It occurred on Fort Bragg in North Carolina. When the MPs arrived they saw a really terrible crime scene with a surviving victim—a military captain saying "quick, check my family and give me mouth-to-mouth." He recognized that he needed resuscitation, because he had difficulty breathing, and they listened to what he said. He was taken to the hospital immediately and, of course, he survived.

Then the military looked at it again more closely, and some parts of his story really didn't connect. But I don't think at that point the local military investigators were that sophisticated to overcome what I believe was his staging of

•

the crime scene. And it was thoroughly staged, as far as I could see, to really make it look like a struggle had taken place. But again, when you look at something like that, you have three males and a woman coming into a place to attack—I mean no property was taken at all, other than McDonald's wallet was missing. It was questionable whether or not someone that was assisting, either an ambulance person or someone like that may have lifted his wallet. I don't know. But when you look at three people, four people, intruding into someone's home in the middle of the night, and then not overcoming the male with a brutal savage beating, when his wife and one of his children took a very serious beating, and the second child was killed in her bed, then why not concentrate your attack on the male? That's something that now stands out quite a bit.

If you recall, over a year ago up in Boston, the Charles Stuart incident. He was taking his wife home from a Lamaze class. She was seven or eight months pregnant at the time. He reported that he was attacked by a guy who jumped in the car and tried to rob him and his wife. He was shot, however, and his wife was executed—I mean she was shot in the head. Now my sensors go off when I see something like that. It's a little too good to be true. When something generally is too good to be true, I find that it very well could be a staged crime scene that we're looking at.

And that's exactly what that case back in Brooklyn was. That water leaking through the ceiling when the nurse came into the clinic. Why was that water there? Well, the guy could have been washing fingerprints from the jewelry box and the knife that he touched. However, it turned out that he was where he should have been at 10:00. So that was done as a cover for him, because the body was discovered then. It was staging the crime scene to make it look like some disorganized person had come in and ransacked the house a bit, as well as turned on the bath and left it running.

Now, to a greater extent that appeared to be what Jeffrey

•

McDonald did down in North Carolina—he staged the scene to make the authorities believe that these four individuals had intruded into his home, in the middle of the night, and attempted to kill him.

What I found very interesting in that case was that Mrs. McDonald's stepfather supported Jeffrey at first. They had a military hearing and he was exonerated. Then the stepfather tried to persuade the military authorities to find these people that actually did it, and when it wasn't forthcoming, he stayed involved in it. He became driven to find the people that had committed this terrible crime. Ultimately, it was he who decided that McDonald was, in fact, guilty of the crime. The stepfather then petitioned Congress to reopen the case and to really look into it. And they did, and that's when an extensive examination of the entire scene was done.

One of the luxuries that the military has that we don't have is that they were able to preserve the crime scene, to seal off that whole residence, for over nine years. So, they were able to go back and recover additional evidence, particularly the blood and fiber evidence that ultimately, I believe, led to his conviction.

If you recall, he was on the Dick Cavett show, and a few other shows, explaining his innocence. Well, I feel that he is such a good con man that he could probably con just about anyone that he was interested in manipulating, which is exactly what he did with the military police that first night in North Carolina.

After he was initially exonerated, he worked for quite a while out on the West Coast as an emergency room trauma specialist. The Long Beach, California police department gave a benefit for him to offset his expenses for going back to trial because he was such a good guy and took care of so many people in the community, as well as the police officers. I'm sure that there are people who have even read Joe McGinniss's book *Fatal Vision* who feel that Jeffrey McDon-

•

ald couldn't possibly have done it. He's now, however, in a federal institution in California. Unfortunately, I think he's going to be eligible for parole this year.

What probably happened was that he and his wife had a fight. The theory is that his daughter had a serious problem with bed-wetting. He came home late. He was working very long hours with a part-time job in another hospital, as well as in military practice. He may have been overtired. He went in to bed and found his daughter sleeping with his wife, and she had wet his side of the bed. And he just acted out in a spontaneous rage. In that spontaneous rage he brutally killed both of them. He then killed the girl that was still asleep in her bed in the other room to cover up the first two murders.

There was an interesting magazine found near the coffee table. It was the current *Esquire* magazine. And there was a story in this magazine about the Manson family.

I'm sure he stabbed himself with this ice-pick type weapon and then disposed of it. And he staged other areas of the apartment. The sophistication is there. The above-average intelligence is there, because under great stress he was able to respond effectively and stage the crime scene. But he is not criminally sophisticated. And with the identification of blood and fiber evidence in the McDonald case, the government was able to overcome his staging.

It was a very interesting investigation, as was the case in Brooklyn.

Since coming back to the NYPD, I've been spreading the word about what I can do to assist other investigators. I don't remember all the people that I've arrested, but I'm more interested in criminals now. Before they were just filed away, put through the system. That case was closed, let's go on to the next. Now, with the training I've received, I'm more interested in what they were thinking. I find that by trying to predict what they would do, based on what I feel they may have been thinking at the time of the crime, it

•

is that much easier to track them. And if you equate it to playing ball, where if you can approximate what your opponent is thinking before the play begins, then maybe they're not going to get that end run on you.

What I find very interesting now, about the work that I do in assisting detectives with their investigations, is trying to overcome that sophisticated criminal. Not necessarily the intelligent criminally sophisticated individual, but the intelligent noncriminally sophisticated offender. Someone like McDonald, who commits a crime in a rage and then tries to cover it up.

Recently we had a case where it appeared that a woman fell from a high-rise building in an affluent area of Manhattan. And one of her shoes was in the apartment, and the other shoe was where she had landed—fifteen or twenty floors down.

When the detectives interviewed the husband he said, "It was terrible. I just saw her, as I came in. She said something and then she went out the window."

The autopsy report came back from the medical examiner's office the next day. They found that her larynx had been crushed. So they were able to determine that she was, in fact, strangled first, and then pushed out—leaving one slipper behind. Generally, people keep their shoes on, or they take them off, but they don't leave just one on.

The husband later on admitted committing the crime in a rage. But he just didn't realize that we would check that much further, or that the medical examiner's office has a responsibility to conduct autopsies in cases like this. So that intelligent person was not criminally sophisticated. And the detectives were able to overcome this, and ultimately a very good confession was obtained.

One of the more interesting cases that came in during the first six months I was back from the FBI was a case from another area of Brooklyn that I had worked in. A sixteen-year-old girl was killed in her apartment.

•

She lived with her mother and a younger sister. It was the day after Thanksgiving. They had been out to a relative's home on Long Island. The younger sister stayed with the relative. The sixteen-year-old victim came back with her mother. Her mother had to go to work the next day. She went to work about 7:00 in the morning. She worked within walking distance of the home, and normally she would come home for lunch. Particularly this Friday she was coming home because her daughter was home from school. At noon she returned, where she found her daughter brutally stabbed to death. She called the police and they immediately responded.

The investigator in the case centered in on three friends of the victim. She had a sixteen-year-old boyfriend, and a sixteen- and seventeen-year-old set of friends from school, and they were all very close. The detective felt strongly that one of these kids probably committed the crime. So, what he was asking for was not necessarily a profile, but an assessment of the personalities of each of these three teenagers, to see which would be the one he should concentrate on, which one would be most likely to be capable of committing that crime. So I reviewed the case.

It was interesting, because everything that I could see in the case indicated to me that it was committed by a much more sophisticated individual than a sixteen year old.

She was found undressed in her bedroom. She had a neckerchief around her neck. Underneath that, her neck was slit from side to side. Very little blood, however, indicating that it was probably postmortem when she was cut. She had two serious injuries in her chest that had killed her. It was a single-entry wound with a knife, and the knife was partially removed and then pushed in again. A single entry, double-track wound that perforated the heart. And there were other superficial wounds around the body, but they were just like little half-inch penetrations of the skin. Nothing really that would do that much damage. And

•

again, the absence of blood suggested they could have been postmortem also.

Based on that information, could these sixteen- or seventeen-year-old kids have stayed and experimented with the body afterwards? Of course, they could have. But there were two other crime scene photographs in the case that really led me to believe that it was someone older than a kid. And I'm talking about someone probably twenty-five to thirty-five years of age. One crime scene photograph was of a jewelry box that she and her sister apparently shared. It was a cardboard laminated jewelry box. It was up on top of the dresser, and there was a television next to it. It had maybe fifteen or twenty little drawers. Each one of these small drawers, maybe they were two to three inches across and four inches deep or so, were carefully taken out and placed on the television or on the bed. They had twin beds in the bedroom.

I recognized that the scene was staged to look like a burglary. Right up on top of this really flimsy jewelry box were different little bottles of perfume and lotion—indicating that the person who took out these drawers was very calm about it. Maybe even very comfortable with her jewelry box. Maybe much more so than a sixteen- or seventeen-year-old boy would be. Putting myself in the place of that sixteen or seventeen year old, if I had just killed a girl I knew, and maybe I had a couple of hours before her mother came home, I think I still would have been out of there. I wouldn't have taken the time to stage that scene. But if I had tried to do something with that jewelry box, I think my hand would have been going about fifty miles an hour trying to pull the drawers out. It just didn't fit.

The second photograph really bothered me. It showed that in between the two beds the girl's nightclothes were carefully laid down. And there weren't any perforations in the clothing that corresponded to the stab wounds in her body, indicating that when she was stabbed she was nude.

•

Then there is the all-important victim information. In this case, we got very good information about the victim from her mother.

She had begun her menstrual cycle the day before, on Thanksgiving. A menstrual pad was laid on top of her underwear. Every layer of clothing was just taken off, and placed down beside the bed, as if she was going to take a shower.

The theory was, at the time, that perhaps some consensual sexual activity was started, and then it got out of hand, and the guy wound up killing her. But in this case it didn't appear to be that way. It was so carefully laid out; otherwise it was staged to appear that a random burglar came in there and held her at knife point, or gunpoint, or something like that, and then attempted to rape her and wound up stabbing her. It just didn't seem right to me.

One of the precautions I take from getting tunnel vision in an investigation is that I'll speak with other detectives. All cases remain confidential. The other detectives don't know where the case is coming from. But I'll give them a summary of the case, and let them observe the crime scene photos. So, I spoke with a female detective about this case. I said, "this bothers me." I'm thinking back about my own life experience. "A girl, sixteen years old, would be a bit embarrassed about anything to do with her menstrual cycle in front of a young boy. What do you think about this?"

She looked at the photographs and said, "I'm thirty-five years old, and if a six foot-five guy stood in front of me in my bedroom with a gun to my head and said take off your clothing, I'd take off my clothing. But if that was my menstrual pad, I'd stand there with my hands up and I'd kick that under the bed. I wouldn't leave it exposed."

I then asked the detective who had the case, "can you tell me some more? You know, there's something missing here. There's a big piece of this puzzle missing."

What he was able to tell me was that the mother had been

•

separated from the father for about four years, and they'd been divorced for two. In no way was the father a suspect. His alibi was quite well verified out in Long Island. And the mother was a great mother. They weren't financially well-off at all. She worked hard, but she didn't make much money, although she provided just about everything the children needed. And it looked like a typical teenager's room. The mother was just devoted to the children.

I said, "well, there's gotta be something. Is there anything else that you can think of?"

He said, "well, the mother's a lesbian."

"That could be important information. Does she have friends who come over the house frequently?"

He said, "oh no. She belongs to some group of women in the area. She goes out, but she's very protective of the children." He went on to say that the younger daughter couldn't deal with her mother's lifestyle, but the sixteen-year-old victim accepted it. Whatever her mother wanted to do was fine with her.

Ultimately the profile that was provided in the case was that the killer would be a woman, twenty-five to thirty-five years of age. There were many things that indicated to me that it might very well be a woman. First of all, the absence of facial battery. The girl wasn't beaten at all. She was contained and stabbed. We can surmise that her arms were pinned and she was stabbed in the chest from behind. The familiarity with the jewelry box. There was a lack of forced entry into the apartment. Also, there was a television on when the mother returned, and there was a huge jigsaw puzzle out on the floor that the girl was working on—it was one of her hobbies.

The weapon was recovered, taken from the kitchen drawer. The drawer had then been closed again, but had no fingerprints at all, and there should have been. It was a surface that we could have found fingerprints on.

There were also several points in the case that suggested

•

it might be a male, but the behavioral evidence and probabilities indicated it should be a female—just that comfort with the jewelry box, and the leaving of the menstrual pad out. I felt strongly that it was a woman. Someone who knew the mother, perhaps a former romantic interest. Someone who had been in the apartment numerous times in the past. Someone who was very comfortable.

What we surmised afterwards was the killer probably made a move on the girl, and she threatened to tell her mother. So the girl was killed, and the scene was staged to look like a burglary and a violent homicide. Except that it wasn't that violent. There was another key in the photographs to indicate that it wasn't that violent. It was a very neat crime scene for what should have occurred.

To continue with the description of the killer, if I'm going to say that it's someone who had been in that apartment numerous times in the past, then probably they were from the mother's and daughter's circle of friends. The three kids she knew from school were all Hispanic. The mother's ethnic background was Hispanic. The mother's circle of friends was also totally Hispanic. And in this country, whites kill whites in overwhelming numbers, blacks kill blacks, Hispanics kill Hispanics, and others kill others. It's a generalization, but statistically I think you'll find that it's overwhelmingly correct that people tend to kill within their same race, because they tend to kill people they know, or from the same area that they're in. So I felt strongly that the killer would be Hispanic, and this individual would be female. And again, twenty-five to thirty-five years of age, because of that sophistication that I saw at the scene.

It wasn't a kid that was able to stage that scene. Even with putting the neckerchief over the slit in the girl's throat. That was supposed to appear as if it was a gag at one time. Except that we checked, and there was never any saliva on that neckerchief.

I mentioned before that the all-important victim informa-

•

tion is just crucial in solving many cases. Well, in this case, the information we had about her was that she was a very experienced swimmer. She had trophies for swimming in school. She had, for her size—which was pretty big, she was five-six—great upper-body strength. Most swimmers do. So, how do you get a girl like that contained in a room unless you're big enough to overcome her? Now, could a sixteen- or seventeen-year-old boy do that? Most definitely. But a very strong woman could do that too. So, the profile went on to read that the killer would be particularly strong. She would have good upper-body strength; probably worked out every day. She might even belong to a health club in the area.

I also said that although females represent—particularly at that time, this was in 1986—a very small population in the military, it's most probable that this killer would have been a member of the military. Probably served as an enlisted person in the military for at least two years.

I also spoke to some friends of mine who had been in special forces. I was in the military, but I only had basic training where we learned how to take people down by putting your arm around them: Like something you see in the movies, where someone will come around the body and come up and cut them for the benefit of the camera. My friends said that if you receive advanced combat training, you wouldn't even bother going around the body and risk having the victim throw up an arm. Instead you would put the knife right through their back. So, I felt strongly that this person may have had military training, but not advanced combat training.

The detective who had the case was annoyed at first that it wasn't one of these three kids. I said, "we can always go back to these three kids."

The other problem that he had with the three children was that they wouldn't submit to a polygraph examination. Their counselor in school had told them not to. The detec-

•

tive was trying to either eliminate two of the three and identify the one person that may have been the killer, or exclude all of them.

So I said, "why don't you take a look and see, from the mother's circle of friends, if anyone could fit this profile."

It turned out that he identified one person from the circle of friends that fit the profile. She was twenty-nine years old, and had access to the house numerous times. I said, "well, good. What about the military?" It turned out she was a former marine. I said, "anything else? Is there a health club close by?"

He said, "no, there's no health club there."

"She's gotta do something. Does she work out?"

"No, she doesn't work out."

I said, "okay, fine."

"But she works in a post office, midnight until eight o'clock in the morning."

"And what does she do in the post office?"

"She loads trucks all night. Throwing mailbags around or whatever."

Obviously she had the good upper-body strength.

We had identified the killer, and the detective who had the case caught her telling several lies. However, there was no physical evidence, such as fingerprints, since everything in the apartment that was disturbed had been wiped clean, to not link her to the crime. Consequently, there wasn't sufficient cause for an arrest or to attempt an indictment. But the detective did warn the mother about her friend, which possibly spared her other daughter from a similar fate.

It was a very interesting case, because just as I was coming back from this training, I was presented with a detective who was looking in one direction, and I was able to refocus his investigation. It was really positive reinforcement for me.

Last week, I was down in Quantico for a week of retraining, which I go down for every year. And that reinforces the

•

entire procedure by going over new cases from around the country—particularly serial murderers, and serial rapists.

We're going to start a research project with serial rapists. We are going into prisons and interviewing them. And not necessarily asking them, why did you do what you did? But, how did you beat us for two months? What did you do to evade detection? Why did you choose that type of victim? The answers to these questions are something that will help us in tracking other criminals in the future.

I think most detectives are like Sherlock Holmes. Maybe my logic has been fine-tuned a bit, and I've had some additional training, but what did Sherlock Holmes do? He observed. And that's what psychologists and the people in the behavioral sciences unit do much more thoroughly than your average detective.

If you ride with a detective or fire marshal down the street, they may be driving and you may be talking with them, but their field of vision is wide. They're looking at people on the street. It's a nice summer's day, and they may be looking at some woman walking down the street, but then they're also looking past her. They're looking for that guy with the bulge in his waistband. They're always observing behavior. It's very distracting if you're out socially with someone to have them constantly looking like this. If you ever go into a restaurant with them, you'll find a police officer doesn't sit the way a normal person would. They don't want to face a wall. They want to be able to look around—they're trained observers. I can remember one case where Sherlock Holmes says to someone, "You're obviously a military man who just returned from . . ." whatever war was in effect at that time in the British empire. And then he tells him exactly where he has been. Well, it was wintertime in England, and the guy had a tan, and he had his arm in a sling, and he was smoking a specific type of tobacco that came from that area where the war was going on. So it was just a logical series of deductions based on ob-

•

servations of what's going on. And that's what every detective does.

It generally takes about three weeks to provide an effective written profile for an investigator. As a homicide investigator going to the scene you can get caught up in the anguish that goes on. Consoling the relative at the scene is part of your job. Securing the scene is also part of your job. You're thinking of many, many things at the time. But I have the luxury of sitting in an office and reviewing the material, and hopefully going out to the crime scene later, if we still have it. But I also have the luxury of having those relatives absent. Although the emotion is still here, I try not to become callous. I can separate myself from that quite a bit now.

We initially take Polaroid pictures. Then our Crime Scene Unit takes the larger photographs and sketches the crime scene for us. In the past, I'd look at them once and say, "yep, that's what I saw." Then I'd put them away in my case folder. Now, I look at them a minimum of ten times. Maybe two or three times the first day I get them. Then I'll put them away for a day or so, before I go back and look at them another couple of times.

Then occasionally I'll consult with other people. There is a deputy chief surgeon within the New York City police department; his name is Martin Symonds. He's a psychiatrist. And he was a police officer before going to medical school. He was in the 1940 graduating class of the police academy. I'll speak to him about a case and get the value of his years of experience, and sometimes it's just as simple as observing something in the crime scene photograph that I missed.

There was a case on the Upper East Side where a woman was killed in her studio apartment. The problem that I had with the case was that she had friction burns on her face, and it looked like she had been beaten but, in fact, they were friction burns from rubbing.

She had a very large studio apartment. Unlike my office,

•

everything was in its place. I don't think she was compulsive, but she was very close to it. Everything had to be in its place, every dish washed and put away.

When she was found she was lying faceup on the carpet of her living room floor. There was a couch on one side of the room. There was no obvious bed in the apartment, but it turned out there was a Murphy bed.

She initially did not appear to be sexually assaulted. No semen was found or anything like that. She was wearing a nice, long nightgown. She was in her late fifties or so. At autopsy, however, there was found to be vaginal trauma. So, she had been penetrated in some way, most probably just before the homicide occurred.

We had the scene for a while. So, I went back with the investigator, and I took the Murphy bed down. Then, based on the crime scene photographs, I approximated where she was found by laying my standard-issue trench coat on the floor. We originally thought that she had been killed in the bed, and then rolled onto the floor, but it just didn't fit. She hadn't been on that bed. I mean, we couldn't get any hair or any fiber evidence from the sheets. The sheets were immaculately tucked in. It looked like they were brand new. Just nothing could be found that was foreign to the scene. So we put the bed back. We just couldn't figure it out.

I then went and spoke with Dr. Symonds in his private office on Lexington Avenue, and one thing that he pointed out to me changed the entire case. He said, "What do you think about that couch?"

I said, "well, it's a nice long couch on the side of the wall in a nicely decorated studio apartment."

"But don't you think that couch was disturbed during the homicide?"

I said, "no, it looks very neat to me."

Then he pointed to one of the photographs in the series and said, "well, what about this? What about that cushion right there?"

•

I looked a little closer. Now, I had never seen this before, but from the couch cushion one of those little tags was protruding slightly. One of the tags that say if you remove this, the pillow police will come after you.

He said, "From what you told me about her, she could never have left that out. It doesn't appear to be within her character to just put a cushion back on the couch like that. Perhaps the killer straightened up that couch afterwards."

So I went back to the scene with the detective, and it turned out that it was a convertible couch. We hadn't checked it before. Now, I again lay my trench coat down on the floor exactly where she was found. And it was apparent that she was just taken from the couch, probably after having semiconsensual relations, and placed on the floor.

We were also able to find that she was cut, in addition to having the abrasions, but it didn't appear to be a laceration from a fist. We then found that down in the mechanisms of this convertible couch there was a little bit of blood where her head had been pushed in there. We surmised that she was strangled to death after her head had been pushed in there on the nubby fiber of the couch, causing the friction burns, and her head hit the metal rod underneath the couch, and that any screaming she had done probably was muffled. So, that really gave us an indication of what was going on prior to the crime, which led to a description of an individual that she had known, and had a consensual relationship with.

Is every case solved from something like that? No—but it demonstrates the power of observation, even by someone further separated from the investigation than I was. I'm not going to tell you that it's as interesting or as rewarding as chasing someone down the street and, after a flying tackle, arresting them. I'd still like to be doing that, though I don't know how effectively I'd do that now. But the rewarding portion of my job is coming up with something extra in a case to pull it out.

•

The criminal population is becoming more and more skilled. People out there are watching shows like "Murder, She Wrote," "Quincy," and all of the different crime movies. I don't really want the enemy to find out all the tricks that we have, or some of the legal maneuvers that we can make that are still left to us by the Supreme Court.

What's going on out in society is a little frightening. But is it that much different from one hundred and fifty years ago? We're overlooking this archeological dig outside of headquarters. That area was known as the Five Corners, in the 1840s and 1850s. It was a treacherous area of town. The police didn't come there unless you pleaded with them. There was supposed to have been gangs running wild, with a homicide a night, including a couple of interesting gangs called the Plug Uglies, and the Rabbit Heads, who walked around with rabbit heads on staffs.

Nowadays, if you're a drug dealer and you have your little empire on one corner of the city, and someone moves in on you, how do you take care of that? Rarely do they appear to negotiate. They just point out the one or two targets that they want to attack on that corner, and if fifteen other people happen to be around, they really don't take that into consideration. And that's one of the reasons why these drive-by shootings are going on.

If you're a drug dealer, you sit in your little fiefdom all day long, and people come in either with the product, or the money, and you just watch your videos of the *Terminator*, one, two, and thirty-seven, or other violent stories that depict people constantly being shot up.

I think when we were kids we saw movies that were violent, but not like the volume of shooting massive numbers of people in these current terror movies. Whether it's *Friday the 13th*, where some horror subject is killing a large number of people, or someone just shooting into a crowd.

I think that they see this, and if it's reinforced every day, what happens? People become objects. I've found it difficult to shoot a person, but it's very easy to go for target practice and shoot at an object. So it's quite different, I think. And when they just see these other people as objects, and they see the target that they want as an obstacle, that's their corner, they want that corner to sell drugs or whatever. So if I shoot at those two or three people, and these other people happen to get hit, well, I'm justified because I'm trying to take over that territory. It's my drug business. When people become objects it's really, really tough. And it's going on not only in our city, but in every major city in the country. That's what I see changing in our society—the coldness of some of these people.

However, homicide is still a very personal crime, so the majority of people who are killed are going to know their murderer. Even in these drive-by shootings, the people that they're actually after generally know them, if the assassination is not done by a hired individual.

Recently, I helped interview an inmate in a state prison. Part of my job is to assist other detectives with interrogations. The prisoner was scheduled to be released on parole in 1996. He was a street robber, but we were trying to get him to confess to a murder that occurred in 1986.

He told us that he was an orphan, adopted when he was eight years old, who lived with the person that adopted him for seven years. The person who adopted him was a single male who had adopted several other boys. He said there was no molestation involved, this guy was just out there helping these previously unadoptable children. As it turned out, he realized that this guy was using him when the man asked him if he'd like to go on different shows and be in different magazines to show that this guy adopts the unadoptable. He said, "it wasn't that bad of a life." But he became a real street kid that grew up tough.

He'd been on his own, in the city, since he was fifteen. He had a heavy cocaine addiction, and he supported himself with minor jobs and robbery. He said his habit was up to about 800 dollars a day.

He had been arrested twelve times over the last thirteen years. His first arrest was when he was fifteen for attempted murder. He is a very violent individual.

He told the detective that was working on the case, Tim Copeland, from the Detective Squad in the 112th precinct, that he would go out and do robberies, but he wouldn't hurt anyone. He had a gun that he only displayed. He said it was a toy gun he kept in his waistband. He'd just hustle people on the subway. He'd come upon a homeless person, and if he realized that this person might have some money, he'd display the gun and say, "well, we're taking everything today." And he'd do this over and over again. He just wouldn't hurt anyone at all. Meanwhile, we knew his record indicated that he was extremely violent.

Our strategy was to talk to him about the robberies he did before we hit on the homicide. He knew that he was doing time for the robberies and we weren't going to pressure him there. What I got from him in discussing all these robbery cases was that he felt entitled to the money he was taking from these people.

I tried to build up his ego by saying, "you know, some of the people that you were involved with in these robberies I wouldn't rob. I'd take off an easy victim, maybe an old lady, grab her purse or whatever and just walk off. But you were confronting men. Most robbers don't do that."

Naturally, he's going to open up and talk a little bit. And in one case that we reviewed he was wrong for going after the guy, because he got arrested. The guy fought back and held him for the cops. The intended victim was a muscular black guy sitting at the end of a subway car. It seems this guy was just loaded with gold, including a five-finger ring. He started talking with him and the victim said, "yeah, I'm up in the East Side. I have my own street. I'm a dealer up there."

•

The subject told us that he said to himself, "that's where I used to buy some of my dope. And I've gotten bad dope up there. This guy might have been selling the bad staff." So he rationalized the attack before deciding to rip this guy off.

Again, this isn't the type of victim that the average robber goes after. Generally, most males in the city over five-eight have a free ride as far as robbery goes. When you think about it, most of the victims are either elderly, infirm, intoxicated, or powerless in one way or another. Not that robbery doesn't occur with stronger adult males, but if you're an animal in the wild, why go after the strongest animal, why not go after the easier catch?

He had a toy gun this time, which was kind of stupid with this kind of victim. I'm surprised the guy didn't have his own gun. But they got into a fight, and someone else called the transit police, and they arrested him.

As we were speaking with him I realized how he rationalized his crimes: That he was entitled. He stressed the fact many times during the conversation that he never knew his natural mother or his natural father. We interviewed him for about six hours. He really felt he was dealt such a poor deal in life, why would he have to go out and get a legit job? He'd keep preying on society. Ultimately, he killed this girl in 1986.

He first met her in the subway. She invited him over to her apartment on a weekend evening, and they just had a couple of cocktails. He was strung out on drugs for quite a while. He had been living in the street for two days, but he brought an attaché case with him because he wanted to impress her. He told her that he had a job.

While he's telling us the story I'm not going to interrupt him, but afterwards we will review the information with him. I wanted to know how, if I'm in the street for two days, how do I impress someone without being steam cleaned before I spend a little time with them in their apartment. He said, "I washed all the time. There are public places where

•

you can wash. I had my attaché case. I wanted to make it look like I came from work." So he was conning her.

Unfortunately, he was so strung out he didn't realize that she didn't have a large amount of money in the house, and money was one of the reasons why he went over there. He did notice that she had 50 dollars tucked in her coat pocket earlier, but that was all she said she had. So he threatened her.

She had a burglar alarm and she threatened to sound the alarm. She wanted him out of the apartment, "but things escalated," as he put it. He said, "I wasn't thinking rationally at the time. I just told her, 'I want your money.' "

She said, "that's all I have. I don't have any more."

So he said, "stay exactly where you are. Don't move."

She was on the couch. But she made a move towards the side of the couch. He felt strongly that she was going to get up and activate the burglar alarm, so he shot her once in the neck. He had a small-caliber pistol.

Then she pleaded with him, "okay, okay, anything you need."

He said, "I just remember shooting her three more times: *Pow, pow, pow.*" And then he remembered that he had five rounds left in the gun. He claimed to have been irrational at the time, but how irrational can you be when you remember that you have five rounds left in your gun?

Then he explained that he did not put the gun in his pocket, (because a good street robber doesn't want to be caught by the police with a gun in his pocket) instead he put the gun in his attaché case, and walked down to the street. But when he opened the apartment door he activated the alarm. He said it was low at first, then he heard the alarm get louder and louder. He said it got louder as he was two blocks away. Now, maybe that was in his mind, but he said it caused him to take the attaché case with the gun in it and just throw it into a city wastepaper basket. The gun was never recovered. I don't know if it was thrown somewhere

•

in a dump, or if one of our sanitation workers opened that attaché case when they found it in the basket, or if he actually threw the gun away. Although there's no physical evidence to link him to the homicide, I do know he is guilty.

6

•

SERGEANT

NELLIE

TORRES

I started working for the police department in 1979, as a 911 operator while waiting to come on as an officer. After I was sworn in and completed the police academy training, I was assigned to Neighborhood Stabilization Unit II, which encompassed the 6th precinct in Greenwich Village, the 9th on the Lower East Side, the 10th in Chelsea, and the 13th precinct in Gramercy Park. It definitely was something that I had wanted to do, and I knew from the very first day on patrol that I had made the right choice.

I was promoted in January of 1987 to sergeant, and I went to the 81st precinct, which is in Bedford-Stuyvesant, Brooklyn. It is one of the high-crime areas in the city, and it was one of the most satisfying assignments I ever had.

It was quite a leap going from police officer to sergeant—that's the first rank in supervision. Before you're used to having supervisors give you orders within the department—what to do, what your different posts are, when your meal is, etc. Your sergeant is the one you would call to make major decisions on

•

big or unusual incidents. Now as a sergeant you couldn't rely on going to somebody. Now you were it.

It was a challenge being out there, especially as a female, especially with my stature or lack thereof—and being Hispanic. All these were factors. The day that I did my first roll call I could just hear the officers in the back of their minds saying, "oh god, we got a girl for a boss."

It was strange, because it threw me back to when I first came on patrol, because that was the initial reaction of the officers I worked with. Now, I'm getting the same reaction, but just not as boisterous, because I'm a supervisor.

I think you have to pay your dues no matter what organization you go into. If you want people to respect you, you have to earn respect. You can't just expect to waltz in and have everybody love you and respect you and admire you. I think it's something you have to work for, and it feels good to accomplish that.

I'll never forget that early in my career I had an old-timer who would never, ever ride with rookies. To him a rookie was anyone that had less than twenty years. And one day, lo and behold, we got paired up, on a midnight tour, no less. I was saying to myself, "Oh my god, this is going to be the worst eight and a half hours of my life. This is going to be miserable." We ended up getting back to the station house late. We stopped to help somebody whose car had broken down, and we started talking while waiting for someone else to come help him. I couldn't believe how well we got along—it was absolutely incredible.

Being a sergeant in Bed-Stuy was a challenge, because we handled a lot of unusual incidents: homicides, shootings, emotionally disturbed people, and a lot of other violent situations. Just to be able to go there, make the decisions to make it work in a positive fashion, was something that was a challenge for me. But I did it.

I dealt with a lot of homicides, but I think there is one

•

homicide that really stuck in my mind the most. We get an anonymous call that there's a dead body at a brownstone. Bedford-Stuyvesant has a lot of gorgeous brownstones. Two officers had responded and then called for me, the supervisor, because indeed they did find a dead body.

I respond to the scene. There are steps to go up to the brownstone, and underneath the steps there's an alcove, and in the alcove is a huge box that a clothes washer had come in. And whoever had killed the woman had taken her, dumped her in the box, and had anally sodomized her, either during her death throes or after. There was still sperm on her. He had put her in the box head down, so that her buttocks were facing us, and you could see that the anus was wide open. The fact that somebody would kill another person and then leave them in such a degrading manner always stuck in the back of my mind.

I was raised in a middle-class family, with the Catholic schooling, so it was quite a bit of an eye-opener to see things like this. The amount of cruelty was incredible. The case was turned over to the detectives. I know for the longest time they didn't have any leads, but I never found out how the case ultimately turned.

Another job that we went on—a thirteen-year-old girl stabbed her fourteen-year-old sister, because the fourteen year old took a Pamper for her child that belonged to the thirteen year old's baby. And then along comes another young girl, who I assumed to be an older sister, and she's their mother. I mean she was a grandmother by the time she was thirty-two.

We saw very little parenting. We saw a lot of kids having kids. And for many of these children, police presence was predominant in their lives, whether somebody called them, or because mom left them alone as children, or because dad might be beating mom.

We had another one, this was something like out of a

•

Jimmy Cagney film, with Pat O'Brien, who always played the priest. I'll never forget this. This was July 3rd, and my driver Al Castagna and I went to get our meal. It was a very, very busy day in the precinct. It was a very hot Friday, and of course heat and humidity have a tendency to add to violence.

The dispatcher calls me on the radio, she says, "eighty-one—Sergeant, we're getting numerous calls on shots fired at," and she gives me the location. We were just a block and a half away. Usually when you hear "numerous calls" you know it's authentic.

In my mind I start to think tactics—what are we going to see? Is the perpetrator still on the scene? How is it going to go down?

We get to the location and there's a huge crowd and, of course, nobody saw anything. It happens to be on the side of St. John the Baptist Church. It's like a cathedral, ornate, imposing, and it's absolutely gorgeous. And here's a young man who was shot in the face. He's bleeding profusely. It looked like he had a volcano erupting out of his face. We called for an ambulance. We knew that he was going out of the picture; there was very little that we were going to be able to do. We had to rope off the scene. This was outside, the projects are right across the street, very expansive area. There's a lot of people hanging out on the street. But as for police presence, it's just myself and Al, because it was a very, very busy day—all the units are out on assignments. They were handling the numerous calls to 911.

We kept the crowd back. We called for additional assistance and the detectives show up. With that, a priest from the church comes over, and he wants to see if he can come through the crime scene to give the last rites. We let the priest through. I mean, there was nothing for him to disturb anyway, it was all out in the open.

•

Somebody in the crowd tells us who the victim is and where his mother is. One of the detectives goes to the mother's house and she says, "yes, so what. Thank god I'm rid of him." And she refused to come down. I mean, we don't know that that's actually him until she comes down to make the identification. But she just refused to come down. It was a very strange scene, that life can mean so little.

I remember once on a Saturday night, I had the desk duty, and this woman walked into the precinct with two children who couldn't have been any more than two and three years of age. She tells me, "Sergeant, I don't know what to do. I was on my way to church when this woman came up to me. She gave me these kids and then she just walked away."

So now we had these two beautiful little kids sitting on the desk. Of course, cops are the biggest soft touches in the world, and these kids were spoiled rotten that night between the candy and the ice cream, and somebody managed to get to a store to buy a teddy bear. We didn't know who these kids were. The woman didn't know who the woman was who handed them to her. She said "she looks like a crack addict." The kids, though, did seem cared for. They did not seem malnourished or anything like that. But this woman just handed her children over to a perfect stranger and walked away.

I came for an interview to work as a police officer with the Sex Crimes Unit a little over four years ago, but then I was promoted and no longer qualified for that slot. Subsequently, a position opened up in the Central Investigation and Resource Division of the Detective Bureau. They needed an administrative sergeant and integrity control officer. Inspector Wrynn, who originally interviewed me, had kept me in mind, and he called me up at the precinct and asked me if I'd be interested. I said, "gee, this sounds like something different." It's always good to do diverse things

•

in your career. So I accepted the position, and eventually I took over the Sex Crimes Unit, which is now known as Special Victims Liaison Squad.

I found the Detective Bureau camaraderie to be somewhat different than patrol's. On patrol officers had a tendency to be exceptionally close to their partners, or a handful of other officers within their precinct. In the Detective Bureau the cohesiveness is bureau-wide.

As a detective, you build a network that no computer or information system could duplicate. As you meet other detectives from other squads you exchange cards. Then when the right case comes along—out come the cards, "Hey, what can you tell me about that homicide? I've got a very similar one." Detectives pay extensive attention to details, and love to pick each other's brain.

If you work in a citywide squad, it becomes more difficult, because now you have to be familiar with so many cases. But the satisfaction is great when you can direct the investigator to the appropriate source of information.

When you're newly assigned to the bureau, the fastest way to learn is by hooking up with the more experienced detectives in the squad, listening, watching, and doing. This apprenticeship is not exclusive for the detective rank. I learned a lot from my former boss, Inspector Wrynn, my coworkers, Lieutenant Walsh and Sergeant Anderson, and other detectives.

In the Detective Bureau you're always learning. When I ran the sex crimes investigators course, I always prefaced the introductory remarks with "we're here to learn from each other." I would have each of the one hundred or so attendees introduce themselves, and gave them plenty of time to network. I know many cases were cleared because of that.

In the Special Victims Liaison Squad there are ten detectives that cover the sex crimes report hotline for the police department, which is staffed twenty-four hours a day,

•

seven days a week. We only have female detectives answering the line, because it was felt that perhaps a victim of a sex crime may want to speak to only a woman at a certain point. We can never guarantee that a victim of a sex crime is going to get either a female detective or a female officer to actually handle her case.

My detectives do a lot of referrals, they'll take cases, they'll do counseling with the victims. Sometimes the victims just call to talk to somebody. It may be 2:00 on a Saturday morning, and they're very upset, there's nobody around to talk to, but they can always call us and we'll talk to them. We give them a shoulder to cry on.

We also talk to the families. Many families don't know what they should do. They're in crisis too. They go, "oh my god, I don't know if I should tell her to shut up and forget about it, or should I let her talk it out." For many of them it's very difficult, because nobody wants to hear that a terrible thing happened to their loved one and, of course, they don't want to hear the details of it.

We keep on hand the phone numbers of numerous groups throughout the city that are helpful to families and to the victims.

We also do training on sex crimes and child abuse investigation for the New York City police department and for transit and housing police. We also lecture to hospitals, doctors, nurses, rape crisis counselors, social workers, and we do the Board of Education, both the administrative staff, the teaching staff, and the students. And for virtually every city agency that you can think of, we've conducted training. Additionally, we give lectures to the public on awareness techniques. We hate to call it *prevention. Prevention* implies that if you do a certain number of things you'll never be a victim, which isn't true. We're a warehouse of information.

We're the contact point for any agency and the NYPD regarding sex crimes and child abuse. So if the FBI needs to make a contact on a sex crime case, they'll come to us.

•

We've even worked with Scotland Yard, Interpol, and other international police agencies.

We also run a one-week long advanced training course on sex crimes and child abuse investigation, which is only open to investigators. We bring in lecturers from different areas: medical, and prosecutorial; we also bring in defense attorneys, and anybody that you can think of who has impact on child abuse and sex crimes. And I'm very happy to say that all of these lecturers, who have outstanding credentials, do it for us for nothing, because they are sincerely dedicated, and want to get the information out. And we get such a positive response from our attendees; it's one of the most sought-after courses in the department and from agencies all over—for example, earlier this year, we had two detective inspectors from Scotland Yard attend. We've hosted the New Zealand police, the Israeli police, and police from Australia. It's very heartwarming to see that other agencies are interested, and that they're trying to make an effort to lessen the occurrence of these crimes and break the cycle of violence.

In 1972 the department had its own Criminal Justice Liaisons Unit. And their function was to ensure that the NYPD was doing things in accordance with the other agencies in the criminal justice system. Well, they conducted their own survey within NYPD to find out why 66.6 percent of all sex crimes cases were being dismissed from court. The study indicated that it was because the women were not being taken seriously, and the investigations were done in a very shoddy manner, if at all. For example, poor evidence handling, poor investigative techniques, insensitive interviewing of the victims, lack of attention to details, etc.

The department undertook measures to remedy this. In December 1972, this unit was started, and it was known then as the Sex Crimes Analysis Unit. This unit took over the interviewing of all sex crime victims, and all sex crimes reports were analyzed to see if there were patterns occur-

•

ring. Supervisors, Lieutenant Mary O'Keefe and Sergeant Harry O'Reilly, developed a curriculum to teach the public to be aware of sex crimes, awareness techniques, and to shatter myths about rape. Subsequently, it was discovered that bringing all the victims up to police headquarters was very traumatic. So it was decided that the department should have satellite squads in every borough, and that's how the borough Sex Crimes Squads were born. And since it was discovered that some of the dynamics in interviewing the adult victims were the same for children, the borough squads were also assigned to do child physical and sexual abuse cases.

The Special Victims Liaison Squad still analyzes sex crime data, catches cases that are referred from the New York State central register, as well as from the hotline.

We've worked up some cases that have become very newsworthy or noteworthy, and have gone on to trials and convictions. For example, we worked the Ralph Bull case, where he sexually assaulted four little girls in a foster home he had access to. The case made all the media after the judge allowed him to go free rather then sending him directly to jail before he was sentenced. Again, a lot of the things that we do are to just keep on top of what's going on with sex crimes and child abuse. We develop new strategies. We also assist the chief of detectives. We apprise the latest crime trends, and research, which may necessitate a change in NYPD policies and procedures. And, of course, he makes his recommendations to the police commissioner.

Some of the cases stick in your mind, not because they are so heinous, but because of the implications. For instance, many times we get calls from hospitals about patients that they've admitted. I remember getting a call from one of the local hospitals about a fifteen-year-old girl who had just given birth to her third baby. She identified who the father was, and we had enough to charge him with third-degree rape or statutory rape. But because she had willingly en-

•

gaged in sexual relations with him, and her mother did not want to prosecute, nobody wanted to pursue the case, and it became exceptionally difficult to even get her some social services. Obviously, the girl needed help.

Eventually, we were able to hook her up through social services to have somebody come in and teach her some basic mothering skills and help her raise these children.

When investigating rape, there are certain principles that you always utilize. The number-one thing is that there is always the victim. In the NYPD, patrol officers are trained at the academy in something called victimology, which is basically helping people who are in crisis. The officers are taught to provide some type of emotional support—psychological first aid, to try to calm the victim down. Particularly when you're dealing with sex crime victims, it becomes a very sensitive area.

The officers are instructed that certain types of questions must be asked in a different way. For example, there's nothing wrong with asking a robbery victim, "well, did you fight back?" because we have to establish that every element that's in the New York State penal law did occur in order for us to label this crime as such. For example, with a robbery you must have force and you must have something stolen. So we have to show that there was some force involved, and that there was property stolen. With a sex crime it's a very similar thing. We have to show that there was force. However, if you ask a victim of a sex crime "did you fight back?" the victim is going to sit there and think, "this officer thinks I wanted to be raped. He doesn't believe me." So we tell them don't ask the victim that. You can ask her "can you tell us what happened next?" or "can you tell us what events led up to this happening to you?"

From a forensic-evidence point of view, if the victim does mention that she fought back, the officer will advise her to undergo an examination, because she might have skin scrapings from the perpetrator underneath her fingernails.

•

Thomas J. Byrnes, the first chief of detectives in the New York City Police Department. (*NYPD Museum*)

above: Lieutenant Phil Panzarella (with a cigar) at a crime scene, where several decomposed bodies were found in plastic bags. (*David Rosenthal*)

Waddel Winston, under escort by Lieutenant Panzarella, after being arrested in the murder of Mildred Green. (*Kim Garnick/* New York Times)

Detective (now captain) John Gorman (with the pistol) capturing a suspect in the kidnapping of detective Tony Vitaliano. (Daily News)

Sergeant (now lieutenant) Nellie Torres, commanding officer of the Special Victims Liaison Unit, which coordinates sex crimes and child abuse cases. (*Nellie Torres*)

Drug bust in Washington Heights as a result of undercover investigation. (*David Handschuh*)

But again, the victim is always first. The officer will encourage her to be medically examined, and will take her to the hospital if she consents. She'll usually be advised that the mere fact that an officer took her to a hospital, or that she was examined by a doctor, or that she consented to letting the doctor use the sex crimes evidence collection kit, does not obligate her to press charges. We realize that at this point in their lives, sex crime victims can't make a choice as to whether they want coffee or water, let alone make a big decision as to whether they're going to press charges.

Officers are also instructed not to use any forceful words with the victims, no forceful actions, be as kind as possible, and don't touch the victim. It's only human nature that when you see somebody crying and upset you want to throw your arms around them and calm them down, but it's the worst thing you can do, because this victim has just undergone forceful touching that they didn't want. You're hitting a raw nerve. It's almost as if the perpetrator is doing it again. We had a veteran sex crimes detective who had felt particularly terrible for a little three-year-old girl who had been sexually assaulted by her father. Inasmuch as these cases are all terrible, sometimes they become more personalized because it just so happens that the little girl was a dead ringer for his daughter. And he just picked her up and the little girl kicked him and went screaming out of his arms. In the back of his head it jolted, "god, I knew I shouldn't have done that, I shouldn't have touched her."

After taking a victim to the hospital, the uniform officer will conduct an interview and will try to get as much information as possible. If it's possible that the perpetrator was still in the area and she's all right physically, he'll ask "well, would you like to come in the police car? We'll cruise the area and we'll see if we'll spot him." If she knows the perpetrator, we'll get his identity. It can be a boyfriend, it can be an ex-husband, it can be her employer, it can be her next-door neighbor, or an acquaintance. We've had cases where

•

somebody who works in her building, someone she knows, has raped her in her own apartment. It can be a whole slew of people.

One of the myths about rape is that women claim rape to get even with men. False allegations of rape happen in very rare instances. Two percent, on the national average, of all rapes reported are unfounded. Most times when a victim comes forth and makes a false allegation of rape, they don't even identify a perpetrator. Most times it's because she's very young and she's out past her curfew, or she's pregnant and doesn't know what to tell her mom and dad, or it may be a cry for help; she wants attention and doesn't know how to get it any other way.

If we get a report of a rape on the hotline, the information is relayed to the Special Victims Squad in the borough that it occurred. The detective will reach out to the victim and make an appointment for an interview. The victim has a choice. She can come down to the precinct to be interviewed, or the detectives can go to her home. If the victim is going to come into the police facility, the interview is going to be done in a private room, which no one else has access to except the detective and his or her partner conducting the interview. Many victims prefer to come into the police facility. Why? Because some victims haven't told their family that they've been victimized. We also ask the responding officers to be sensitive to that. When he initially responds, she may not want her husband or her boyfriend or her parents to know. And we tell them you have to respect the victim's privacy. Often it takes victims a long time to tell a loved one that they've been victimized. So that can be a touchy situation. The detective interviewing the victim has to let her know from the onset that he is going to ask her many detailed and intimate questions. If she's going to come down to the precinct, we encourage her to come down with a friend, a support person. We also tell the detective to let her know that he or she would prefer to interview her

•

without that support person being present in the room, because the interview is going to be very emotionally draining for her, in that many times victims will relive the incident just by telling us the story, number one, and, number two, the detective is going to have to ask very, very intimate details of the attack. It's very necessary for the investigation.

We find that serial rapists rarely change the way they operate, so we have to know every single thing that happened, other than what he looked like. For example, did he have an accent? and things of that nature. We also need to know, what did he say? How did he say it to you? Exactly what were his actions? What did he do first? If he did multiple sexual acts, we want to know the sequence in which he committed them. Did he use a condom? A lot of different things are going to be asked of the victim. We have to let her know that we need to know this information for the investigation. There may be other open cases out there where this man has done the same thing, and your information is going to help us find out whether or not he's the one who's done other cases.

We find that the term *serial rapist* is pretty much redundant in that most rapists rape again and again and again. We've seen studies that indicated that many of these men have raped at least ten to twenty times before they've been arrested for the first time.

From our viewpoint it doesn't appear that these people get cured because we see them time and time and time again. On the other hand, we are only now seeing experiments in treating sexual offenders. Sometimes we have offenders call us on the rape hotline, and it's very difficult to try to track down a place to which we can refer this person for treatment. For some reason it seems that in our society we don't give precedence to treating offenders. It could be a catch-22 situation: Well, there is no cure because there's nobody out there doing cures, because there's nobody funding cures.

•

The recidivism rate is incredibly high. I'd say it's about 80 percent. For instance, a couple of years ago in Upper Manhattan a man was accosting children as they were coming home from school in the housing projects. He had them do sexual acts upon each other and then he did sexual acts to them. Whenever there is someone doing something like this we try to publicize it. Well, a lieutenant in the housing police, who was assigned to Staten Island, read about this case in the newspaper, and notified Manhattan Sex Crimes that when he was a rookie cop up in that area he had a very similar case. He arrested the perpetrator, who was convicted and in prison. A detective from Manhattan Sex Crimes ran the perp's information through the computer. He had been released from prison about two weeks before the attacks started. Same guy. That's very frightening.

It's not unusual for us to get information from parole officers telling us, "listen, we have a sexual offender who's on parole and we think he might offend again, so we're letting you guys know that he's out in the area." Because it happens, the recidivism rate is just absolutely incredible.

Initially, when psychological profiling of criminals was initiated, there were five different categories in which rapists could be classified. Such as "the assaultive rapist," said to be the most common type. He's the person who doesn't preplan the rape. He's a person who's motivated by anger. He's getting even with this woman for some real or imagined wrong that another woman in his past has done, or is still doing in the present time. We're not too sure exactly what sets him off or why he chooses a particular victim. Maybe she has some characteristic that reminds him of the woman he feels wronged him, or she looks like the woman. But there's something about this woman that angers him. He just approaches her by doing an assault, which is why he's called the assaultive rapist. He may hit her from behind, or he may choke her from behind. He'll use whatever weapon he finds handy. He's unpredictable. He may tear at

•

the victim's clothing, he may punch her, he may slap her, he'll curse at her, and he'll rape her.

Another category is the "sexually inadequate." Now, he's the only one of the five categories that is really viewing this as a sexual act. And in his mind the victim is doing this willingly. He's doing a role-play with her. He may break into a home, perhaps stalking the victim so that he knows she's by herself or home alone with children. Not an unusual ruse for him is to tell her that she either submits or he's going to kill her children. When he breaks into the home he will have her dress up for him. Sometimes he'll bring lingerie with him. He'll have a script for her to read. He'll make her tell him that he is wonderful, "oh honey, you're the best," because again in his mind she's doing this willingly. He is not usually a violent person, because if he starts assaulting her then there goes his fantasy that she's doing this willingly. Which is why breaking into the home late at night, when the woman is alone, and waking her out of a deep sleep, is a very intimidating ploy. A woman home alone with her children will feel very threatened from the get go. Oftentimes, when he is arrested he does confess. He feels very guilty about it afterwards.

The third category is the "predator." He's the type who commits one crime and decides to commit the rape as an afterthought. Sometimes it becomes a little difficult to differentiate between the "predator" and the "sexually inadequate" because the "predator" might have broken into a victim's home and then raped her, but usually once we start asking about what his actions were towards the victim, we are able to make the differentiation. The predator, of course, will not be living a sexual fantasy. Usually what the predator likes to do is engage in psychological games with the victim, hanging a threat over her head that he's going to either kill her or rape her, and this can go on for a period of time.

The fourth category, one that we don't see much of, is the

•

"sadistic rapist." His motivation is not so much the sexual act. (For most rapists, their motivation really is not so much the sexual act, with perhaps the exception of the sexually inadequate rapist. For a lot of them their prime satisfaction comes from humiliating and degrading somebody else, and from the idea that they have all this control over someone.) The sadistic rapist's motivation is more the victim's reaction to pain and torture. The more reaction she has, the better fulfilled he feels. He's someone who's usually a very intelligent person. He will preplan the rape down to the last detail. He'll bring everything he needs with him. He'll almost never rape a woman he knows because in his mind he's not going to get caught.

We're seeing an increase in the use of condoms. Some of the perpetrators are using the condoms because they don't want to get AIDS from their victims. Others are using the condom because they think that the sperm can be evidence and they take the condom with them. That creates another problem, because now people are going to say, "you mean you just sat there and watched him put on a condom?" People forget about that deer with the headlights in the eyes phenomenon. Yes, people can be immobilized by fear.

Some of the sadistic rapists will go too far and kill their victims. The sadistic rapist usually approaches the victim with a con, and before the victim knows it she is being attacked. Many times a car is involved. That's the way he can get the victim to an isolated area. Bondage is often involved. He may bring handcuffs. He may bring ties. He may tape-record or videotape what he does to his victims, because he'll often relive the experience.

Probably those perpetrators that would fit under the sadistic rapist category are the most difficult to apprehend, because these guys truly don't want to get caught, and they make it very difficult. They read up on police procedures. A lot of perpetrators do follow their cases if they get any publicity in the media. Some of them keep scrapbooks. It's

•

not unusual when you make arrests to find police-related material on investigation techniques and forensics in their homes.

We did have a really, really terrible case that would fit under this category. It was unusual in that he took the victim back to a motel room. He stripped her completely naked, cuffed her with his hands behind her back, and placed her face down on the bed. He took out a knife and he told her "I'm going to stab you to death." And for the next hour she just lay there waiting for the jolt of the knife. But it never came. All he did was trace lines on her body.

She had to use the bathroom. Subsequently he told her "yeah, you can use the bathroom." He made her go in the sink while still cuffed. It was very strange. Eventually he was tracked down and he did have some pornographic materials dealing with sadistic practices. I guess it was just to relive the fantasy.

The last category of rapists is the "polymorphous perverse." Only because if you can't fit them into any other category, this is probably the category they belong under. Most rapists will usually stick to certain types of activity: They'll either specialize in doing solely rapes, penis to vagina; or they'll do oral sodomy, penis to mouth; or anal sodomy, penis to anus. The "polymorphous perverse" will have done every sexual act imaginable. He may have indulged in bestiality, necrophilia, he may have assaulted children as well as adult victims, or adult male and female victims. Usually when he's arrested we find that he's done a whole slew of other crimes.

Most rapists we find will stick to the sexual crime and/or any other crime that can facilitate the sexual crimes, such as burglary to get into the home, or robbery. For example, in the robbery-rape, he sees a woman coming out of a shopping mall late at night, he goes to rob her and he finds that nobody else is around, so he rapes her as well. But we don't usually see them committing a whole slew of other crimes.

•

This is the difference. When the polymorphous perverse rapist does gets locked up, he may have done homicides, robberies, burglaries, grand larceny of autos, narcotics, illegal gun possession. You name it and he's probably done it. He is usually someone who's very transient and has no roots in the community.

The biggest obstacle in doing these investigations is society's attitudes about sex crimes and sex in general. One of the examples I use when I teach detectives occurred a couple of years ago. The Pennsylvania state treasurer had been accused of embezzlement. He holds a press conference—"I did not steal any money. I did not embezzle any money." Well, the press conference is about over, but for some reason one of the press cameras is still rolling. With that he reaches into his pocket, pulls out a gun, puts it to his head and shoots himself dead. This segment was aired on television—prime time. I mean people who were home with their children saw this on television. If we changed the scenario somewhat, and instead of pulling out his gun he pulled out his penis, none of the stations would have carried it.

You have a victim, and she's ingrained with those attitudes also. She feels that it was her fault, or that it was something that she did. It was the way she dressed. Why was she there? She'll start blaming herself.

Then you have to deal with the victim's family and their attitudes. They're like "what the hell were you doing there, dressed like that, nice girls don't—maybe you're not a nice girl after all."

Finally, you have to deal with the judicial system if this thing goes to trial. Now the prosecutor has a big job ahead of him or her, because not only does he have to prosecute this case, but also he has to educate the jury and sometimes even the judge. Many of them have these deeply ingrained attitudes about sex crimes. Number one is nice girls don't get raped. Well, rape victims range from one month old to one hundred and two years of age. I would say 98 percent of our victims were not dressed in a manner that society in general would consider provocative or sexy. Then again I can't talk for the rapist. In his mind, perhaps a nun's habit is seductive. Perhaps a nurse's outfit is seductive. But society in general doesn't see these things as being seductive attire. Number two is that the rapist is a Freddy Krueger type, he has scars, he has a raincoat. We've had rapists ranging from doctors to elected officials to drug addicts to pillars of the community. Anybody is a potential rapist. Men can't be sexually assaulted. Yes, men can be sexually assaulted. Little boys can be sexually assaulted.

For little boys, the generally accepted statistic is one out of eight to one out of ten have been sexually assaulted. The figure holds pretty much the same for adult males. Personally, we're seeing an increase in it. I personally don't buy the one out of eight to one out of ten figure in boys. I think it's much higher. I think the figure is probably closer to 50 percent. With adult males it probably could be about the same.

The reason for the discrepancy in the statistics that you see on sex crimes is that they're based pretty much on conjecture or educated guesses. Only approximately one out of ten cases is ever reported. For women it's painful and difficult to report, again, because of society's myths. For a male it's even worse, especially with male adolescents, because they may feel that if they say something this means I'm a homosexual. Not that there's anything wrong with being a homosexual, but at this time in their lives the child might be very confused about gender identity.

The biggest increase we're seeing, and again this is based on the phone calls that we get through the hotline and on information we get from hospitals, is adult heterosexual males being assaulted by other adult heterosexual males. Many times it is in conjunction with assaults on females. For example, a man and a woman are going through a park when they are set upon by a group of youths. She gets raped or sodomized and he gets sodomized. And the psychodynamics behind that are quite interesting. Mental health professionals have told us that these actions predominantly have to do with the control aspect in these cases being more attractive for the perpetrator. Not only did he control the female, but he did it in front of somebody who should have been able to protect her—an authority figure, and since males in general are viewed as authority figures, this causes a greater exhilaration for the perpetrator.

Many times victims of acquaintance rape will say, "my god, I knew him for a long time, he's a friend of the family, he's a professional, but he was like an animal, I couldn't believe what he did to me. Even when it was going on, I said to myself, no, I must be imagining this. I mean this can't be happening."

Some psychologists have told us that they feel that victims of acquaintance rape are more psychologically damaged than victims of stranger rapes. So many times the victims of acquaintance rape feel they can't trust anybody at all now. They can't trust their father's friends or their brother's friends or someone whom they've dated.

I recall one young woman who was living with somebody. He had to relocate out to the West Coast. She went out there with him for a while, but her job would not permit her to relocate, so she came back to New York. Her first night back in her apartment, she's fast asleep. She hears these strange noises, wakes up, and finds the superintendent of her building in bed with her. He used his passkey to get in. And throughout the entire act he was telling her that there was nothing wrong with what he was doing.

We had a very unusual case. A woman who called us worked at a bank and she didn't know what to do. She wanted to remain anonymous. She had been at a party. Her boss had gotten promoted and they were all celebrating. They all had a couple of drinks. It was getting kind of late and she had stayed longer than she thought she was going to. Now she's a little scared about taking the subway home. He offered to give her a lift and she says, "oh, great, I really appreciate this."

They get to her house and he says, "listen, I really have to go to the bathroom. Can I use your bathroom?"

She says, "sure, no problem." So they go into the apartment. She shows him where the bathroom is. He goes to the bathroom and he comes out and just *boom*, he attacked and raped her. There was no emotion on his part. Then he put his clothes back on and just walked out without saying a word to her throughout the entire thing. She was stunned.

Now she's telling us, "well, you know, I guess it was my fault. I let him into the apartment and I shouldn't have done that." And we're telling her, of course, that this is absolute nonsense. It's never the victim's fault.

The next day he calls us up. I don't know whether she had said something to a friend of hers that she had called us, or if something else precipitated this phone call. But he starts to tell us, "she wanted me. She let me buy her drinks and she invited me up to her apartment." He's rationalizing his behavior: He did not commit a crime because she voluntarily had sex with him because she was coming on to him. She let him buy her drinks. He went on to say, "you know how these women are. They try to use their sex to put us in our place."

We really don't know what happened with that case. Our phone line is not on tape and we tell the victims the decision is theirs whether to pursue it or not. This woman didn't.

We can perfectly understand why women would not want to prosecute. It's a very, very difficult thing, especially if the perpetrator is somebody who is a professional or is well-known. It creates a big problem for the victim because it goes from being a criminal trial to being a media circus.

Unfortunately, certain things do come out in a trial, and once publicity surrounds these trials we find a decrease in the reporting of rape and other sexual assaults. We had vic-

•

tims calling us up and telling us, "well, I wouldn't want to prosecute. Look what happened in the case of the Central Park jogger, or the St. John's case where everybody got to read the victim's past sexual history, where everybody knew the last time the victim had sexual intercourse."

We never reveal the name of a sex crime victim or a child abuse victim, because we feel that the victim's identity should be protected. The NYPD had this policy long before the state legislature made it law. No victims of other crimes have to undergo such intense scrutiny. I mean, when someone is a victim of a robbery people go, oh my god, that's terrible, you got robbed. Or your car gets stolen: Oh my god, you know, my car got stolen last year too, I can sympathize. But someone comes forth and says, I was a victim of a rape, and people say, god, what did you do to provoke it?

The National Victims Center did a survey of the American public, and it was discovered that something like 85 to 90 percent said that if they were to find out that a woman that they knew had been the victim of a sex crime she would lose all credibility with them. And then people wonder why victims don't come forth. She is being chastised by society, she is being chastised by her family, and she might become the subject of adverse publicity.

It gets very, very difficult oftentimes to deal with these cases, because you're trying to focus your energies on conducting this investigation, and now you're being sidetracked to shield her or him from the family, or from friends, or from loved ones, who may not be as sensitive. Many times the families don't mean to be insensitive, but they'll say things without thinking, and these statements can really hurt the victim.

Compared to other countries in general, we're a society that emphasizes violence. And I think when you mix violence and sex, you get a very fatal mixture.

A lot of kids grow up with very little respect for themselves. Many of them are just latchkey kids, they have no

•

authority figures in their lives. They virtually raised themselves. They get into the violent subculture. It's not unusual for them to have seen death and violence in front of them at a very, very young age, or to have been the victims of violent assault themselves very early on. So this carries on, because now violence becomes the norm, and they don't see anything wrong with a statement like, "hey, just because she said no and I did it, doesn't make it rape." Because they don't know that. They think it's okay. Violence is okay. Instant gratification is okay.

One of the problems is that sometimes there's a lack of positive male role models, and the boys that are growing up will just latch onto any kind of male-oriented stereotype that appears to them. And in many neighborhoods the children grow up feeling that they all must have guns—a phallic symbol—and it has to be a big gun.

I remember in Bedford-Stuyvesant the kids would kid each other. "You don't want to carry a faggot gun, like the police do." I mean they had to carry big guns. And, again, that's part of it—the violence and macho symbols, because they don't know any better.

Kids are very confused. We see a lot of streetwise kids today; but a lot of them are not emotionally mature. And they will see mixed messages. Young girls see a lot of the commercials for diapers, and think, oh isn't that great. Well, I'm going to get pregnant and have one of those, because the babies are always fun and they're beautiful. And when these girls do get pregnant, they say to their peers, look what I did, look what I accomplished. But now after they give birth it's like, oh, I've got to feed it. Oh, I got to change it. Well, I can't—no, I gotta go hang out with my friends. They don't see that there's a responsibility with having children. So these little children end up getting victimized and abused. They become subject to the wrath of their parents, who are children themselves.

It wasn't unusual for me to see fourteen-year-old girls

putting soda in the baby's bottle. They don't know that you don't feed babies soda, or that kids that age cannot eat potato chips. They're not aware of nutrition. The baby has a temperature; they may not even know the baby has a fever. They don't even know what kind of symptoms to look for in a child. They don't even know the basics of child care. The fact that, yes, children have to be changed constantly or they'll develop rashes—they don't know these things. You just don't remove the dirty diaper and put a clean one on, you have to wash the child's private areas. They don't know that.

Some of the abuse comes from their own frustration that now I'm saddled with this thing that I thought was going to be so easy. Some of it comes from the totem pole—I get abused by mom, so what do I abuse: my child. Some of it comes from the way they were raised. They were raised that it's okay that if your kid plays with matches, you take your child's hand and put it over the stove and turn on the flames. And there again they perpetuate the cycle of abuse.

I would probably say there is more physical than sexual abuse. The kind of people who tend to sexually abuse children runs the whole gamut, and it changes constantly. That's why we try to keep aware of latest research. We saw a study recently that indicated that young girls who are sexually abused will go through puberty a lot faster than girls who are not sexually abused.

Another thing we're seeing now is more sibling-to-sibling sexual abuse. It concerns us; we take a very good look at the background, because oftentimes this behavior is learned. We had a case of a twelve year old who was inserting objects into her four-year-old stepsister's vagina. We were notified by one of the hospitals. The father called us; he was very upset that there would be police intervention. We explained to him that there has to be police intervention because we're talking about criminal activity. He was very concerned, he wanted to get psychiatric help for his daugh-

•

ter. Of course, we didn't want to broach the subject with him until we looked into it further, but where is this twelve-year-old girl learning this behavior? Is it happening to her? We didn't know whether something was happening to her.

The families often do get very upset when they see police intervention, and sometimes they get mixed messages too, because the public has such stereotypes about police. They feel that we're all brought up in vacuums, we're all Robocops, not sensitive, and oftentimes they're so shocked by our reactions.

For example, right now, we're making a film that's being sponsored by the Junior League and the Long Island Hospital rape crisis center aimed solely at law enforcement officers on how to facilitate their encounters with sex crime victims. The film acknowledges that many times law enforcement people are secondary victims, because we have to deal with the broken pieces day in and day out. It addresses techniques to help victims feel better, to facilitate the reduction of the stress that law enforcement officers are going to be dealing with when you're investigating this type of case.

The film was started because four years ago two young officers were on patrol in a radio car in Brooklyn. It's January, it's late at night, it's very cold out, snow is on the ground, and they see somebody staggering in the street. They get closer to take a look, and they thought she was emotionally disturbed. They see that she's virtually naked, but she has Hefty bags tied on to her. They wonder what the heck is this. She tells them, "I was just raped." They get her into the car and she tells them, "please, please, he said he was going to go upstairs and rape the woman upstairs from me." So they call for more assistance. They cover her up. Then they go upstairs to the apartment. They knock on the door. Lo and behold, who opens the door? Someone who answers the description of the perpetrator the victim just gave them. The man tries to get back into the apartment and

•

shut the door on the officers. They call to have the victim brought back, and they ask her just to take a peek inside the apartment. She does and she says, "that's him. That's my stereo. That's my VCR." That was the perp, and that's where he lived, right upstairs from her, with his wife. And his wife was sitting there saying, "what's going on?" She sees all these police officers coming in.

The perp was arrested and later convicted.

But this was the very first rape case the two officers ever handled. And the rape victim was new to New York, so they spent a lot of time with her. They helped calm her down. They made notifications for her. They called her family for her. She wanted to speak to her family and they suggested, "why don't we help you do it, because you might get a little too emotional." And she was so impressed with how well they handled her case, but yet she could see in their faces how stressed-out they were by this.

She was a member of the Junior League. She went to the League, and they decided this was a worthwhile effort, and they raised all this money. The film should be in its final editing stages anytime soon.

She's since relocated outside of New York, but she came back to New York when we started filming. We're in the "green room" waiting to go on tape, and we got the two officers back to be part of the film, when she walks in. Well, the tears were coming down like you wouldn't believe. It was an emotional reunion. So we're very excited about this project, because many cops are very sensitive to the needs of the victims, and people oftentimes don't see that. The public often sees only what's depicted on television or in the movies. I know, having dealt with many victims. They tell me, listen, you guys have been so great, so supportive, I can't believe that I even thought twice about calling the police. We've testified at City Council hearings where the district attorney was asked if he ever had complaints about the police, and the response was no. The bulk of the victims have complained more about their own families than they do about the police.

I think child cases sometimes generate even more sympathy, especially when it's someone who's really very, very helpless. I mean the things that people have done to children are incredible.

I remember we had one little three-year-old boy who was sodomized and virtually tortured. I dislike the term "child abuse." I prefer "child assault," and to get even more accurate, "child torture." He had been tortured, both physically and sexually, the whole three years of his life. He had healing fractures. We were notified by the hospital. It ended up being an M.E.'s case—he died. He had been used as a punching bag for his father's frustrations and angers and aggravations. He had been continually orally and anally sodomized. He tested positive for all types of sexually transmitted diseases, including genital warts. It is just absolutely amazing to think of the pain that he put up with for those three years.

The father was arrested. He was found guilty.

These cases can be very disheartening. I think a perfect case in point is the fabulous documentary done by "Frontline," entitled "Who Killed Adam Mann?" It is an absolutely wonderful documentary by a woman who eight years ago focused on the workers at special services for children. She went out on a couple of cases with them, and one case involved the Mann family. They made numerous visits to the Mann family. There were allegations of child abuse. Different things were tried, the children were removed, the mother was removed, a lot of things were done. However, eight years later she suddenly gets numerous calls from the media; they want permission to use her documentary, because it turns out that Adam Mann, who hadn't been born until after she filmed the original documentary, had just been the victim of a homicide. When the medical examiner performed an autopsy on this child, the medical examiner

•

said into the tape recorder, "I just can't keep documenting because, at one point or another, every bone in the child's body had been broken." The cause of death was determined to be a punch from his father that severed the liver.

We see that even with the continuous abuse that these kids put up with, they still internalize that guilt or that shame: Oh, it's my fault, it was something I did, it's not my mom's fault, I'm bad, I'm the one who causes my mom to do this, I'm the one that causes my dad to do this. It's the same psychodynamics with children of sexual abuse: I'm a bad girl, that's why my father does this to me, it's not my father's fault.

The torture that these children undergo is absolutely incredible, yet society doesn't like to believe that it happens. They like to believe that the police trumped up the charges, or that the investigators led the child on, that it's impossible that parents do this to their children.

Some of the cases are very difficult for the doctors too, because they're very difficult to diagnose. Because of the rising health-care costs many people don't have a private physician, so they have to go to the emergency room. And you have social workers present there, so the likelihood that you're going to get a report coming out of an emergency room is very great. Many people, including some private doctors, however, are going to believe that a wealthy person or someone from the upper middle class wouldn't hit their kid. A lot of the people who abuse their children just don't have "I'm an abusive parent" stamped on their forehead, or they may not exhibit violent tendencies; they fit very well into society. And the parents do come up with stories. "Well, the kid fell down the stairs. You know, he's accident-prone." And it's easy to buy the story. I think it's a lot easier for those who have money to obscure the problem than those who don't. But child abuse cuts across all lines. A former Miss America came out with a book about how her

•

father had sexually assaulted her. It happens in New York City, and it happens in the small towns across America.

We had Ken Lanning of the FBI do a presentation for us. He showed us a slide that the FBI originally used when they spoke to the public about child molesters. In the slide you see the man with the dirty raincoat, hiding behind the tree, and the little girl with the pigtails skipping down the street. And he said, "well, this was forty years ago. Now, let me show you what we're doing." And the screen was white. "There is no slide, because we find that it runs the whole gamut. Anybody can be a sexual offender, and anybody can be a child molester."

Until society starts to accept the reality of child abuse, I think we may not stop these crimes and the people that do these will continue to get away with it. Yes, grandmothers can sexually molest children too. Yes, lawyers can do it. Yes, crack addicts can do it. Yes, most child molesters are hetero-sexual.

I have ten detectives working for me, and all ten of them fight to take cases. The satisfaction in this job comes from the sense that you've done something nice for people. Many times, and I tell the detectives this over and over again, we forget to emphasize the positive work that investigators do. These detectives often are the first persons that have ever done anything nice, especially with the children. They can be such a positive influence with the victims.

Often the victims can't come forth to say, gee, thank you, because they're in such trauma and shock. But we'll get calls months, even years later, from victims: I want to do something nice to thank that officer, or I want to know where he is now, so I can call him up and thank him. It took the woman a while to do the Junior League film, but on tape she says that until the day she dies, she'll never forget these two officers. Sometimes we do things and we don't realize how much of an impact they make on people. I just keep emphasizing to the detectives, I know sometimes it feels

•

like it's a hopeless situation, sometimes your caseload over-whelms you, sometimes you feel like, my god, what am I doing this for, this probably won't go anywhere, this guy is probably going to walk—but you did something positive. And that's what counts. A lot of the victims tell us, even if their case didn't go anywhere, that they were just so happy for the support that the officer provided, or the counseling that the detective did, or just to hear someone be positive about it, or the fact that somebody cared and tried to do something for them.

I think it is probably because we deal with cases that are of such an intimate nature. We deal with people's lives. That's the bottom line.

•

7

•

CAPTAIN

JOHN

GORMAN

When I came on the police department, I did four years of foot patrol in Midtown Manhattan: Forty-second Street, Broadway, and Times Square. I made my first arrest on the same street that my son made his first arrest twenty years later. I arrested a fellow who had robbed a cabdriver, and my son arrested a guy who mugged someone at an ATM machine. So I guess the tradition goes on.

I had an opportunity to go into plainclothes in what at the time was called the Public Morals Administrative Division. They basically were a citywide unit that investigated gambling, prostitution, pornography, and similar kinds of things.

In 1971, I was put into a specialized team investigating pornography. There were five of us and a sergeant—and we had citywide responsibility for enforcing pornography laws. Most of our work was done in and around Forty-second Street, but we really were interested in the production plants and storage facilities.

It was complicated, because the laws are very complex and they are different from the normal en-

•

forcement procedures. We worked very closely with the DA's office. You had to have judges review material, and search warrants were necessary for everything, because you could easily have a problem with the suppression of First Amendment rights if you took too many copies of a particular item. And there were always new decisions coming out of the courts in the early seventies.

It was a very dynamic and an interesting way to learn investigations. You learned a lot about doing paper chases and interviews. Normally you do that much later in your career; usually you first do enforcement work at the street level. But we traced down corporations and we did a lot of civil forfeiture proceedings.

I spent about six and a half years in Public Morals, although in April of 1972 it became part of the Organized Crime Control Bureau (OCCB), which was formed when the police department reorganized itself, following the Knapp Commission hearings. The Knapp Commission was an official government body headed by Whitman Knapp, who was appointed by Mayor Lindsay to look into police corruption as a result of Frank Serpico's and Dave Dirk's revelations.

We basically just changed our name and continued doing what we were doing, only now we answered to a deputy commissioner, and other controls were put in place. What had been revealed by the Knapp Commission wasn't going to happen again. And it hasn't.

The Organized Crime Control Bureau was just a way to take all narcotics, public morals, and auto crime, and put them under one bureau. At the time the philosophy was to concentrate your enforcement effort at the distribution points—particularly with the organized crime groups that controlled narcotics. Rather than arresting addicts on the street and prostitutes, and that kind of thing, let's find out who really is behind it.

We worked one or two levels off the street. We worked

•

the production facilities, the actors and actresses, and the people who finance the pornographic movies. *Deep Throat* was one of the movies where the producers, the actual people who financed it, were brought to court.

In the pornography industry, organized crime acted basically as copyright enforcers. The people that made the films were independent producers who, along with the actors and actresses, were just trying to make some money. After they made these films, the producers would need to go to a laboratory, which is very expensive, to have the films reproduced by the thousands. What happened was that the organized crime people would find legitimate factories, the ones that were servicing ABC, NBC, and the rest of the television industry, that might be closed at night, and they would open them up with their own crew by paying cash to the owners. Then they would make copies of these pornographic movies for distribution on Forty-second Street.

The stores on Forty-second Street were mostly fronts owned by organized-crime people. You couldn't distribute any movie on Forty-second Street without somebody's permission. They generally got, at the time, 10 cents a copy, sometimes 25 cents a copy, depending on the movie. And if you were distributing somebody else's movie in your store and didn't have permission to do so, somebody would come in and take it off the shelves and just throw it in the garbage. So it was a very tightly controlled industry, and there was a lot of money in it.

Star Distributors, one of the big distributors, was controlled by a fellow by the name of Robert DeBarnardo— "Bobby D." or "De-Be" they used to call him. And he distributed most of the pornography. He was killed a couple of years ago, allegedly on John Gotti's orders, for not showing up for a meeting.

A little side story: Star had their offices on Lafayette Street—I don't remember the address, but it's the building that Congresswoman Geraldine Ferraro and her husband

•

allegedly owned, and later on became a big cause célèbre. But Star Distributors had been in that building for years. They had their executive offices there. And almost all sexually oriented publications, including *Screw* magazine, were controlled and distributed by them, and if you tried to distribute them yourself you had a problem. It just wasn't done.

There were other firms that primarily distributed legitimate magazines; about 80 percent legitimate and about 20 percent pornography. When we took one in Queens, a place called GI Distributors, they had a separate section that was caged off where the pornographic stuff was kept, and that was controlled by an organized crime family who used the legitimate distributor's trucks and distribution system, but were paid through separate accounts.

Sometimes somebody would just take a film, copy it, and distribute it through his own network, the producer didn't make a dime on it. So the organized crime guys acted sort of as copyrighters. If you had a complaint you say, Mr. Organized Crime Person, here is X amount of dollars, my film is showing up on Forty-second Street and I didn't arrange it. They would go and take it right off the shelves for you, and they would tell the clerks on the street, who were responsible to them, "if anybody comes in trying to push this line of film, call me." They would then send somebody over to talk to this maverick distributor and see where he got it, and if he was with anybody. Maybe he was with another one of their cohorts. Then they might have a sit-down and split the profits, and the person who actually made the movie would be the one that lost out in the end.

Most of the movies they sold were called loops, and they were sold outright. The organized crime guys just bought the masters from somebody, and reproduced and distributed them. We figure it cost about $3.25 to make a reel of film, and they were getting 25 dollars or more for them at the time. Nice profit. They used to have the peep show ma-

•

chines. The machines were in the back of the store. People would put quarters in, they'd watch it—about two or three minutes of a pornography movie, and then they would have to put in another quarter. It would cost them maybe 2 dollars, $2.25 to watch the entire movie in the machine. Marty Hodas controlled most of that industry. He was convicted.

We worked massage parlors too. At the time massage parlors were brand new, they had just opened up. It was like a new way to have a prostitution operation. A Greek fellow by the name of Nicky started the massage parlor business. But as soon as it became profitable, organized crime people moved in and told him, "you're out of the business," and they burned down a couple of his parlors. We had a couple of arson investigations on Forty-second Street with Tommy Russo, a fire marshal. We convicted some people of arson, and we tried to find out who really were the organized crime people moving in. But they moved in so fast, with so many different places, that massage parlors popped up like mushrooms all over the city. You just couldn't keep up with it. Plus, it was difficult to get enough legal corroboration to get it into court. So we worked on the angle of extortion, where we tried to open up "legitimate" massage parlors, not connected massage parlors, to see what was happening with them.

Basically what that case was about, it started out as an investigation into organized crime taking over massage parlors. There was a group of people from Brooklyn who thought of themselves as wanna-be organized crime people. They were sort of connected to a fellow named Tony Dots, who was an organized crime person. Dots was his nickname. They were pretty much a wild gang of guys who went around sticking up massage parlors and slapping people around, and taking extortion payments from them to protect them from this type of activity.

We were working a case in which Detective Tony

•

Vitaliano was undercover, working against massage parlor owners. He was passing himself off to them as a bad cop. He was taking money and they wanted something for their money, so the massage parlor owners went to him for protection. They said to him, "hey, you gotta get these guys off our back." So the idea was that Tony would be introduced to the extortionists as an organized crime person, to sort of scare them, or find out who they were with, or find out what could be done, and if he could be involved in a sit-down with them.

But they, being as wild as they were, when he went to make a second or third payment, thinking he was an organized crime person, they kidnapped him. They were going to hold him for ransom from these other organized crime people. He was kidnapped off the FDR Drive. He was taken into Brooklyn, secreted in a house, and threatened and beaten. When they then discovered he was a police officer they didn't know what to do with him. Now they had a tiger by the tail. Later on, it came out through tapes that they were probably going to take him out and shoot him.

But by this time, the entire New York City police department had mobilized to find him. We had surrounded every address where these people had ever been arrested, or their girlfriends had ever been arrested, every place that they ever made phone calls to. We were all over Manhattan and Brooklyn. Everything was pretty much covered. It was really a massive manhunt. They were going to start a door-to-door search pretty much. It must have been six to eight hours long. But to him it seemed like sixty-eight hours.

There was a team out in Brooklyn. They saw these guys bring Tony out of the house, and they jumped them and arrested them. Tony's still a member of the New York City police department; he's in charge of the Bronx Homicide Task Force.

I characterize organized crime as disorganized crime. There's a myth about them that they are all *Godfather* types.

•

It's almost like life imitating art. They went to watch *The Godfather* to see how to act with each other. And after the movie came out, they all started kissing and hugging and paying respect, and doing all these other silly things you see in the movie.

Basically, most of the guys that we worked on were just nickel-and-dime thieves who got organized. They worked in a structure, whether it was what they call the Mafia or organized street gangs, and they answered to people and paid tribute to other people.

One of the things I'd say is that they must have been working for below minimum wage, because these guys worked twenty hours a day, seven days a week. We followed them from place to place, and they were constantly going around trying to make a buck. Sometimes they were rich, and when they had plenty of money in their pocket they'd go to Las Vegas. Sometimes they were broke. I think the best characterization of them is a scene in a book by FBI agent Vincent C. Teresa called *My Life in the Mafia*. He pretty much hits them right on the head when he observed that they were grown men who are sort of arrested adolescents—dangerous, arrested adolescents. They have a real skewered view of how things worked, and they were going to make them work their way. They're pretty ruthless. They're not mythical Robin Hood types—they would beat up innocent people—that fellow who owned the bar, maybe a guy who's trying to make a living at a grocery store, or whomever they wanted to extort by putting their machines in the store. Anybody that got in their way they would either terrorize or kill without any compunction. I think some of the revelations we're seeing now with Sammy "the Bull" Gravano, who killed his brother-in-law and committed some fourteen or fifteen murders, are very telling. These people are like a Roman emperor. In their own little group they can just say anything, and do any-

•

thing—kill this guy, or kill that guy—and the group responds and has to do what they say.

If they're judicious and they're good businessmen, they make a lot of money, and they don't cause too much trouble. If they're egotistical wackos, they hurt people and they do a lot of damage.

I don't like them. Over the years working against them I don't find them to be anything like the books or the movies that depict them as being noble men of honor, and all these other appellations that they give each other. They're not nice people, and most of the time they're also not very good businessmen. Whatever they touch they destroy. They take over a business for free. They don't put a dime in it. They got it from gambling debts, or loan-sharking, or whatever, and they destroy it. Even if they try to run it right, they don't know how to. They're not the type of people who go to work on a steady basis and do what has to be done to make a living. They want everything to come to them. So if they take over a legitimate restaurant, you can be pretty sure that it's going to be out of business, because they're going to steal from the suppliers, they're going to steal from the register, they're not going to pay the taxes on the employees' withholding. They're going to just do everything they can to make a quick buck out of it, walk away, and let it collapse.

Some of the people who have been successful in O.C. have run businesses over long periods of time, and have worked very hard at it. They might have been organized crime people who had an edge using the tactics they use, but when we followed them we found out they were spending a lot of time at the business.

I worked undercover against one guy in particular. It's funny how years later you find out things that you didn't know at the time. He was a pornography distributor who was also a murderer and just a general lowlife.

He thought we were bad cops. We had arrested him a

•

couple of times before and had gotten friendly with him, and he made a bribe offer to us to protect his business, and we went along with it. After telling it to the DA, the DA said, yeah, what we'll do is make a case of bribery and then we'll see where we can go with it.

So we were meeting with this fellow. He was giving us money and we were vouchering it, but we were also going out to dinner with him and hanging around with him. He was showing us the business.

He wanted us to eliminate his competition for him. That was to our advantage, because he told us where all the factories were, where the warehouses were, where other people were distributing, what line was being distributed by who, and who was shooting film at a particular location. So it gave us an opportunity to really make a lot of inroads into the pornography business, and at the same time we were going to take him down—because halfway through the investigation he admitted a murder to us.

Even though we knew what he was, we were out with him two or three nights a week, and I had a certain amount of rapport with him. He wasn't the bad-guy type. But I knew what I had to do.

Years later, when I became the head of the Hostage Team and took a lot of training, I found out about transference. That also takes place with undercovers. You have a certain identification with the person as a human being, and even though the guy is going down the tubes at the end of this thing, you have certain ambivalent feelings towards him, both sympathy and dislike. The transference happened the other way with him, because he basically became a junior G-man. He wanted us to do well in our careers, so he was giving us a lot of information he didn't have to give us. He gave us an assassination murder case, because he thought, for some reason or other, that my partner and I could get promoted if we solved this case—which was a notorious killing on the West Side of Manhattan, where a fellow who

•

was a politician for the New York state conservative party was shot and killed over a business dispute. He gave us the whole case, basically. Laid it out to us, because he wanted us to do well in our careers. Even when he was arrested, he wouldn't tell the DA or anybody that he had ever paid us money. He kept saying, "no, I never paid them money. I was their informant. I had no relationship with them other than that."

Finally it became obvious we had to come in and tell him, "hey, look, you know, we were never taking the money. Here's the tapes, and here's the money." Then the guy finally broke down. He wound up going to jail over a lot of this stuff, and he was really disappointed that things weren't the way he thought they were. He really kind of liked us.

I think undercover work should be analyzed a little closer, I found it unpleasant. I did it a couple of times against a fellow who was a police impersonator. He was probably one of the best police impersonators that I've ever seen in the United States. He was an older man; at the time he was in his early sixties. But he could walk into station houses and sign blotters, and he could talk police jargon. He had been doing it since the thirties. His name was William Burke. He should be dead by now, either that or he's in his eighties.

Bill Burke was basically a fellow who made a career out of impersonating police officers. He hung around in police bars. He hung around policemen. He picked up all the jargon. He used to go down to court and get forms, search warrants, arrest forms, and type them up. His specialty was basically harassing homosexuals he would catch in bathrooms back in the forties and fifties, and then he would shake them down for money. He had some really very unique schemes for getting money from people.

When I got to work against him, I got introduced to him as a laid-off police officer, around the time of the layoffs in

•

1975, who had kept his shield. Burke had been looking for people who had police identification. So I'm introduced to him, and I'm bitter about being laid off. So he tells me that we can make some money by doing this, this, and this. We'll go down to the public bathrooms and we'll shake these guys down. He was basically trying to make some money doing a younger man's type of police scam work. And it's funny, when I met him he told me how to dress. He said, wear a sport jacket, you have to wear plain black shoes, and you have to look like a detective—at least what he thought a detective should look like.

Then he told me how to deal with the people. He would send a young kid into the bathroom to solicit sex from homosexuals who were hanging out. Then he and I would come in. We would pretend to be from the Youth Squad. I would take the kid out. Burke would then talk the mark into giving him money, so he wouldn't be arrested. He was making money like that all over the west side of Lower Manhattan.

One of his real big moneymakers was catching a tourist. He would have a tourist set up with a kid, a boy. They would wind up having sex. Then the boy would steal the tourist's wallet. When the guy went back to Iowa, or wherever he came from, about a week or two later Burke would show up at his door with the wallet, pretending to be a policeman who found the wallet. The wallet was being returned to him. Burke would ask him some questions about how he lost the wallet. But as soon as the guy took the wallet back and acknowledged that it was his wallet, Burke would take out a picture of the kid and say, "look at this boy—and his parents are making a complaint against you, that you had sex with him, and that you abused him."

He would always go early in the morning before the guy went to work, so that the guy could get to the bank and get money. He would have a bogus warrant for the fellow's arrest and take him in a quiet area of his house. Oftentimes

•

the guy was married or he was living with his family, and he didn't want them to know what was going on. He would tell him, well, look, if you give me this much money, the bail on this thing is 10,000 dollars or whatever figure he had in there. "I can go back, and I'll change a few numbers on the warrant and it'll just get lost in the paperwork. They'll never call you again." And the guy would usually acquiesce, and give him the money. He would then go back to New York, call the guy up and say, "look, it's all taken care of. You'll never hear from the police again. If you want I'll send you your warrant in the mail and you can rip it up, or you can do what you want with it, but you'll never hear from us again." The guy would be happy, he would think, oh boy, nothing happened to me. And then for the rest of his life he would think a policeman came and had taken money and fixed the case in New York. Burke had been doing this for years. It was one of his main scams.

So I worked undercover against him, but I just didn't like it. I was successful at it, but it was a lot of tension, and I never felt comfortable. I never really lived the role. I was always afraid if the guy said to me "you're a cop" my face would turn all red and the whole case would fall apart. You got too close to people. I was up in Burke's room, and he was showing me his scrapbook; he kept a scrapbook of scams and of things that he did. He had a whole community of police impersonators that he worked with, along with kids that he would train how to act, and other people who were his backups, his other police partners. He knew the whole scam.

Burke was arrested and charged with attempted extortion. We had the entire bathroom thing set up—they were all policemen in there. Other people came forward, because we had made an appeal to the gay community, urging anybody who had been shaken down to come forward.

Burke disappeared into the recesses of the criminal justice system. I don't know what happened to him. He had some

•

fake identification on him. My feeling was he was also working for other government agencies as an informant, or working in some capacity for some other government agency, because we tried to trace this identification down, and we were coming up against fronts and phony mail drops. It was the type of thing that an individual wouldn't be able to do. He looked like he was part of some organization. But this was my opinion at the time. I'm not sure exactly what I assumed that he was playing at—maybe an FBI informant or some other government agency informant— and they had either interceded on his behalf in this case, or were using him for some other purpose, I don't know. Undercover work is like that, a hall of mirrors.

My career moved on, and I got a so-called normal investigative assignment. I was assigned to the 77th precinct Detective Squad where we did traditional investigative work. In a suit and tie, no undercover, basically you're assigned to investigate crimes that the uniforms report. I worked there for three years, basically doing homicides, robberies, family disputes, domestic stuff.

When I went to the 77th it was a shock. I was coming from an Organized Crime Control Bureau, where you worked in teams and you worked on big investigations, to work on these very narrowly focused investigations. You were handed a case, and it was your case.

At the 77th precinct we had one of the police officers who was on station house security, standing in front of the station house in uniform, stuck up. He was shot in the stomach and his gun was taken. The precinct covers the Crown Heights-Bedford-Stuyvesant area. We had a case where people came into the station house and for no apparent reason started stabbing one of the clerks, and the desk officer wound up shooting him. There was constant, ongoing violence.

It was just chaotic. I mean for me it was chaotic. The other detectives took most of the stuff in stride. It was like, okay,

•

another day at the office. It took me about six months to adjust to the work schedule and how things happened there.

The cases included a lot of children, under seven or eight years old, missing overnight. You'd find them at an aunt's house, or some other friend or relative's place. After a while you got to see what the pattern was.

There seemed to be family disintegration, a lot of the inner-city type problems that people have. People were getting murdered over sneakers, basketball games, just anything. I was going to people's houses and telling them that a family member had been killed.

But the thing I learned working there was that as bad as it appeared when I first got there, there was a community there. There were people there. The average person was going to work every day trying to make a living. I used to look out the window of the station house at 8:00 in the morning, and the bus stops were packed with people going to work. The A train that came through the neighborhood was loaded with people going to work.

It was basically a hardworking community of people that really needed police service, maybe more so than another community. Maybe a community has, for argument's sake, 1 percent of the population who are criminals. Whereas in this community maybe 3 percent were criminals. That's a 300 percent increase in criminals, but it's still only 3 percent of the population. And the people were really under siege there. They'd go to work and they weren't making much money, they'd come home and find their apartment ripped-off. The television set they're buying on time was gone, their furniture, which didn't come out of Sloane's, and was being paid off on time, was destroyed. It was a community that needed a lot of police attention. You felt like you could do something for people. You felt like you were doing something when you finally got over the initial, what you might call, cultural dissonance of being dropped into the middle of this place.

•

One case that does stand out—it was kind of an odd case, but it gives you a flavor of some of the unrealities in that precinct. There were two police officers sitting in their car by the old St. Mary's Hospital. All of a sudden a guy comes up behind the car and starts firing bullets into the back window of the car at the police officers. One dives under the dashboard, the other guy also dives down. Thank god, I don't think they were hurt. Then this man comes around to the side of the car and shoots into the window of the car. He runs away. Later on he's captured. He was an escapee from a mental institution. I believe he might have been the same guy that stuck up the police officer in front of the station house. I asked him, "what were you thinking about? Why did you come up to a police car? They didn't do anything to you." He says, "oh, I thought they were going to be like Starsky and Hutch—the doors would fly open and they would come running out of the car firing shots—'cause I wanted to commit suicide." That was the first time I ever heard of suicide by police, but later on I found out more about it. Then he said, "now, I come around the side of the car and they're hiding under the dashboard. What kind of cops are they?"

He got sent back to wherever he came from. But his whole, his whole idea of firing into the back of the radio car, was that he thought they were going to be like on television, and come rolling out of the car firing shots, or whatever the heck he expected them to do, and shoot him and kill him because he just wanted to die for some reason. That was the reason I think he stuck up the guy in front of the station house. He thought the guy would whip his gun out like in a Western and shoot him, but it didn't work out that way. He wound up sticking him up and taking his gun away and running away. There were a lot of crazy chaotic cases that went on in the 77th precinct and throughout the city. I'm sure every station house has its stories.

In the 77th there were some outstanding detectives.

•

Looking back on it now, I consider myself on a scale of one to ten probably a 7.5 as a detective. I did what I could do, and I did it better than your average guy. I got my cases solved. I was concerned about them, and I worried about them. But I was amazed when I worked with some of the really good guys—the guys that could just see beyond what was happening and were lifelong detectives. I was a detective, for maybe seven or eight years, doing a lot of OCCB work, and I was thrown into this regular detective work with almost no experience. I think I was a very good OCCB investigator. When I went on to regular detective work, I realized that there were a lot of holes in my training, so I hooked up with some second-grade detectives and learned a lot from them during the three years I was there, and it was nice to see them work.

After the 77th squad I got a little bit of a break. I was on the sergeants list, and I went to work in the chief of detectives office in headquarters. By this time I had fifteen years on the police department, and I was in the field the entire fifteen years. Now I was in a job that supported the field investigators. I took care of confidential funds to pay for undercover operations, like renting stores to be used as fronts in sting operations. I took care of homicide statistics: Where, when, and how people got killed, and what type of weapons were used. I assisted in personnel assignments, and I got really a flavor of how the administration of the Detective Bureau works.

•

8

•

DETECTIVE

FIRST GRADE

BRUCE MEYERS

I was first assigned to the Narcotics Division Undercover Unit. I found that what I saw on TV, and actually
doing it, were two entirely different things. I thought it
would be very exciting. I thought it'd be a little bit more
cloak-and-dagger, sort of a romantic type of situation. I
came to find out it was dirty, scary, and almost like playing
Russian roulette with a derringer. It was enough to keep
your adrenaline going.

The people I worked with were a very close group. To
this day, we're all still very close. It was a small unit. We
worked all over the city, and we did a lot of work. We had a
very high conviction rate.

We had some ups and downs in the unit with personal
things—one guy I knew killed himself. I don't know if it
was a result of family problems, or the job, or a combination
of both. But we lived hard, worked hard, and played hard. I
guess we were often very close to being taken
out, so we thought we should have a good time at
least.

I had a lot of the street operations. And the street

•

operations were, I think, the hardest. When you work undercover you're going out there making these 5 dollar, 10 dollar, 25 dollar buys, and you're dealing with people that are very, very spontaneous in their actions. The fight they put up against you is like trying to put a cat in a bag or trapping a rat. They would be the most violent of the people that you deal with, because they are trying to get away from you at all costs. And a lot more cops have been hurt doing these small buys than with major buys. Most of my early time in Narcotics involved standing around the barrels of fire that they used to set up in the street to stay warm, drinking wine at 10:00 in the morning, and being with a lot of smelly, undesirable people. We were taken to some very, very dirty places to make our buys. In my early days, heroin was very prevalent; there was not as much cocaine.

I remember making a buy in Brooklyn. It was around Christmastime. It was snowing out. There were people to escort me into the apartment to make the buy. And you have to play the role as they would play it. I walk into the house. I'm following these other people in, hoping that they don't stick me up, or when I buy the drugs they'll take the drugs back and hand my head to me. In this apartment there is no heat—it's like living outside—but there are two little kids sleeping on a mattress on the floor, with only a sheet and their clothes on. The kids looked hungry and cold, and here we are doing a drug deal. I have on work boots that are covered with dirty snow. These people I'm with walk right across the mattress where the kids are sleeping. In my mind I'm saying, "you don't want to do that." I almost hesitate, but you can't hesitate in a situation like this. You have to do like they do.

Another time I had made several buys that day in an operation that we were wrapping up. We were making fresh buys to locate the people that were still out. I had gone into the bars and had a beer or two so I could generate enough conversation to identify my subject and make a buy. Then

•

we were going to arrest these guys. The last guy I was after, I needed fresh probable cause to see if he was still dealing, and to see if he was still at this particular location. I also needed to get a look at the location, because we were going to make application for a search warrant, and certain things were needed to satisfy the warrant, such as, have you been inside the apartment, and what does it look like.

So, after making these three or four other buys in these bars and drinking beer, I go to this guy's apartment door. I knock on the door. He opens it and he has a spike in his hand. He was getting off. I knew he was a speedballer, a coke-and-heroin shooter. I said to myself, this doesn't really feel too good. I would have preferred if we could have just done the business right at the door, because I'm figuring he may be a little irrational. But he invited me in, so I was committed. I was still trying to make the buy, but also trying to get a full view of the apartment so I could come back and draw a diagram of the place for the search warrant.

We're standing in the front room. I asked him if I could use the bathroom. He says, "wait here a minute," and he walks into the next room. He calls me from this room, which I think is going to lead me to the bathroom. As soon as I go to this other room he puts a shotgun in my face, and I knew I had a major problem. I was only carrying a derringer with two shots, and I had some loose rounds in my pocket.

I ask him, "what the hell you doing this for?"

"You're the police. I know you're the police. I'm going to kill you."

I was wired, and I'm trying to choose my words carefully because I really didn't want my backup team to know right then that this guy had a gun on me, because I really didn't want them to come through the door, since I'd have to kill him or he would have killed me. So I tried to ignore it to some degree, and I said, "look, let me just go into the bathroom and take a leak."

•

It was a very short period of time, but it was like hours for me. I'm saying to myself, should I close the door to the bathroom, and then come out and try to shoot this guy? I'm trying to analyze all of my options. How could I take this guy down? I opted to leave the door open, because at least I'd know where he's at and what he's doing, still remembering that this guy just shot up. So I don't know how rational he is.

I really had to go to the bathroom, because I was drinking all of those beers prior to this. But I was standing over the toilet bowl and I couldn't even find it, let alone really try to take a leak. I was still thinking, how effective am I? When I qualified with this weapon at this distance, how accurate was I? If I hit him with a round, even though it's a magnum round, is it going to stop him cold? I'm trying to evaluate all of these things. I'm trying to tell myself, "maybe the gun isn't actually loaded and he's just bluffing me." Because a lot of times we've taken guns off guys, and they've had one or two bullets in them, or none at all. I couldn't know. I guess I was trying to build my confidence up. Then I said, "well, maybe I could fire my two rounds and quickly reload this derringer with the loose rounds in my pocket and use the tub for cover." But thinking of the ballistic characteristics of what he may have had in his shotgun, I began to wonder if it was going to penetrate this tub or not. A million things are going through my mind. But this is all like in a matter of seconds. I realized that I couldn't take him out from a distance. I figured I had to get closer to him and try to aim for a vital area that I think that's going to make him stop immediately. So I came out of the bathroom. My plan was to get close enough to him to deflect the shotgun and do what I had to do to take him down. But he never allowed me to get close enough to do that. He maintained a distance that would have been too hazardous for me to try to reach him and get his shotgun out of my way. I figured I had to get in closer to him to actually make the buy, and at that

•

time there might have been a very slight window of opportunity. But to this day I don't know, because I didn't go through with it. I did consummate the buy, and we did do the exchange. I kind of regretted it after we did do the exchange of money and drugs, because I figured now I still have to get out of here and I have to walk to the door. I said to myself, how do I do this? I can't turn my back on this guy because he may shoot me and take the drugs back.

But I walked with him to the door, and all the time he was still saying, "you're the police. You're the police. I know that you're the police."

My palms were sweaty. I kept trying to reassure him that I wasn't the police. My hand was on my gun that I carried in my back pocket at the time. Finally, I just walked out, although I wanted to go right back in there and do this guy.

My boss probably knew that I was a little upset with this guy, so when they went back the next day to arrest him, he wouldn't allow me to go. I had a little too much personal interest in what happened in there. I guess he probably did the right thing, because this was one guy that I would have liked to treat the way he treated me that day.

The guy went to jail for some time, since he was a predicate felon when we arrested him.

I remember a night in Brooklyn with a female partner of mine by the name of Stephanie. Actually, I was going in just to back her up because her regular partner was away at court that day. They had a buy set, and the boss did not want her to go alone. They like to send someone in with you for safety purposes and for corroboration of what was going to happen.

We had a confidential informant, a CI, with us, who she previously knew. Before we got there the CI told us, "this is an easy buy, in and out, one, two, three." With us you have famous last words, such as, "easy buy," "easy buy." There are no easy buys. If there's an easy buy, then something is wrong and you're waiting for something else to happen.

•

The CI went on to say, "yeah, the guy's going to have the stuff. Go over there and I'll do the introduction, and tell him what you want."

But for whatever reason, maybe because it wasn't my case and I was just filling in, when we pulled up I asked the CI, "This guy have any guns?"

"No, no, no. He never has any guns, never has any guns."

I said, "You're sure?"

"No guns. No guns."

I also want to know why this CI is giving the guy up. Because things can happen, and they may be eliminating their competition or whatever. For example, he could have taken this guy's girlfriend, and now you can be the instrument of his removal.

We get there and get out of the car. The CI whistles up to the window. The guy we're looking to make the buy from opens the window and in a very agitated state says, "What the fuck do you want?"

I say, "nice guy."

He's one flight up. We go into this vestibule to wait for him to come down the stairs. A cold rain was falling. I think weather has a lot to do with things. It seems like I've always had my worst experiences in inclement weather.

As a detective, you learn to observe a lot, like the subtle things that people do: How they dress, how they walk, and the look on their face. As he came down the stairs he was still very agitated. His eyes were bulging like he was pissed off at our CI. As he's walking only one arm is swinging. So I sense he had something in his hand. I'm saying, "uh oh."

He snatches the vestibule door open and points a gun in my face. I'm looking at a .22 revolver. I look in the cylinder and I can see a silver-colored bullet, a gold-colored bullet, another silver-colored bullet, while he has it in my face. And I look at my partner. We have a certain nonverbal communication, because we work that close. I'm thinking, "no fucking gun, huh? The first thing this guy does is points a gun in

•

my face. And here I am just going to back her up on her case. Well, how can I get out of this?"

I had a Walther .380 that I used to carry down in my pants. So I'm getting kind of ready with this thing. The informant is on my right, the guy with the gun is in front of me, and my partner is on my left. But me being right-handed, I said to myself, if I get into a tussle with this guy I have to deflect his gun to my left, which is where my partner is standing. What can I do now with this one?

She's looking at me, and there's no place else to go, because we're just in a vestibule. We're just trying to think of how we're going to get out of this, but there comes a time when there's nothing else you can do but wait it out.

I got out of getting shot with just conversation. Having the informant there agitated the situation. I had to tell him, "get the fuck out of here and let us just do this deal." We don't like them to witness the buys anyway, so he had to disappear so we could consummate the buy. I want to take the informant out and whack his head in.

We made the buy. It was actually my partner's buy to make. As soon as she completed the deal we came out of there, with this informant, who assured us so many times en route to this location that this guy had no gun. I wanted to take his head off. "No gun, huh, no fucking gun . . . the first thing I knew I was counting rounds in this gun." It is kind of a strange feeling to have a loaded gun a foot away, knowing that you're less than a second away from taking one in the face.

There was a very good possibility the informant was trying to set us up. Believe me, we went back to collar that dealer, but we couldn't find him. They move or whatever, and they don't leave forwarding addresses. He's still out there. To this day, he's gotten away with it. He might have gone to jail for something else or someone else got him.

There's so many times that you go out where things can happen to you, and it's just bad situations that you're con-

•

stantly involved with. And how do you deal with it? I don't really know, but like I said earlier, we worked hard and we played hard.

I had another case I was working with an informant where I'm going out to buy pills on Suffern Boulevard in Queens.

I ask the informant, "Why you doing this?"

He says, "oh, I want to be a good citizen." Well, I come from the streets and I know good citizens from shitheads. He didn't fit the profile of a good citizen. I knew where he hung out. A lot of times they think that you just jumped off the turnip truck, and you don't know anything about what they're doing or about the places they go, but I know all the spots out in Queens, especially in the black areas. And he would go to this place and that place, so I knew he's living large. He's in the fast lane. He was a well-dressed guy, like he had some office job, but something wasn't right.

I had a Volkswagen at the time, and he's riding next to me. I give him instructions. "When the guy comes in here, you'll sit in the back and the guy will sit in the front next to me on the passenger side, because I don't want any bad guy in back of me." He screws that up first of all. He has the guy get in the back. Then when the subject gets in the car, he starts insulting him, calling him a bunch of "mother-fucker"'s and "asshole"'s.

I said to myself, this guy is crazy. What the fuck is he doing this for? This fucking guy is setting me up. Then the subject takes out a knife about a foot long. The team is down the block and they're looking at this. I was wired, because I guess there are some days you're braver than others.

I come to find out that the subject stole the informant's girlfriend, so the informant wanted him either locked up, or for me to kill him. And the informant knows I'm still a cop, I can't let the subject kill him, and I have to defend him.

I say to myself, I'm going to upset both of their worlds right now. I get out of the car and I take my gun out. I tell

•

them, "hey, I'll kill both of you in there. You know, I'm not going to get fucking hurt. What the fuck is the matter with you fucking guys?"

The subject selling me the pills was a better guy than the informant. The subject said, "I bring the fucking pills and whatever this motherfucker told you ain't shit."

I said, "like, man, just give me the fucking pills and take your fucking money." To the informant I said, "You—get the fuck out."

The best thing that I've found with informants is to have a guy we have a case on. The motivation is that you will not go to jail if you do the right thing for us, or there will be consideration for you. Then they're going to be fairly honest. They can't jerk you around. The guys that work for money I don't really trust, because they're mercenaries. And some guys make a very good living doing that.

But the thing with all of these informants is that they can get you in there. My thing is, if I'm going to lock somebody up I'm going to do it right. I've had sixty or seventy trials, and I've only lost two. And one of those I thought for sure that I won, but I think the judge let the guy walk.

We locked up the subject, but the pills turned out to be beats. They weren't any type of scheduled drug that was against the law to sell. It was like buying aspirin. The other guy is gone. He was no good as a CI for us.

One morning, I made a buy of marijuana in the South Bronx, then in the afternoon I bought quarters in Harlem, which is a particular weight of heroin they used to sell at that time. That night with one of my partners, Bobby, we went out and I backed him up on a buy of a kilo of cocaine. All in one day, playing different roles, with different clothes and different scripts, but not scripts that are written down. For example, when I made the first buy I was playing the role of an opportunistic thief, a small-time convict, a con-man type. Someone who would probably like to impress upon other people that they're more than what they are.

•

The medium level—you're still bigger than what you are. A quarter at that time was 50 dollars and it was about an eighth of an ounce in scale weight, but they called them quarters—I don't know why. With those quarters you were going to become an entrepreneur. If they were supposedly of a quality and quantity that you could take and hit it and at least double it, and then you would make a profit on it. So you would try to buy several of these, and your story would be I'm going to take them to Jersey, or I'll take them to Queens, or I'll take them to Brooklyn, and make some money.

The 28th and the 32nd precincts in Harlem were where most of the quarters were sold. One particular place up there for copping was the Shelton Hotel on 116th Street. One of the Kennedy sons went there. I believe the story was that the Kennedy son said he was there because he was experimenting with cocaine, but, from all of my undercover experience and the street intelligence, there was nothing but heroin at the Shelton Hotel.

We went looking for a guy named Watusi. Watusi was a street name. We had information that Watusi was selling drugs in the Shelton Hotel. My old partner, the one who made that kilo buy that night, and I were working together on this one.

So we go into the Shelton Hotel, and they have a booth where you go pay your dollar to get in. The place is somewhat like a catacombs; the hallways go ways that you wouldn't normally think they would go. We luck out asking for Watusi. We get his room number.

He's in there with what we initially thought were two women. We tell him that we want to buy some heroin. He says, okay, he will be back with the drugs. He leaves myself and my partner in there with these two.

One of them was getting off. I don't know if you've ever seen someone get off, but they make sure they have a vein, then they draw some blood into the syringe and it mixes

•

with the drug, and they inject it all back into their vein. I tell you, they know as much anatomy as doctors about veins, especially the females that are in the drug business. They wanted us to get off in there. I said, "okay, this is good. Let me use your works, 'cause I just got out of the hospital. I had hepatitis."

"No, you better go get your own shit. I don't want you using ours." So that got me out of that one.

Then we had this long conversation in which they were talking about when they were in the Queens House of Detention, and how they almost got raped by the boys.

I'm saying to myself, where were they in the Queens House of Detention to have male-female contact for them to be raped by these guys? I just kind of dismissed it because that's not my immediate concern. I'm trying to focus on what the layout of this place is because I need to get the team back to this room if we consummate this buy.

We're working with a team headed by one of the senior sergeants, Al Ingram, who's now dead; he got shot uptown while he was working on another case. He was Mr. Buy-and-Bust. His team was unusual since it was all black. This was good for us up there because they would be right up on us, and we had a lot of protection and a lot of corroboration when we did things.

Watusi came back with the drugs and we made the buy. When my partner and I were out of the room I said, "good, we got this guy. Let's get out of this place."

In a little while we're ready to go back in there and arrest Watusi. We are now with Ingram and the four guys on his team. We hit the place. We go in and knock on the doors. Twenty people are in a room shooting heroin. We go to another room; there's another twenty people in there. In a short while we have over sixty people, and your gun feels like it's getting smaller and smaller and smaller. And I'm saying, "this place is absolutely crazy." It was just a drug den.

•

At that time it was all black. However, sometimes white guys would come up there. There's no prejudice in the drug business at all. White, black, Hispanic, Indian, Asian, whatever you are, if you want to get high there's no problem. It's unbelievable. But I don't think we need that kind of community to get rid of prejudice.

We arrested Watusi for sale of drugs, and we also arrested his two female friends. We had to get a female officer to search these two. The female officer comes back to us and says, "These aren't for me, they're for you."

I said, "What are you talking about?"

"They're guys."

They had breasts and their voices were feminine, but in all the excitement I kind of forgot that maybe they could have been guys. Well, I guess they were going back into the House of D, this time for acting in concert. Actually, when I think about it, Watusi may have had some kind of desire for these two people. Watusi was also a halfway pimp, and I think he may have been pimping them. It's a kind of dirty world.

Some people may say, it's okay, but the war on narcotics is a dirty business to be in, because you work in a lot of dirty places, with a lot of dirty people. I mean, you've got to strip search some of these guys, because if there's a place to hide something like a weapon, or narcotics, they're going to hide it. I didn't do much of it, because I was undercover. I would just go out and make the buys to maintain my cover, but sometimes I did the searches when I did some of the investigative part.

You would take guys' socks off that you'd have to peel off their feet, because they hadn't changed them in months. I had one guy who we put in the car in the dead of winter, and he smelled like a chicken coop. You ever smell a chicken coop on a rainy day? We got back to the precinct, and we had to strip-search him. He had gauze wrapped around ulcerated sores on his legs, and the sores are oozing

•

pus and the gauze is stuck in it. I asked him, "When was the last time you saw a doctor?" He told me it was the last time that he was in Rikers. I said, "well, I'm doing you a favor, because at least you're going to go back in the medical at Rikers."

Many of these guys literally haven't taken their cloths off in a month. And if you have a steady diet of this day in and day out it will work on your nerves, and everybody becomes a skell.

We were out working an overtime day up in the west side, in the 24th precinct, in an abandoned city-owned building that these drug guys just took over. Because it's city-owned we don't need any court papers to go in there. I just go in and make a buy. Then one of my partners goes in and makes a buy. When he comes out we hit the place.

I kick one door open, and I see what I think is a guy and girl laying on a mattress on the floor with a blanket over them. So I yell at them, "get your fucking hands up! I want to see your hands! Kick that cover off of you!" Because I'm thinking they may have something under there. I go further into the room, and I see they don't have any clothes on, and they are having anal intercourse.

The guy says, "don't hurt me. Don't hurt me. This is my wife, my wife."

I'm saying, "get the fuck up."

It was pay week. We get paid every two weeks, on a Thursday, and we hung out that Friday night. Now it's Saturday day, and it's cold. It's the winter, and it's snowing. After you've been drinking for a while you don't get warm the next day. And I'm in a fog, from being tired and cold. I'm looking at this guy, and he's still laying there with this person, and I say to myself, what's he's doing? Then I get him up, and I see that this other person has a penis. "What are you doing? Like what are you doing here?"

He says, "this is my wife. This is my wife."

I'm telling him, "wives don't have dicks. They don't have

•

dicks." But you could not convince him that this person wasn't his wife.

I'm looking at one man's in another man's ass, at 10:00 in the morning, and it was just disgusting. I said to myself, what am I doing in this slum? Oh my god, it's just crazy.

We had people from other arrests out in the street, and we were getting them all together before we transported them down to central booking, and they were looking at his so-called wife, because it's a common thing in jail—if you want to be a girl, they're going to treat you like a girl. But he's trying to defend his wife, and I'm saying, "the world has turned upside down."

Now, when you buy a kilo you are a money person. You're living large, and you have a tremendous ego. Oh my god, I have on this million-dollar suit and a speck of dust from you came and hit my suit—that becomes a major occurrence. But it's a hard game to play.

At that time, it was okay to sell heroin and use coke, because the thought was that cocaine was not addicting, and crack was not yet around. We used to call it "musician's coke." They would tell you there was nothing better than good coke snorted off a hundred-dollar bill. And they were very, very hyper on coke, so they were going fast and they were making fast money.

When they went out to a place everyone knew them, and they would sport their people and their women, and they'd spend a lot of money. They would buy nice cars. They had certain hangouts, that in a sense, they took over. They developed a taste for champagne and cognac, Rémy preferably. They would drink a lot of that, and so that's what you'd drink.

I think they were intelligent in a very narrow scope. They knew what they were doing, but they didn't know a lot of other things. But if they did learn something new, they wanted you to know it and they would constantly talk

•

about it. I think it was an If-I-do-this—it-may-add-class-to-my-life type of thing.

With them, being very vain, and with these super egos, you couldn't be so overbearing as to turn them off. If you came off smarter than them, you would be embarrassing them, and they would get pissed off and they could do something violent. They're very impulsive that way. They use the term "dis" to mean that you disrespected them in some way with their woman, or you made someone laugh at them. You had to walk a very narrow path to consummate a buy. It was like a game of chess to me, which was more interesting than doing the street buys. You could do a hundred street buys, and it wasn't challenging enough, and you might get your head handed to you just as easily. I probably was in more danger with the kilo dealers, but I felt more comfortable doing "operations," which was the term we used to refer to buying keys, or some substantial weight, of heroin. And I wasn't standing around a fire in the middle of Eighth Avenue, drinking cheap wine at 10:00 in the morning—I was drinking some cognac or champagne, since these deals would go down in bars or in their apartments, and some of them had nice apartments in very nice areas of the city, like Riverdale.

It always amazed me how they got these apartments. I go looking for an apartment and they want nineteen references. Money talks, bullshit walks, and they had the money.

These cases were interesting in that they would carry you further than the confines of a precinct investigation. And I think that makes you develop a little more.

I did Colombians, in the early days, up in the 34th precinct. The Colombians were controlled by the Cuban OC people. Then, as time progressed, the Colombians did their own thing with the cocaine trade. They were very, very vicious, and we had a lot of homicides. Eventually the Dominican community, up in the Northern Manhattan area, monopolized a lot of the crack-cocaine trade.

•

When you're dealing with the blacks, or the Colombians, or the Dominicans, or the Italians, there's a difference in terminology, and there's a difference in attitude. The Italians are very businesslike. Their packages and their weights were good, they were always on.

With some of the blacks, depending on who you would go to, there was always a problem with getting the right weight, or doing it on time, and it was always much more dangerous. I mean, just from the areas where you do some of the deals. With the Italians it was at the Rainbow Room, or some other nice location, and it's not a problem. No one's just going to go crazy and start shooting at you.

With some of the blacks and Latins you would do business in the bathroom of a bar. Most of them were dives. Somebody's holding the door so nobody else would come in while you're conducting business. The room is half lit. The floor's pissy. It smells. It's dirty, and it was crazy. You gotta try to make the buy and then you go back out. Everyone in the place knows that you conducted some kind of business because of who you're with. You have one, or two, at the bar like nothing happened, because that's the role that you have to play.

The Colombians would say "spoon weight or scale weight?" You always want to buy scale weight, because drug people, being dishonest people, shave the spoons down on you. Each time they would fill a spoon they'd wipe it with a card, and that's your spoon weight, but they would dip the card to cut a little deeper into the spoon and the spoon would be shaved down a touch, so they'd say fifteen spoons would make an ounce, when actually eighteen spoons made an ounce. It was more for them. And the Hispanics used to deal in kilos, while the blacks always dealt in pounds. I guess in Colombia they were used to using the metric system.

The blacks and the Hispanics are also more dangerous because they do a lot of macho things to intimidate you, but

•

you can't take any shit because you are the Man. But if you blink, you're not the Man anymore, somebody else is the Man. Someone's constantly jockeying for the top of the heap, and it's so fleeting.

You have to negotiate your way through all of these obstacles and come back with a package. But you can't be perceived as a chump either, because if you're going to be the chump, yeah, I'll sell you the drugs, but since you're a chump just give me your money and I'll keep my drugs, or I'll put one in your head. It's a very thin line that you have to learn to walk. You have to be many things at all times. I guess it's almost like being a politician. You have to tell everybody exactly what they want to hear in order for you to survive.

I never considered myself a great undercover. I'm more like a blue-collar type of undercover—I just get the job done, and I think that's what gave me my longevity. I tried to understand a lot of what was going on around me, because I felt that the more I knew the more armed I would be.

We want to arrest as many drug dealers as we can. But I had this guy, Shorty Kinkaid, that I started dealing with, and every time I was in his area Shorty was there, and he'd serve me. He wouldn't let any of the other guys sell to me. He would tell me "that guy has shit, this guy has shit, that guy has shit over there. My stuff is so good it'll make you bend over and suck your own dick, that's how good my shit is."

We finally had to take Shorty off the street. We lock him up and we go to trial. I had made about twelve buys off the guy. He has a prior criminal record that we can't reveal to the jury, but in the middle of my direct examination he jumps up and starts saying, "your honor, your honor, he's a liar. He's a liar. This man is not a cop, because I know him. I know him, because we did time in Sing Sing together." I had to laugh, the judge laughed, and the jury laughed.

Kinkaid had his lawyer come up to examine my shield

•

and my ID card. The lawyer said it was all fake. So I guess his lawyer's investigators tried to find out who I was and where I worked, but according to our records we don't exist.

What Shorty did, however, was great for us, because it opened the doors for the ADA to say, "well, Sing Sing; so you were in jail? What were you in jail for?"

"Robbery." We killed him on the stand with that, and the ADA got a conviction.

So Kinkaid thought for sure that I was just someone on the street impersonating a police officer, and that's why he went to jail. Although he never denied that he sold me the drugs; he just denied that I was a police officer. But when he left the courtroom he said, "well, at least you didn't flake me."

Just like you have a job that you go to five days a week, the dealers have to be out on the street, or wherever they're doing business, or they don't have any money. And money is the thing that ultimately gets to them. It makes no difference how much money they make, they still want more.

One day we hit a place. We thought we were going to have to break the door down, but I said, "what the hell, let me try the door." I tried the door and the door was open, so I go in. I have my gun out. I'm looking around. The team is with me. We hear the shower running. So we crashed the bathroom door. Now, here is this guy in the shower with five mad guys pointing guns at him. You know that people in the nude are a little intimidated anyway. There in the bathroom was a one-foot by one-foot window, and this guy's trying to jump out of it while he's crapping all over the tub. He was a big guy on the streets—so bad he knows that people are after him, so he's thinking that we're the bad guys and we are going to do him in.

Many times they're relieved that it's the police who're holding a gun on them, and not one of their adversaries, or

•

someone that's looking to go up another rung on the drug-business ladder.

Guns and drugs—there is just too many of them, too many. Now, with crack we have more violence. I don't know, maybe it was a little more honorable when it was just the heroin thing, and the junkies were the junkies. You could always recognize a heroin junkie because of their poor complexion and their nasal voices. You knew when they were using drugs because you could see them on the nod.

The dealers we're involved with now would go and shoot other people for little things. I think it's life imitating art. This is what's done in the movies, so this is their conduct.

You talk to some of these young kids out in the street, which I do, and you ask them about what happened to so and so, they'll say, "he's away getting strong." That's the term used for being in jail. He's away getting strong—physically and mentally. What a thing to believe.

I think we've just about lost a couple of generations of minorities with drugs and guns. Hopefully, through education, they can learn how detrimental using drugs is.

The other thing we have to do is lock the drug dealers up. We're going to have to really hammer them.

I was transferred into the intelligence section of OCCB where I worked on the Nicky Barnes case. He was a challenge.

Nicky Barnes was a big-time Harlem drug dealer who was called Mr. Untouchable because he beat a case the feds had against him. He was like a success story—he was a drug user who created this big empire. At the time, him and the Lucas brothers were the main black drug dealers in Harlem.

We had a white sergeant, and he sent a team of us, five black detectives, up to Harlem to find out what was going on. And we worked this operation for seven months up there.

•

We started hanging out to collect information on who was going where. Who was meeting with whom? Who was driving what car? We went every night, to all the spots, and all the parties.

I had a female partner who happened to be a very good-looking lady, and she would get a lot of invites. She'd say, "okay, I'll bring my friend," and I'd go. We got a lot of information.

We were invited to the renaissance opening of the Apollo. They had the show, and it was a good show, and we went to the party afterwards. We also had two other guys in there to back us up.

I'm not a person to wear jewelry, but through our property clerk I had all of this gold on when I went out that night. I also had this salmon-colored suit with no shirt on, and I caught bronchitis right after that.

But who do I run into? One of my old subjects that knew me. He was a very, very cruel guy. He had quite a few bodies on him. Our intelligence information was that he either carried an attaché case with a sawed-off carbine in it or a .9 mm.

I immediately remembered him—normally you don't—but again, it was on a cold winter's day when I was arresting him. He went for his .9 mm, but I had mine out first, so I beat him to the draw. We got about forty-four pounds of pure heroin as a result of that investigation. It was one of the largest seizes of heroin in the country at that time. It was the first time we made the connection between the Cuban and the black organized-crime drug trade, and we were not even looking.

Well, I see him first. I believe he saw me, but I disappeared on him.

I had to get word back to my team that I may have been compromised, so I had to get out of there. If he would have given me up inside there I would have had a major problem. I had to let my team know without burning them out,

•

and then get out myself. So I'm trying to get the word to them in this big ballroom. I'm scooting around, trying to keep this guy out of my sight, even though I also had to point him out to them so they could follow-up and see who he's socializing with.

Eventually it led to some other investigations. But things get a little crazy like that. Ultimately they got Nicky Barnes. He got life without parole. A lot of people were involved with him.

Besides doing the Nicky Barnes case, we used to debrief informants at the time. When there was an arrest made, the arresting officer would ask the perp, do you have any information on certain outstanding cases? If they said yes, the officer would call our unit out, and we would go there and interview them. Because we would have much more intelligence information on the cases; a person that's working in Manhattan North may not necessarily know what's happening in Brooklyn South. We were central repository of all that information.

I was also working the electronic surveillance detail, because before I worked in the police department I worked for the telephone company. I was doing the wiretaps and the bugs. My partner, John Murray, and Don McGuire and I did some of the first bug jobs and pin register jobs. We had a lot of antiquated equipment. Now we have all new high-speed equipment, but in the old days you couldn't do electronic surveillance remotely. You had to be in close proximity to the subject, and everything was dependent upon identifying a safe place to leave this device. So we had to survey the areas, and make friends with people, and ask to use their basements in locations that wouldn't compromise the investigations. We had these things all over the city and we did it quite well—we never got compromised in any of our jobs.

The bug jobs were hairier than the wiretaps. You would actually do a break-in, when they weren't around, secrete

•

the device, and get out. And the bugs were always the best to do, because we used to get the adrenaline going. It was like being a cat burglar. It's as tense as making a buy in narcotics, because if you're caught, or compromised, a lot of work is going to go down the drain and it's going to jeopardize the entire investigation. And possibly jeopardize the lives of some agents. So it has to be done right. It's very hard, and it's very demanding.

In fact, one of the DEA guys, Jerry Smith—he just died a few months ago—was trying to get this bug in. They tried all kinds of exotic methods of doing it, but they couldn't, and the court order was going to expire because you only get a wiretap order or a bug order for a certain amount of time. But it had a few days left to it, so Jerry calls me up and says, "can you come down and give me a hand with this one?" It wasn't the first time he had called me for a job. So I said yes.

There was this group of guys called Black Sunday, and they were doing a lot of heroin in Harlem and in the Bronx. They had an apartment. I mean, talk about a strong place to get into—the guy had nine locks on the door, it was just impossible. If it was a house, or something like that, you could bypass the locks, but with nine locks in that type of setting, with the traffic and everything else, no way. I did the thing, but I won't say how. In fact, I put two bugs in there.

It worked out well. It was in the paper. They locked everyone up and they made a good seizure of guns, money, and drugs.

Then they went to trial. I go to federal court to testify. I was up the whole night before, because I had to wire up a room in a hotel and we seized a lot of cocaine. So I'm tired. I haven't had a shower or anything. The prosecutor was an assistant U.S. attorney, Mary Lee Warren—in fact, her grandfather was Chief Justice Earl Warren. I give my testimony and bang, we get them. Then the guy who was in the apartment when I put the bugs in comes back and says I

•

poisoned them. He wanted me locked up because, he said, I slipped him some poison and he was sick and he had to go to the hospital. I said, "I wished I had."

Another time I was doing a guy for Jerry Smith, and this guy was the nastiest individual that I have ever met. A guy named Trees, at least that was his nickname. They call him Trees, because he was as big as a sequoia. And he was involved with Italian organized crime.

I gain entry to Trees's apartment, but he is very, very cagey. I say, "I have come here to fix your phones."

Trees responds with, "you fucking motherfucker."

I say, "hey man, I'm here to fix your phones. You want me to fix your phones, or not. I don't really give a shit."

He grabs me by my arm and says, "get the fuck out of my place." I mean, he has me by my arm, but he has me like almost off the ground and he was getting ready to throw me out. But I knew he had gout really bad in his feet, so I fucking came down and stepped on his foot. I could feel his grip just loosen up. Then he said, "just get the fuck out of here."

So I said, "okay," and left.

He needed his phones fixed, it was just a matter of time. So he complains again to the phone company. I have to come back in.

I had to go back in there a third time, because we still didn't have this bug working right. This time he says, "well, you're always working around here."

I say, "yeah."

All of a sudden he brings out some debugging equipment, and says, "you know anything about this?"

"Yeah, I know about it. I learned all that shit in the military." So what he wanted to do was put me on his payroll to go around and sweep all these areas where he was doing bad business in. But it didn't pan out. What happened was he had a number to reach me at and he lost the number.

We went to trial with him and six other codefendants. It was one of the toughest trials that I have gone through in

•

federal court; seven defendants, each with their own lawyer and with a technical expert. So the cross-examination, needless to say, was a lot. It was pretty much a week of torture, because everyone was asking questions for each of their clients, and in a different way. So I may have answered the same question seven different ways.

Trees got life, no parole.

In 1982, I went into TARU, the Technical Assistance Response Unit, where I'm presently assigned.

TARU provides the technical support for investigation that the Detective Bureau conducts and any other unit needs. We do a lot of work for the chief of department's office; we provide technical assistance in hostage situations, kidnapping; and we respond to major disasters like plane crashes.

With the major disasters, we set up communication nets and document what happens as far as the emergency response goes.

I'm one of the TARU people who is also a hostage negotiator. But in hostage situations, we usually provide technical information and technical intelligence. We set up secure communications. If they're negotiating over the phone, we'll make it a secure phone. We'll deny incoming and outgoing calls, because we've had instances where the news media has called in to people. For example, we had a situation at an H&R Block tax preparation office on Eighth Avenue. A guy was holding hostages in there. We negotiated some of the people out, but he was holding one last person in there. The newspeople wanted to get an exclusive story. They see the phone number, because it's right outside on the window, and they were calling in, "do you really have the gun at her head?" We don't want things like that to happen, so we take control of the lines, and if they're going to talk they're only going to talk to us.

We do probes. We have different types of electronic devices that enable us to see what might be happening in the

•

room. We support the Emergency Service people going in there, and give them the intelligence that we gather. Because even if the guy in there says he only has one hostage, he may have two or three other people in there; and if ESU assaults the place and they have to get into a shooting situation, then everyone else is a bad guy as far as they're concerned. So we try to develop intelligence that will aid in the situation if it goes tactical.

Kidnappings are some of the hardest things that we do, because you're talking about someone's life out there, and you're almost totally at the whims of the kidnappers. You can't do anything but just wait, wait, wait. They're pulling the strings. "We want this sum of ransom." "We want it dropped off here," but we don't know if we're paying for a dead body. So we try to get information. I can't get too far into the methodology, because if somebody learns what we do then it's hard for us to protect against it. But we track them down electronically and with good-old police work, like doing good record checking and things like that. And we do a lot of surveillance. Normally in kidnapping we're usually the first and closest platform of surveillance to the situation. We're usually on the drop locations, and consequently we've gotten into a couple of shootings.

In fact, I wound up shooting two guys. It was a long incident; we wound up working all night. It was a Brooklyn kidnapping. This guy was kidnapped from like the 70th precinct. Probably they thought that he had drug money. They broke into his house armed to the teeth—Uzis, .357 magnums—snatched the guy, and took him out to Queens. They're holding him out there and they start demanding his ransom. We get information that these kidnappers were calling from an area out in Queens.

They made arrangements for a courier to come in and pick up the money. When the courier came in we had to take a gamble and jump him, and then convince him to tell us where they were. So the courier told us where they were, and we responded out to that area. Our information from the courier was that they had all types of exotic, high-powered weapons. We pick the kidnappers up on our surveillance. They were in a car waiting for the courier to come back, and it looked as if they probably figured something was wrong, and they were leaving. So we decided we're going to take them down now. Shots were fired. The whole thing lasted about five seconds, maybe. I thought I fired three rounds; I fired six. I wound up shooting two of the guys with my Colt Detective Special.

The guy they kidnapped had already escaped, but I didn't know that at the time. One kidnapper I thought for sure was dead. But he had only superficial wounds. He was treated and released by the hospital. It was amazing.

After a shooting there is always an investigation. The guys who conducted this investigation come back and say the fragments of the bullet weren't identified, but who had the Colt? I was the only one with the Colt, everyone else in our team was using Smiths. The bullet turns a different way than the Smith.

I say, Jesus Christ, if anything goes wrong, the only one they can say anything to is me, because I was the only one with the Colt.

So here we try to rescue this guy, and we get into a shoot-out with the kidnappers, one of whom had been locked up a few months before for attempted murder of a police officer. And here I'm going to a grand jury, and I may be going to jail. And the kidnappers want to sue me for excessive use of force. I thought I was the good guy. But those are the things that you have to go through. I went down to the grand jury, but they didn't return a true bill on us—we were exonerated.

In another incident, this guy was kidnapped in the Bronx. I think in his kidnapping drugs were also involved. He was living large. He had a very nice-looking girlfriend. She was really very attractive, and, this amazes me, she was a decent girl—but she knew what he was into, so I can't really have any sympathy for her. The guy had a high-speed apartment in a very nice area, over in New Jersey, right around the George Washington Bridge.

We go to the ransom drop, it was down by Eleventh Avenue, in Manhattan, right by the Lincoln Tunnel. We have two of our guys who are going to pay the ransom. They're out there and they're wired. I'm monitoring the wire. Again, we're the closest unit to whatever's going to happen. We're on the west side of Eleventh Avenue and our two guys are on the east side. The next thing I hear is our guys saying over the wire, "put that gun away. Put that gun away, you don't have to—" I tell my partner, "Bobby, let's go, something's not—"As I'm saying, "let's go," I'm jumping out of the van. I'm getting ready to run over to them.

Pow, pow, here we go, another shooting. I'm in the middle of the street running over there. They're shooting back and forth over there. I can't take any shots, because our guys are right in the middle of it. Now the kidnappers start shooting at me, *zing, zing, zing.* I'm saying, "holy shit!"

They had a .32 and .25, and they just ran out of bullets. The avenue actually smelled like the range from all the shots that were fired. We chased the guys. Then it became a fistfight between us.

We were so lucky that at the time of night there weren't cars going fast and there were no pedestrians in the line of fire, because that's the biggest thing on my mind. I don't give a shit about the shitheads out there, but I would just hate for some innocent person to get caught in the middle of something like that. That's the only thing that was on my mind.

It was just amazing that at that time of night there was still traffic, but it was just like nothing happening when this whole thing went down.

•

Another kidnapping we did in the Bronx went on for about a week. We electronically intercepted information that "the police were close, shoot him, cut him up and take him out and put him in the garbage pails." We were fifteen minutes from that happening when we rescued this guy. We located where the guy orchestrating the kidnap was at electronically, and he told us where the others were. But he had already sent that message to do away with the victim. So we had to get the team up there fast. In fact, four guys were arrested. One guy jumped out of a fourth-floor window and wound up with compound fractures of both legs. He was in bad shape.

The victim, who was a tough guy, shits all over himself because they were going to kill him. Quite a few things like this have happened with these kidnappings.

The kidnappings I would say are the most interesting thing I do, because I still like the hunt. They're good, they're different, and it's a challenge trying to figure out who these people are and then locate them. And that's where I think I really earn my money. So far, every new variation that the bad guys have come up with I've been able to decipher, counter, or develop a way into what they've been doing. This year's been a little slow, but in the last four years we've averaged about fifty kidnappings a year.

We don't want them to make the news because then we have to start explaining too many things, and divulging methodology could hurt us.

I've been on 350, close to 400 kidnappings, about 95 percent of all that we've had in the department unless I was away on military leave.

One kidnapping, which was the most interesting, turned out to be almost like a comedy. He was a working guy at an auto body place in Queens. They stalked him, kidnapped him, and took him to Connecticut. We get a ransom demand, and then we don't hear anything.

We were getting all types of crazy information, but we

didn't really have a clue as to what was going on. We're going through a tremendous amount of information when, after about three days of looking, I find one little thing. And starting from there, it opened up the entire case to what these guys were doing in Connecticut and upstate New York.

We get a repeat of the ransom demand from them. The drop was on the Koskiusko Bridge. The victim's brother was going to do it. Well, he gets up there and parks the car, he's all wired up and is ready to drop the money, when the next thing we know a sector car pulls up, "get your fucking car out of here."

Our guys are coming in, we're trying to get the sector car out of there. I'm saying, "holy shit, this captive's dead." The whole thing goes bad.

Three or four days later they call back up again, they're going to have another drop somewhere up in Westchester. The brother goes up there, and he does everything he's not supposed to do: He drops the money when he's not supposed to, and nobody makes the observation. The kidnappers are gone, and they got the money and they got the victim. Now we just have to hope for the best. Luckily they released the guy in Mount Vernon, and he made a call and we got him.

And then we had success with the investigation because we had a lot of information. We were also working with the federal drug enforcement agencies up in Connecticut. They had a narcotics case on the guy behind the kidnapping and locked him up along with a few others. They got kidnapping charges, and we got good physical evidence up in their place. And the victim could ID some of the people that kidnapped him, which was lucky. The mastermind had a very large organization. He was making over 100,000 dollars a week in drug money. He had a fortress that he had built with drug money—it was like a bomb shelter. He would go out with point cars and tail cars and crash cars. They had their own radio frequency and they would talk back and forth to each other. But we got good evidence of where he was at. And three of the people that were involved with the kidnapping got killed by other drug dealers. So it all kind of worked out.

But it was always unclear to me why they want to snatch this auto body guy in the first place. It may have been mistaken identity. We found no real criminal involvement in the guy's past.

There was another kidnapping we did, right around Christmas, six years ago. A little girl was taken. She was the daughter of a world-renowned psychiatrist.

We got a call from Jersey that there's a kidnapping in New York at this address. The normal routine is for the squad guy to go over there. "Is anybody kidnapped here?" "No, no, no." The detective leaves. They call back, "it's my cousin." The guy in Jersey was calling for his cousin. It seems the doctor was going to pay the money, but he needed 30,000 dollars, which he didn't have in ready cash, and he called his cousin. And his cousin called us, so the cops go back to the house, and again the doctor's wife was there. So the detectives say to her, "something is wrong here, where's your daughter?"

The wife finally said, "yes, she was taken. We got this ransom demand."

The doctor was upstairs under the bed. He was hiding under the bed and he would not talk to us. He would not come from under the bed. That's how he handled it.

But they made the drop and one of our teams, being the closest unit, spotted the guy that got the ransom, and they followed him back into Brooklyn. Now when we work kidnapping we do twelve hours on, twelve hours off, and it was Christmas eve. Everybody's saying, what a shitty Christmas. However, no one is going home, everybody's just like hanging around. Because maybe there's one other thing you could do, because it's a young girl.

•

And it was a very good thing that our guys had followed him back to Brooklyn. He lead them to the house, and they rescued the girl. It was the maid, who the doctor's family had fired, that orchestrated the kidnapping. And since that girl knew who she was, they were going to have to get rid of the kid. That kid would have been dead for sure.

It's a terrible thing having your child kidnapped, but I just couldn't believe him hiding under the bed. He just lost it.

I like doing this work, but you have to understand that you can get killed doing it. You can't lose that perspective. And every time before I do it, I get butterflies. I tell myself, that's good, because I recognize what I'm doing.

I can see TARU doing a lot more for the department. I think there's definitely a need for it. And with the technology that's out there now, I think we can support police investigations in a better, more effective, and much more accurate way.

•

GLOSSARY

ADA   Assistant district attorney.

ATF   Bureau of Alcohol, Tobacco and
                       Firearms. It is a division of the
                       U.S. Treasury Department.

BCI   Background criminal investiga-
                       tion.

BEATS   Bogus imitations of psychoactive
                       drugs.

BOMB BLANKET   A blanket composed of multiple
                       layers of Kevlar, with vent holes,
                       which is wrapped around a
                       bomb to help trap shrapnel in the
                       event of an explosion.

CI   Confidential informant.

COLLAR   Police jargon for an arrest.

•

COP A PLEA	To plead guilty to a lesser charge with a lighter sentence, rather than risk a longer sentence if convicted in a trial.
DEA	Detective Endowment Association—the detectives union.
DOA	Dead on arrival.
DO HIM	Short for "do him in."
DROP A DIME	Short for dropping a dime in a pay phone to inform the authorities about someone's criminal activity.
EMS	Emergency Medical Service—they run the city's ambulance service.
ESU	Emergency Service Unit—the police department's elite tactical unit, which has both a special weapons assault team and a rescue function.
FALN	Federales Armed Forces Liberation National—a radical group advocating the independence of Puerto Rico from the U.S.
FLAKE	To illegally plant narcotics on a suspect in order to justify an arrest.

•

FELONY	Any offense punishable by death or imprisonment for a term in excess of one year. They are designated as A, B, C, or D, with A being the most serious.
GET OVER	To fool someone.
GRAND JURY	A group of citizens impaneled to determine if enough evidence exists to indict someone for a particular offense. The standard is that there be enough credible evidence to prove it more probable than not that the individual committed the offense.
HIT	1. Slang term for murdering someone, often as part of a contract. 2. To raid a place. 3. To dilute heroin with a substance such as manatol or quinine before reselling it.
HOUSE OF D	A contraction of House of Detention. They are interim prisons, with one in each borough.
HUNTLEY HEARING	A pretrial hearing to determine the admissibility of certain statements made by the defendant that may be used as evidence against him or her.
KELL	A small hidden transmitter, worn on the officer's body, that allows

•

the police to listen in on conversations from another location.

M-80   A very powerful firecracker.

MINI-14   A .223 caliber semiautomatic carbine, manufactured by Strum Ruger.

MIRANDA WARNING   Prior to any custodial interrogation a person must be warned that: 1. They have the right to remain silent. 2. Anything they say can and will be used as evidence against them in a court of law. 3. They have the right to have an attorney present during questioning. 4. If they cannot afford an attorney, one will be appointed for them by the court at no cost to them.

THE MAN   Black slang for a police officer, or someone important.

MIRAQUIC   The criminal identification unit in each borough where the files of mug shots are kept.

M.O.   Modus Operandi—a Latin term used by police to mean the consistent way in which an individual repeatedly commits a crime.

MP-5   A Heckler and Koch .9 mm submachine gun.

•

NAGRA	A very high-quality recording device used by law enforcement agencies. It will record up to three hours, but the person wearing it usually doesn't know how to turn it on or off. The tape requires special equipment to be played back.
NIGHT WATCH	The midnight to 8:00 A.M. shift for detectives.
OC	Organized crime.
OCCB	Organized Crime Control Bureau—the branch of the NYPD responsible for narcotics, public morals, and auto crime.
PBA	Policemen's Benevolent Association—the patrolmen's union.
PDU	Precinct Detective Unit.
PEDIGREE	Identification and criminal history of a suspect.
PIN REGISTER JOB	A way of determining what numbers are being called in or out on a telephone.
PREDICATE FELON	A designation given to an individual convicted of a prior felony that increases the sentence on the present charge.

•

POPULATION	The general population of inmates in prison.
PROBABLE CAUSE	A set of facts and circumstances that would induce a reasonably intelligent and prudent person to believe that someone had committed a specific crime.
RICO	Racketeering-influenced corrupt organization. This federal statute has made it easier for prosecutors to go after individuals for taking part in a criminal enterprise.
RIKER'S ISLAND	New York City's primary municipal prison.
SCOTT AIRPACK	A self-contained breathing apparatus.
SIXTY-SIX	A complaint taken by a uniformed police officer and given to the detectives for a follow-up investigation.
SKELL	From "skeleton": Police slang for a dirty, disheveled, lowlife individual.
SOP	Standard operating procedure.
SPIKE	Drug culture argot for a syringe.
STROLL	The area where streetwalkers ply their trade.

•

TARU	Technical Assistance Response Unit—the New York police department's electronics experts.
TEN-CARD	A record of a policeman's assignments in the department.
THREADS	Slang for clothes.
TRUE BILL	An indictment handed down by a grand jury.
WALTHER .380	A small semiautomatic pistol. In fiction it is the type of gun James Bond uses.
WANT CARD	A notification to other police officers that an individual is a possible suspect in a case, and they should notify the detectives handling the case if they have this individual in custody.
WISEGUY	A member of organized crime; specifically, someone connected to the Mafia.
WORKS	The equipment used by a junkie to shoot (inject) heroin.
WPA	Works Project Administration.

•

ABOUT THE AUTHOR

Peter A. Micheels is a staff psychologist at Bellevue Hospital and is the author of *Braving the Flames,* an oral history of the Fire Department of New York, and *Heat,* an oral history of the Bureau of Fire Investigation. He is an honorary fire marshal and an honorary battalion chief. His articles have appeared in *Firehouse* magazine and *Daily News* magazine. He lives in Manhattan and is currently at work on his next book.

•